A Wild Life

A Wild Life

MARTIN HUGHES-GAMES

corsair

CORSAIR

First published in Great Britain in 2015 by Corsair

1 3 5 7 9 10 8 6 4 2

Copyright © Martin Hughes-Games, 2015

The moral right of the author has been asserted.

A CIP catalogue record for this book
is available from the British Library.

ISBN 978-1-47211-443-3 (hardback)
ISBN: 978-1-47211-445-7 (ebook)

Typeset in Adobe Caslon Pro by SX Composing DTP

Printed and bound in Great Britain by CPI Group (UK) Ltd, Croydon, CR0
4YY

Corsair
is an imprint of
Little, Brown Book Group
100 Victoria Embankment
London EC4Y 0DY

An Hachette UK Company
www.hachette.co.uk

www.littlebrown.co.uk

This book is dedicated to Jake Drake Brockman,
with whom I was lucky enough to share much
of my life and many of these adventures.

CONTENTS

CONTENTS

1

FLYING WITH FALCONS

Ultimate Killers, BBC1, 2001

It was all Lloyd Buck's fault.

It's curious how a chance remark can sometimes have incalculable consequences. We were strolling around Lloyd's spacious garden, surrounded by a fabulous collection of birds of prey, all immaculate on their perches, talking about things we might do for the new BBC1 series I was about to produce, *Ultimate Killers*. Not only is Lloyd Buck phenomenally good with the birds he shares his life with, he's also great at coming up with filming ideas, but this time it appeared he'd lost his marbles…

'Well,' said Lloyd in his strong Essex accent, 'we could see how fast Lady' (one of his peregrine falcons) 'can actually stoop' (dive through the air, generally after prey).

'Really, Lloyd?' I said, genuinely very interested. 'How on earth could we do that?'

'I've been thinking: we could go up in a balloon, and then if we jump out, with an air-speed monitor, she'd stoop after the lure, and if she caught up we'd know how fast she was flying.'

I laughed. 'What a fabulous idea, Lloyd! I love it! Brilliant! But obviously totally and utterly impossible, ha-ha-ha…!'

So here we were, six months later, at 10,000 feet in a hot-air balloon, high over the Spanish countryside near Segovia. Steve Leonard, our presenter, was perched on a bit of board outside the basket with a parachute and vertigo. Our slightly crazy but brilliant extreme cameraman Leo Dickenson was teetering on the edge of the basket holding on to a support wire, squeaking 'I'm ready! I'm ready! I'm going to jump!' in a high-pitched voice, and Lloyd was just about to unhood Lady the peregrine falcon who was perched on his fist – madness!

It had taken a fair bit of work to get us all to this point, and even in those last few seconds we had no idea if it would really work…

The peregrine falcon is the fastest creature on earth. When it hunts, this bird enters a physical and sensory world we can hardly begin to comprehend. It is said a hunting peregrine will attack its prey at speeds of up to and perhaps beyond 150 miles an hour. There is no doubt it is shatteringly fast – but 150 mph? Really? How could it get up to such a speed? And if so, how could it manoeuvre and accurately hit its prey going so fast? How fast, in fact, is a peregrine? In the spring of 2000 that was what we set out to discover.

Evolution has provided the peregrine with a series of wonderful adaptations to enable it to reach, and hunt, at prodigious speeds. Its eyesight is extraordinary – a peregrine can pick up the white flash of a wood pigeon's wings from perhaps two miles away – the eyes take up over 50 per cent of a peregrine's skull. Potential prey is often a bird that's flying more weakly than others in a flock: the peregrine can detect fractional differences in flight patterns that might identify an older or injured bird – easier to kill.

Once locked on, the peregrine will 'ring up', gaining height rapidly before flipping over and accelerating at a seemingly impossible rate, turning into a lethal, feathered bullet. In full stoop a peregrine goes into what's known as the 'mummy position', wings tucked tightly in. And here's an odd thing: if you dropped a stuffed peregrine in the mummy position it would only get up to around 70 mph, yet clearly a living peregrine can effortlessly exceed this speed – so what's going on? No one really knows. Somehow the bird is using its body as an aerofoil to continue to accelerate way beyond any theoretical maximum. They also seem to pump their wings slightly to add more speed.

And they have to be going fast, because a healthy wood pigeon, for instance, is also a powerful flier. If the pigeon catches sight of its nemesis it may try to take evasive action and high-speed aerobatics will ensue – there have been reports of pigeons using moving traffic on motorways to try to thwart their pursuer, jinking between high-sided lorries in an effort to throw it off.

If the peregrine has timed its stoop right it comes hurtling in, flips its talons forward at the very last moment and then – well, what happens next is a source of much speculation. Some experts say it rakes its back talon up the prey's back before embedding it in its brain like a lethal dagger. Others say the peregrine simply hits its prey so hard it can break a wing, or rupture essential organs. One well-known Scottish bird called Storm – who we'll meet later – specialised in killing grouse, which it always hunted in the same way: rolling underneath the fleeing prey and disembowelling it in mid-air. Whichever method a peregrine uses, there is generally a puff of feathers and it's all over. Post-impact, the peregrine often binds on to its prey and flies down to earth to pluck and feast. All this happens so fast it's hard for us plodding humans to comprehend what's going on.

Yes, peregrines are breathtakingly fast – but could we, on *Ultimate Killers*, put a figure on exactly how fast?

After Lloyd's ridiculous suggestion I'd gone away and given

it serious thought. After some financial calculations I knew it was going to be very, very expensive – but if we could pull it off, I thought, what an amazing bit of television! Fortune favours the brave and all that…

Originally we thought about using a small aeroplane for the jump, but cameraman Leo Dickenson suggested a hot-air balloon would be much less unsettling for the peregrine. Lloyd was worried about launching Lady from an aircraft with such a lot of forward motion: a balloon would provide a more user-friendly start point, not just for Lady but for the whole team, and actually, it quickly transpired, we would need quite a large team. An expert balloon pilot, an expert sky-diving 'tandem master' (who would be attached to Steve Leonard, our presenter), an outstanding aerial camera person, a ground-based team to find Lady when she came down, another camera person in the balloon basket – it was going to have to be quite a big balloon.

And then, how would Lady, Lloyd's peregrine, react to the din of a hot-air balloon burner going off? I don't know if you have ever stood next to a balloon while it is being filled with hot air? The noise is deafening, to say nothing of the huge gouts of flame that would turn Lady into a small roast dinner in an instant. Would she be OK with the sound, and would she steer clear of the flame itself? As a trial, one cold winter's morning we tethered a balloon in the garden of a pub in Gloucestershire – to the surprise of the regulars – then fired up the burner. Lloyd unhooded Lady, who didn't seem at all bothered as she sat calmly on his fist. Then Lloyd began to fly her around the burner. Lady darted back and forth with spectacular grace, always avoiding the flames and clearly totally unfazed. We, or at least Lady, had passed the first test.

Now we had to see how our presenter Steve Leonard would take to sky-diving. It had to be a tandem jump, meaning he would be physically attached to an expert parachutist. A small percentage of the population suffers from a curious affliction – known in the USA as Total Sensory Overload, or TSO. People suffering from TSO become paralysed by extreme situations, like sky-diving, and cannot take any instruction, which is bad if you need to pull something in an emergency, or simply extend your legs to land. We had to be sure Steve did not suffer from TSO. Soon we were all up in a tiny aeroplane bumping around in the sky above Devon. Worryingly, we noticed the pilot was also wearing a parachute – did he know something we didn't? But the main danger turned out to be the frightful stink in the cabin. Be warned: if you go for a charity sky-dive, leave your self-respect on the ground – an unpressurised cabin at a few thousand feet gives you the most appalling wind. We were all blowing off like hippos – ghastly. It was thus, for a short space of time at least, a blessing when the wobbly metal door (it looked as though someone had been at the plane with a tin opener) slid back, and we shuffled forward to sit on the edge of the aeroplane with our legs in the slipstream, peering out through rather silly goggles, each wearing a hat that looked like the tip of a cucumber.

For some reason Leo Dickenson, who was running this part of the project, decided we should all jump, to make sure none of us suffered from Total Sensory Overload. I never was sure why this should be, as only Steve was going to jump from the balloon. However, soon it was my turn. Just as I thought, 'Actually, I'm not sure I really want to do this', and was turning my head to mention this to Andy Montreau our tandem master, to whom I was strapped, my head was forcibly snapped back, and I was thrown out of the perfectly good plane into the empty sky. This was my first parachute jump, and I had made the mistake of agreeing to be filmed on the way down, so instead of the emptiness of

Devon stretching out ahead of me there was a chap with a camera, falling at exactly the same rate and smack-bang in my eye-line all the way down. My advice, for what it's worth, is to forgo the film of your jump and just soak up the view. Turned out none of us were suffering from TSO. Test two successfully negotiated.

Of course, everything ultimately depended on Lady. When people talk about peregrine behaviour they often generalise: 'under these circumstances peregrines will do this'; 'peregrines never hover'; 'peregrines never kill their prey on the ground' – and so on. It's a dangerous thing to do, because, like us, animals are individuals, and what holds good for one may not be at all true for another. This is especially true when it comes to their instinct to hunt.

Falconers will take their birds out to fly every day to keep them fit and healthy. Lloyd is not a falconer: he is a bird trainer, and does not want to train his birds to hunt. In fact, unlike the falconer, his main aim is to try to channel the birds' innate hunting instincts into working effectively with him for film and TV.

But just like a falconer, Lloyd uses a swing lure to keep his birds in peak condition. The swing lure is whirled around on a length of string and, if all goes well, the flying peregrine will keep returning to try to grab the lure (known as 'binding on') in a series of breathtaking dives, swoops, flicks and turns.

As the bird makes its approach, the falconer whisks the lure out of the way at the very last moment, and the peregrine sweeps up into the sky once more. It's a highly skilled business, which in Lloyd's case is accompanied by a constant stream of energising and encouraging yells. On a cool day a peregrine may make 150 dives onto the swing lure, fewer if it's hot.

Finally – and the bird knows this will happen – the falconer does allow it to bind on to the lure, and then it will be given carefully chosen pieces of meat as a reward.

Because a falconer will use the lure to train his bird to hunt, it is often made to appear rather like the prey itself, complete with wings and feathers. Lloyd, on the other hand, uses a cricket-ball-sized bag of brilliant yellow, upon which the bird becomes totally focused, without ever making the connection between the lure and live prey. By using this brightly coloured lure (his own innovation), Lloyd can encourage his birds to fly more or less wherever he wants them to go.

But overcoming the hunting instinct is not always that easy. I was flying with Lloyd recently: he has a feisty new peregrine called Moses, and it's a tense business flying Moses! He's young, and has a powerful hunting instinct. Moses is very interested in all the birds around Lloyd's house, especially the crows. Once Lloyd unhoods him (peregrines are carried on the fist with a beautifully made hood over their eyes which keeps them calm), he sits on Lloyd's fist and looks around with his phenomenal eyesight, carefully clocking every slight movement for miles around to see if he feels like killing something. This is the tense time. Then he takes to the wing. Now, will Moses be interested in the swing lure or has he got other ideas? How strong is his instinct to hunt today? On my visit he immediately flew off to investigate a group of jackdaws in an oak tree. Panic! Mercifully, he returned, and started to put on a fantastic display of acrobatics, Lloyd teasing me by getting Moses to whisk past, just an inch over my head, down by my feet, just past my face again. The skill and speed at which the peregrine does this, even flying at the swing lure, is mind-boggling – you clearly understand what it could do if it really started to hunt.

A few days before my visit, while out exercising, Moses had suddenly flown off. He'd climbed up to around 300 feet, hovered for a split-second, then, folding his wings into the mummy position, hurtled downwards. What was he up to? Lloyd just had time to notice a crow hopping along on the ground. From two fields away he heard a smack like a hammer blow. Moses had hit the crow. By the time Lloyd got there the crow was dead and the bones of its wing were jutting out, gleaming white, shattered by the force of Moses' impact.

Sometimes the instinct to hunt makes individual birds difficult to work with safely. Lloyd kept his peregrine Storm 'at hack', which means the bird is released to go and fly free almost all day (in fact she chose to go and fly with some juvenile wild peregrines). At four o'clock prompt Storm would return to Lloyd. But being 'at hack', coupled with her innate personality, made Storm a really formidable hunter: she became less and less interested in the swing lure, and only interested in killing. This is dangerous, because if such a bird starts to kill game birds it may fall foul of farmers and gamekeepers. Fearing for Storm's life, Lloyd gave her away to friends in Scotland, where she proceeded to become the best hunting falcon they had ever known, dispatching a total of 247 grouse in her lifetime, before dying naturally of old age.

Clearly, if we were to have any chance of working with Lady for our balloon jump we had to know she would be completely focused on Lloyd and his lure, and not decide she'd actually rather go off hunting on her own, leaving us sat on the edge of a very expensive hot-air balloon all ready to jump off, looking rather foolish. But there was a problem immediately: peregrines are trained to swoop and dive at the swing lure as it whirls around, but we couldn't swing a lure in the balloon. What to do? Lloyd's wonderful wife Rose solved the problem: simply remove the brightly coloured lure from the string and get Lady to associate just the lure itself with a good meal. OK in principle, but would Lady be 'into it', as Lloyd put it? On the ground she showed interest: now it was time to get airborne.

Very early, on a clear, windless morning, a hot-air balloon containing pilot, Lloyd and Lady rose gently to 100 feet and stopped, tethered to the ground. We had arrived at a critical moment: would Lady follow the lure if it was dropped from the balloon? She was unhooded, the lure waggled, dropped and…One moment Lady was there perched on Lloyd's fist; the next she was on the ground, the lure gripped tightly in her talons. Success!

There was one more essential test. Would Lady follow a lure she could see was being held by a human sky-diver, rather than it simply being dropped? The minimum height for our expert skydiver Andy Montreau to jump from was 3,000 feet. So this time, when Lady was unhooded, she was higher than she'd ever been before in the balloon. Once again this remarkable bird locked onto the lure in Andy's hand and shot after him as he fell to earth. It looked as though Lady was indeed 'into it'!

Somehow, all the elements clicked into place. And at the end of March 2000 the team gradually coalesced in Segovia in Spain, because of its balloon-friendly authorities and perfect weather. Guaranteed.

It rained hard all the first week. The wind fairly howled. I sat in my hotel room with indigestion. I had spent a very large portion of the entire programme budget on this – if it didn't work I would have some rather awkward questions to answer. Lloyd told me he too sat nervously in his room, watching Lady on her perch, one talon comfortably tucked up in her feathers, thinking how cheerful she seemed to be, enjoying her adventure without a care in the world. But finally the weather cleared, we could leave the hotel, and put a halt to our Spanish fixer buying endless bottles of hotel wine to while away the hours. At last, it was time for our first attempt.

Apparently it was my fault: I was too heavy. As Series Producer I had pulled rank and insisted on going up in the balloon. I had set up a chain of command before the jump. First, the pilot had to say he was happy with the balloon, altitude and stability. So was he happy? Check! Then Leo our cameraman, wearing the special helmet camera with which he would try to film Lady in free flight – was Leo ready? 'Yes, yes, yes!' he squeaked. Finally Andy Montreau, our monumentally calm tandem master, currently teetering, with presenter Steve Leonard strapped to him, on their small wooden perch outside the basket – was he happy, and could he identify a safe landing area?

Er, no.

'We cannot jump,' said Andy. 'We've drifted over some mountains, and I can't guarantee a safe landing. We have to abort. Sorry.' We had taken too long to gain enough height, and by the time we'd got above 10,000 feet we had drifted too far.

'Well, I'm going to jump! I'm going to jump! I'm—'

'Calm down, Leo! No, Leo – please – get back in the basket!'

Awash with adrenalin, Leo had to be talked back into the balloon...

It was gently explained to me that my extra bulk, though not enormously excessive, was enough to jeopardise the success of the mission, and so it was resolved that for the next attempt I should stay on the ground.

This was perhaps the most difficult time for Lloyd. He knew he would have to keep Lady 'in Yarak' for nearly two weeks. This lovely expression means the bird is at its absolute peak of both fitness and keenness – it's a bit like an Olympic athlete timing all his or her training to build to one perfect moment – the event itself. To be in Yarak a bird of prey has to be three things: super-fit, super-strong and utterly focused. To achieve this, Lloyd had to feed Lady with incredible precision. This part of the peregrine's life has always fascinated me. No falconer worth their salt is ever without scales to weigh their birds: it's a critical part of the daily routine. Each morning Lloyd would give Lady her bath, and afterwards he weighed her. Her normal, comfortable flying weight was 1 lb 15 oz, and at this weight she was strong and fairly interested. But this was not in Yarak, not by a long chalk. Before we left for Spain Lloyd had gradually reduced her food. Her weight fell to 1 lb 14 oz: now she was very fit and very keen, but still not quite perfect. Finally, at 1 lb 13 oz, Lady was there – at her absolute peak. Just half an ounce heavier, and she would not be quite keen enough to fly with certainty. 'Half an ounce makes a huge difference,' says Lloyd, 'but I'd never take her below 1 lb 13 oz, 'cause I'd worry about her being strong enough.'

By the way, these figures were absolutely specific to Lady, and vary greatly from peregrine to peregrine, particularly as there is usually a big difference between males and females, with the female being some 15 per cent bigger than the male. The problem for Lloyd was going to be keeping Lady at this precise weight and in Yarak for the whole two weeks it would take us to try to film the jump, what with multiple balloon launches, waiting for weather, camera faults, etc. We could not afford for Lady to be at all perhaps-I-will-perhaps-I-won't: when the hood came off at 10,000 feet, all that had to exist for her was that lure…For our second flight Lady was certainly in Yarak, but we made one tiny error. It was embarrassing for all, really. The balloon was up (sans producer – I was watching nervously through binoculars on the ground), and at height; the tiny figures of Steve Leonard and Andy Montreau perched vertiginously on their little platform; Leo was standing on the basket ready to jump. Somewhere inside the basket, out of sight, were Lady and Lloyd.

Suddenly, the balloon shot up, the tiny figures were tumbling through the air – but something was wrong. Walkie-talkies crackled, the tandem parachute opened, Leo was nowhere to be seen. What was going on? If I'd had more powerful binoculars I would have been able to see a peregrine circling, but actually above the balloon. There had been a split-second glitch.

By now you're probably getting the idea that every peregrine is very much an individual character. Lady had a particular routine to go through once she was unhooded and before she would fly: she had to 'mute and rouse' – in other words, have a poo (mute), then sort of wake herself up, shaking her feathers and really becoming alert. Interestingly, Moses doesn't do this – with Moses it's just hood off and he's gone – but Lady had her routine, and on this one occasion Lloyd had got it fractionally wrong. Everyone had been ready, he'd unhooded Lady and sure enough she muted, but she did not immediately rouse. Even so, Lloyd thought she was ready, but at the precise moment he had shouted 'Go!' and the sky-diving team had left the balloon, Lady, still sitting on Lloyd's fist, decided to rouse herself properly. This only took a second or two, but it may as well have been an eternity. The team were gone, hurtling through the sky in free fall hundreds of feet below, and the moment had passed. Having roused, Lady now took off, had a look around, flew up above the balloon and began to circle. Impasse! Lloyd didn't want to call her in – there were too many wires and potential issues in the basket – and after a while she calmly flew off, eventually to be retrieved by the ground-based team (she was carrying a tiny radio transmitter clipped to the base of one of her tail feathers, so they could find her).

Over supper that evening we re-grouped. Clearly we had to wait for Lady to mute, and then absolutely and definitely rouse!

What with poor weather, technical glitches and various other difficulties, trying to get this sequence took a total of ten balloon flights. But then, at last, on a clear and sunny Spanish morning, a bright red balloon could be seen rising smoothly up into the sky. At 10,000 feet our by now well-practised chain of command swung into action.

Pilot: 'I'm happy.'

Leo: 'I'm ready.'

Andy: long pause, peering down around Steve, thoughtfully: 'Yes – we're good to go.'

Now, finally, it was all up to Lloyd and Lady: how would she react today once she was unhooded? The hood came off. She sat calmly on Lloyd's fist.

'Wait!' said Lloyd. 'Wait – wait!' Lady muted – but still Lloyd held back. 'Wait…wait…' Then, at last, she ruffled her feathers and looked keenly around. She leant forward. Lady had roused. 'Waggle the lure,' said Lloyd. Andy waggled the lure. Lady's eyes locked on. 'Wait…Camera!' yelled Lloyd. 'Ready…steady…*go!*' The balloon lurched as first three humans, then, a split second later, one bird, left the basket. All the cameras were running. It wouldn't get better than this.

Lady was stooping after Steve and the lure. She folded up her beautiful wings, tucked everything in to form a perfect teardrop, the mummy position. She began to accelerate. 80, 90, 100 miles an hour…

Steve and Andy were hurtling towards the ground faster and faster…but Lady was closing in…

120, 140…

At 158 miles per hour, the humans reached their maximum speed in free fall, yet Lady had effortlessly caught them up and was now manoeuvring around the falling skydivers, at nearly 160 mph, looking for a chance to grab the lure.

We got it all: as the balloon basket recedes up away from the falling camera, Lady comes screaming down at us. The normally stoic balloon pilot can be heard ejaculating, 'Bloody hell!' Even the generally unimpressable tandem master Andy, who has pretty much seen it all, made a note in his logbook that day that reads, 'The most amazing thing I have ever seen in free fall'. When we landed, the astonishing Lady was happily tearing bits of meat into chunks having been relieved of the lure. The entire team were ecstatic. That casual remark of Lloyd's, walking around his garden all those months ago, had turned into an extraordinary sequence of film.

I don't think we could ever do it again – budgets have been cut to the bone, and it would be hard to assemble such a unique team of skilled adventurers. Lloyd told me recently he'd been approached by another film company, and the encounter went like this. Very excited telly person: 'Hey! We want to film that balloon jump again, only in high-definition!' 'Great,' says Lloyd, 'I've got a fantastic new peregrine, Moses' (sadly, Lady is no longer with us), 'we'll need to go to Spain, in the perfect weather window, probably early April. We'll have to hire in a large balloon for the three weeks it will take to film, and we'll need a team of around fourteen different experts – pilots, sky-divers, animal handlers, recovery team, camera crew and so on – is that OK?' Pause. 'Oh. We were thinking – could you film it in a day?' Yeah, right!

You can still see the sequence we filmed ('Peregrine falcon dives at 180 mph – *Ultimate Killers*') on YouTube – it's had over a million hits. Despite all my fears, the then-controller of BBC1 was so excited by the balloon jump – 'Oh, when he looked down over the edge of the balloon! I couldn't bear to look!' – we got another series commissioned off the back of it.

2

SAILING THE SOUTHERN OCEAN

Steve Leonard's Extreme Animals,

BBC1, September 2002

Refreshments?' asked the air hostess.

I started awake. It wasn't an air hostess at all, but a squaddie in green ill-fitting fatigues. 'Refreshments?' he repeated.

'Oh. Er, yes – yes, what have you got?'

'Orange juice, mate.'

'Er…'

'It's very nice.'

'Well, in that case… I'll have an orange juice, please.'

We were well into the eighteen-hour flight to the Falklands islands aboard an RAF Tristar. Unnervingly, in a reminder of fairly recent events, the whole of the front of the plane was fitted out with hospital beds. But from the moment the crew and I had set foot on the airfield at Brize Norton the organisation had been superb. Thanks, RAF. The 8000-mile journey was uneventful, and after a brief halfway stop-off at Ascension Island to re-fuel (it took two attempts to land – 'Runway a bit short'), we were nearing the Falklands.

As the Tristar lined up for its final approach I glanced out of the window. What was that? Closing in on us, out of the low clouds, was a fantastically businesslike RAF fighter – closer and closer until the plane was almost touching our wingtip. I could wave at the navigator, who waved back. Actually, there were two fighters, one on each side just feet away. Transport planes in combat zones are highly vulnerable as they slow to land, so we were being escorted in as practice for the RAF. Eventually we were just too slow, and the fighters lit their afterburners, flame burst forth and the planes blasted away – simply disappeared. Extremely impressive.

Meanwhile…

A thousand miles away from the Falklands, over a mile under-water, a huge seal is cruising. There is no light down here: it is pitch black. The seal has already been underwater for an hour, yet it will not surface to draw breath for another twenty minutes. And then it will only spend two minutes on the surface before diving once more to immense depth. Although it is a youngster, the bull elephant seal is over fifteen feet long and weighs nearly three tons. As it dives, its heart rate of 110 beats per minute on the surface begins to fall: 40 beats at 1000 feet, down, down, 20 beats – still its heartbeat slows. By the time the young bull levels out 5000 feet below the surface its heart is ticking over at just three beats per minute. At this depth the seal's blood supply is now cut off from its extremities, and is mainly flowing between its brain and heart. All seems to be shut down. Yet the seal is fully alert, and occasionally puts on a burst of speed to catch passing prey.

The young bull was seven years old. Despite still being over 1000 miles away he was heading, with unerring accuracy, towards a tiny island in the southern ocean, South Georgia, which was also, you will not be surprised to learn, where we were headed.

The seal was covering nearly 200 kilometres each day. He was feeding as hard as he could: he needed to build up his strength.

Meanwhile, having landed in Port Stanley, we were already making preparations for the next leg of our journey. The trip from the cozy familiarity of Port Stanley to the extreme isolation of South Georgia is quite a serious undertaking – around 900 miles across the Southern Ocean. None of us in the film crew really understood what we were about to take on.

The storms that sweep the southern ocean are legendary. This is because there are no land masses down here to slow their passage. We were told of a Royal Navy frigate that had recently taken ten days to cross from South Georgia back to Port Stanley (normal travel time four and a half days), an ice-breaker whose entire bridge was smashed to bits by towering waves, and other ships in the past, lost and never seen again. I was expecting our transport, the *Golden Fleece*, to be something pretty substantial. The small sailing boat, with its slightly explosive French skipper Jerome Poncet, was not at first confidence-inspiring.

Jerome Poncet is an Antarctic legend. He first arrived in the Southern Ocean in a tiny boat he and his friend Gerard Janichon had built themselves. It was kitted out with second-hand navigational gear and out-of-date tins of food donated by an admiring but tight-fisted benefactor. Having entered the Southern Ocean they then got hit one night by a massive storm, which turned their 'uncapsizable' boat upside-down. Jerome recalls being furious as the boat began to fill with water and started to sink – how could he have got the design so wrong? In the blackness of the upside-down cabin, lurching around in the storm, surrounded by floating debris, Jerome and Gerard solemnly shook hands to say goodbye and wish each other good luck 'on the next adventure' – i.e. death by drowning – when the boat, having taken on a lot of water, now became unstable in the upside-down position and, much to Jerome's surprise, suddenly righted itself.

They spent the rest of the night bailing, and at first light, observing a white gleam on the horizon, realised they were still, just, within striking distance of South Georgia, rather than on the way to New Zealand many thousands of miles away. The mast was gone, but they jerry-rigged a small sail, and after a very long time the shattered boat and crew approached the harbour at King Edward Point. On sighting the wreckage, a concerned team of British Antarctic Survey (BAS) members rushed out to see if they could help, and were somewhat surprised when Jerome immediately refused. An instinctively suspicious Jerome thought the BAS team might be after the salvage rights on the wreckage of his boat – rights BAS could have claimed if the offer of a tow was accepted. 'Oh, come on!' said the BAS team. 'Don't be so pig-headed! We don't want your boat!' Jerome, thus reassured, graciously accepted the offer of rescue.

No one knows the Southern Ocean better than Jerome. So it was a bit surprising that as soon as the *Golden Fleece* left Port Stanley he became very seasick. We should have been suspicious when our fixer, Dave Roote, also went to his cabin, with armfuls of rations, magazines and bottles of colourful tablets, and said, as he shut the door firmly, 'See you when we get there.'

The next four and a bit days were, as they say, character-building. We were all hoping for a jolly cruise. Wrong. It was nearly impossible to stand at any time on the *Golden Fleece*, so violent and unpredictable was the boat's movement. First up, then sideways, then down – no…up again, slithering sideways the other way, and then turning halfway around to the right, up again…On and on…Nearly everyone, except me, I'm proud to say, was extremely sick. If I'm honest, it was really frightening. To be thrown about on this huge and violent ocean, far from any possible rescue: once you're out of helicopter range of the Falklands, around 200 miles, you're pretty much on your own. I don't ever recall feeling quite so vulnerable and utterly at the mercy of the elements. Jerome advised us not to bother with lifejackets. 'In this water, if you fall in without the jacket you die quickly,' he shrugged. 'With the jacket you just die more slowly.'

Meanwhile, the young bull seal was still homing in on South Georgia. He had changed the nature of his dives. Now, instead of spending time hunting at depth, he dived down, then fairly quickly curved up again, then down again. Up, down, up down: a series of deep U shapes. The dives lasted about twenty minutes but were still deep, down to over 300 metres. These were just 'travelling' dives – twenty minutes underwater was nothing to him: if he wanted to, he could stay down for two hours. When he was going to dive, instead of filling his lungs with air at the surface, as you might expect, he emptied them, and then headed down. If he had any gas in his lungs at the depth he was going down to, it would dissolve into his blood, and then might bubble out as he returned to the surface – what human divers call 'the bends'. While deep underwater his lungs were crushed by the enormous water pressure and no bigger than a pair of oranges.

When scientists investigating the dive abilities of elephant seals first fitted them with depth recorders they thought the results were an aberration. Surely it was not possible for an air-breathing animal to go so deep – over two kilometres – and stay down so long? Elephant seals, it soon became apparent, were somehow doing what was theoretically impossible. How? Even now they still seem to break the rules of mammalian physiology, but the basics are clear. The human body is around 7 per cent blood. An elephant seal is over 20 per cent blood. That blood is very thick, because it's stuffed with oxygen-carrying red blood cells. Elephant seals saturate their blood with oxygen before they dive – even their muscles store oxygen. If we hold our breath we lose consciousness when we still have a quarter of our oxygen supply left: an elephant seal can continue to operate with its oxygen reserves at very nearly zero.

Now the pattern of his dives changed again. He came up to the surface very briefly, then dived, but this time, instead of immediately going deep, he just drifted down, gliding towards the dark like some huge torpedo. He did not move; his fins hung limp; all was peaceful: he was asleep.

We were not asleep, and all was not peaceful on the *Golden Fleece*. I was holding on to a ladder with one hand and clutching a small video camera with the other. Presenter Steve Leonard was holding on to the side of the boat shouting above the roaring wind, attempting to give some idea of what it was like and why we were here. The boat pitched and yawed sickeningly; spray drove across the decks. 'Hold on!' yelled Jerome. 'One hand for you, one hand for ze boat!'

The wind eased. It was still terrifying, and the movement of the boat sickening, but now wonderfully beautiful. We began to see icebergs. Pretty soon we were surrounded by them, in every shade of white and electric blue imaginable: vast, majestic, carved by wind and water into fantastic shapes. Little ice shelves on the bergs were sometimes occupied by a huddle of penguins. Jerome took us in very close. The normally vociferous film crew were stunned into silence by these gleaming towers of ice.

Icebergs are formed when a section of freshwater ice breaks away from a glacier or an ice sheet and floats off in the sea. Once in sea-water they begin to melt. Most of an iceberg is hidden underwater: only about a tenth of the whole thing is visible topside, hence the expression 'tip of the iceberg'. A berg is in a constant state of flux. Sometimes as it melts it becomes unstable in one position, and will roll. This can be extremely dramatic, and if a berg weighing thousands of tons decides to roll, you really don't want to be nearby, because of the danger of being hit by it, flattened by falling ice, or being capsised by the huge wave created by its roll. They say birds perched on an iceberg can be a useful guide. If an iceberg is about to roll, they sense subtle movements and all take off, allowing the wise observer to beat a safe retreat. I have not had the opportunity to test this particular nugget of Antarctic lore.

We had been on the *Golden Fleece* for four days, and it was a blessed relief to come in to our first safe harbour on Bird Island, an outlying speck of land at the far end of South Georgia.

For the first time in four days the *Golden Fleece* stopped lurching around. We were all a bit unsteady as we stood on dry land once more, which was unfortunate, as we were instantly attacked by bad-tempered and very aggressive fur seals. We had arrived during the fur seal breeding season, and they had claimed many of the beaches to use as nurseries. They didn't seem to like us at all. Fur seals are not very big, but can move surprisingly fast. They have extremely sharp teeth and a very bad attitude. It was quite a battle to make our way up to the small collection of huts that comprised the British Antarctic Survey station on Bird Island.

'Fancy a game of rugby?' said a wild-eyed Dafydd, pointing to a set of rugby posts made inexpertly out of bits of old scaffolding back out on the fur seal beach. He had a ball in his hands – he was serious. He was perhaps a tiny bit unhinged. It would not be surprising if the young researchers did go a bit off the rails – they will live on this small island for two and a half years, three young people on an island measuring three miles long by just 875 yards wide, visited only very occasionally by boat in order to be re-supplied. We were the first visitors Mark, Jane and Dafydd had had for six months. While the rest of the crew had coffee and swapped stories with the BAS researchers I slipped out for a wander.

It was lovely to feel solid earth beneath my feet. I was soon dodging the blasted fur seals again, even quite high up amongst the grassy tussocks, surprisingly far away from the beaches where I expected them to be. Looking behind at a particularly aggressive individual who was coming after me, I turned around only to discover I had come face-to-face with a real live sea monster. Sleek, grey, maybe twelve feet long, black spots. The sea monster yawned, revealing exactly the sort of teeth a sea monster should have: lots, very pointy, big. I remember being struck by its lack of ears, which just added to the overall impression of smooth sleekness. Now I was stuck: fur seal behind, sea monster to the fore. I turned around again – no fur seal, which, as I later found out, was not surprising, as 58 per cent of the sea monster's diet is … fur seal.

This monster was a leopard seal. Not your average sort of seal at all, most of which look to me like underwater dogs and thus seem somehow friendly? Except the fur seals, of course, which are the badly behaved Jack Russells of the seal world. The leopard seal is something entirely different: an infinitely more serious proposition. Huge, streamlined, subtly menacing. This one exuded that quiet air of extreme confidence I have noticed in nearly all top predators, from harpy eagles to tigers. It comes across as a calm curiosity and a total absence of fear. Here it was again. The leopard seal made no move, just observed me with a relaxed curiosity.

'Hello,' it might have said (in a deep voice). 'Can I help you?'

'No, no – just going for a walk.'

'How are you finding Bird Island, then?'

'Er, fine, fine – nice to get off the boat for a bit.'

'Yes, it is a nice little boat – I've seen it around here before.'

'The, er, fur seals are pretty aggressive, aren't they?'

'Are they? I don't find they bother me much, really...'

All too soon, after our brief pit stop, we were back on the *Golden Fleece* and leaving the relative calm of Bird Island, heading down the coast of South Georgia for our primary destination, St Andrew's Bay.

Apart from some whales, no animal on earth dives as deep, or stays underwater for as long, as an elephant seal. The maximum depth recorded is some 2133 metres. So the question has to be – why? Why has the seal's entire physiology evolved, over aeons of time, to enable it to do things underwater that science still cannot explain? Why go so deep and stay down so long? There must be a reason. And of course there is.

To unravel this natural history mystery we have to go back in time, to 1942, aboard the research vessel the USS *Jasper* off the coast of Baja, California. Ever since underwater SONAR (SOund Navigation And Ranging) was developed in the 1930s, operators had noticed something strange. They kept coming up with a 'false bottom': for some reason the sonar would insist the sea-bed was around 400 metres down, when they knew it was much deeper. The worry was that German submarines would know about the false bottom and be able to hide in it. But what was this anomalous signal? In 1942 three scientists, Charles Eyring, R. Christensen and Russell Rait, had set out aboard the USS *Jasper* to solve the mystery. And solve it they did. The false bottom was actually a massive agglomeration of sea life: fish, jellyfish, krill, all hanging out in the dark at around 400 metres down. This layer of living creatures was so dense the sonar pulses bounced off it and created the illusion of the false bottom.

At night, this layer of sea life comes up to the surface, only to retreat back down at first light. Clearly the billions of creatures creating this illusion were hiding away from predators during the day, and coming up to feed under the cover of darkness. To begin with it was called the ECR layer after the three discoverers (Eyring, Christensen and Rait), but is now called the DSL or Deep Scattering Layer. The DSL is found everywhere in the deep ocean, so its total biomass is almost beyond comprehension.

During the day the animals making up the layer are safe enough from most predators hidden away 400 metres down. But they are not safe from elephant seals. The elephant seal's amazing biology allows them to take advantage of this immense food resource. The seals dive down into this dark zone where so much life is hiding, and stay there for very long periods, hoovering up the delicious seafood cocktail. No wonder elephant seals get so vast so fast.

Oh, and by the way, how do they find the food in the pitch-darkness? Well, many of the animals making up the DSL, the squid and jellyfish, are bioluminescent – flashing gorgeous blues, purples and greens in the dark – trying to attract mates and communicate with each other, not realising they are also saying to an approaching elephant seal, 'Here I am, come and eat me!' What a fantastic scene this must be. Anyhow, thanks to the pioneering work of those three American scientists back in 1942 we can now see why the elephant seal has evolved such spectacular underwater abilities.

That's a lovely bit of science, but how the elephant seals find their way back to the breeding beaches on South Georgia, from hundreds, thousands of miles away, does remain a mystery. Whatever magical sense he was using, our young bull was now just a day's diving from the beach in St Andrew's Bay, his target destination. Over half the entire world population of southern elephant seals, 200,000 or more, will haul out on to the beaches of South Georgia. It's the largest gathering of mammals, by weight, in the world.

He was nearly there, and so were we. On the way we stopped off at King Edward's Point, the capital of South Georgia (population eight!), to get our passports stamped.

'Do you want a penguin or a seal?' said the postmistress.

'Both, please.'

Past King Edward's Point we sailed on down the channel to Grytviken, population – when we arrived – two: Tim and Pauline Carr. Tim and Pauline lived their dream, sailing the world in a tiny wooden boat, the *Curlew*, for twenty-five years, but when they found South Georgia – 'It may be cold and rugged, with savage winds, but to us this is an icy paradise' – they parked up for five years. On our arrival they kindly gave us Pauline's home-made yoghurt (surreal!) and showed us around the small museum. I wonder where they are now? Back on the *Curlew*, sailing quietly into history?

Grytviken is a gigantic graveyard. The hulks of half-submerged whalers list drunkenly in the still, greeny waters of the harbour. Empty whaling sheds are rusting slowly away, and the shore is strewn with whalebones – grim reminders of how man's greed and over sixty years of brutal exploitation brought many whale species to the brink of extinction. The slaughter didn't end until 1966, and not because anyone thought it might be wrong, but because there were simply no longer enough whales to make it financially viable. There is another grave at Grytviken, too. I took my camera and walked up the path. Peeping up above the snow was a simple granite stone: 'To the dear memory of Ernest Henry Shackleton'. I stood there for some time paying my respects to this flawed but supremely loyal and courageous man. In 2011, the ashes of Frank Wild, Shackleton's second-in-command, were brought to Grytviken and buried beside his great friend. The inscription reads: 'Frank Wild 1873-1939 Shackleton's right-hand man.'

Finally we moored the *Golden Fleece* off the beach at St Andrew's Bay. We loaded all the filming gear onto the small tender and came ashore. This was what we had come for. Hard to take it all in really, it's such an assault on your senses.

The first bull elephant seals arrive mid-September and lie about leerily. In early October the females, who may be up to ten times smaller than the bulls, appear, and almost immediately give birth. The females suckle the pups, and around three weeks later will mate with the bulls. But not just any old bull: only around 2 to 3 per cent of the bulls who come to the beach will get to breed. These are the controlling 'beach masters', and what an ugly, smelly, hideous bunch they are! But indisputably impressive. The young bull in our story is big, at around three tons, but he's going to have his work cut out to breed successfully when he's up against beach masters who may be twenty feet long and weigh up to four tons. The biggest elephant seal ever recorded was shot (such a brave thing to do) on 28 February 1913 on South Georgia. He was 6.85 metres long and weighed five tons.

I genuinely think the elephant seal is an astonishing and fascinating animal, but... it's not a looker, is it? Be honest: the beach masters just don't conform to any of our human notions of beauty. First, they are fantastically fat. As they move, their entire body wobbles like a monumental trifle wrapped in cling film. The long snout that gives them their name flobbers about and may be shredded by fighting into gory, dangling lumps. Their fishy breath comes in steamy, smelly streams, and during display it becomes half a roar, half a staccato belch. They also fart all the time. I wonder if the poor females actually fancy them? Or do they simply put up with it because having one huge stinky male to put up with is better than the rough attentions of dozens, which is what would happen if the beach master didn't see them off.

As we filmed a beach master lying drowsily amongst his harem of some fifty females, steaming in the chill air, the young bull, the one whose story we had been following, appeared out of the surf. Yes, he'd made it. His 1500-mile journey was over, and there in front of him was a roly-poly paradise of blubbery fat birds. We filmed him bouncing up the beach, his whole demeanour suffused with what seemed expectant joy. Of course, he hadn't yet seen the torpid beach master. Up, up he came, and bounced into the first female, who began to complain loudly, as did her half-squashed pup. The beach master awoke.

'Wha—' Where was he? What was going on? Where had all the fish gone? 'Hang on...' Suddenly it all seemed to rush back into his brain. He rose up – at full stretch a bull elephant seal can raise himself up a seriously impressive eight feet. He turned towards the commotion, and began to roar. The earth shook.

All the books say bulls can get a good indication of the size and prowess of another bull by the quality of the roary belch alone. It certainly brought our young bull up short. He stopped. You could see him thinking: fight or flee? For a moment he stood his ground, but then, as the vast beach master approached, flattening screaming pups and scattering belching females in all directions, discretion became the better part of valour, and the young bull turned and wobbled back to the sea without a blow being exchanged. He would not, could not, win this fight. Peak breeding age for a bull is between nine and twelve, so at just seven, although already vast, he still had some growing to do. Remarkably, the average lifespan of these huge animals is just fourteen years – that's for the bulls; the cows live up to twenty-two. Somehow it feels as though such a big animal should live for longer?

We filmed some titanic battles between other more evenly-matched males. Fights are gory, but there is so much blubber they rarely seemed to end in really serious injury. Also, in fifteen minutes or so both fighters appear to be on the ropes, apparently exhausted, and probably overheating – an animal designed to survive in the freezing Antarctic waters will quickly overheat if it exerts itself out on land.

Once mated, the females slip back into the sea, abandoning their pups, who soon swim off themselves, guided toward feeding grounds by some miraculous internal GPS we still do not understand. By November the beach will be empty.

Mission accomplished, we set off on the *Golden Fleece* on the four-day trek back to the Falklands. The boat lurched and slid sickeningly over the heaving ocean. Jerome watched the weather map come out of the printer. It was covered in black circles. There were three discrete foci. He shook his head, fiddled with his ragged moustache, and looked quite concerned. 'Hmm…three storms. Maybe zey are coming together…'

'Is that bad, Jerome?'

'Well,' he said with grim satisfaction, 'if they do, it could be zee storm of the century.' It was properly frightening.

It got dark. Something occurred to me. 'Jerome, how will we avoid hitting icebergs in the dark on the way home?'

'Don't worry, Martin. I set zee radar. If there is a berg the alarm will be sounding. I stay on watch, OK?' I went to bed and fell into a fitful sleep.

Suddenly I jerked awake. Up on the bridge the radar alarm was sounding urgently: iceberg. Thank goodness Jerome was on hand to deal with it. The alarm continued.

Where the heck was he? *Beep-beep-beep.* I stumbled up the swaying ladder on to the bridge, which was lit by a dim green light. Peering out into the blackness ahead I could see nothing. The engine rumbled. *Beep-beep* went the alarm. Where was the iceberg? Dead ahead? Where was Jerome?

A sonorous breath made me turn. I hadn't seen him when I came up – the bloody Frenchman fast asleep on a little sofa, all snuggled up under a grimy blanket, apparently completely oblivious to the alarm. What to do? Wake him up? His opinion of me as a miserable coward would be confirmed, but then I probably couldn't fall much lower in his esteem anyway. I stretched out my hand to give him a shake, his moustaches trembling as he snored. No, I just couldn't do it. I spent ten minutes peering fruitlessly out into the Stygian gloom, occasionally looking at the eerie green sweep of the radar. Loads of dots – what did it mean? Jerome slept on. Hopelessly indecisive, I finally crept back to my cabin, the alarm still bleeping, resigned and fatalistic. On reflection, I'm certain Jerome knew exactly what he was doing – after all, how could he not, having survived so long in these wild waters? If there had been real danger he would have taken appropriate action, but to a simple TV producer none of this was particularly conducive to a good night's sleep.

When we got back to the Falklands we found gold-embossed cards waiting for us, inviting us to supper at the Governor's residence with the deputy governor and the heads of the armed forces. We washed and tidied ourselves as best we could, and went out for an absolutely delightful evening. The dinner was delicious – even special food for the vegetarians. As the port went around the conversation was lively. I realised I was very tired. My mind began to wander, out through the walls into the darkness, across the tussocky ground, past the moored-up *Golden Fleece*; the warm, cozy room and the sound of conversation left far behind. The wind began to howl as I raced across white-flecked waves and spumy sea, whipped up by yet another great storm. On and on in the dark, and then suddenly – *splash!* Underwater, down, down, down, until – there he was once more, the young bull, cruising along a kilometre down, lungs crushed, silent, calm, already 800 kilometres from South Georgia and, using instincts and navigation systems we may never understand, heading unerringly towards – where? He knew exactly where. He had not bred successfully this time, but he would be back.

3

THE INCONTINENT SOCIETY
OF MALLAIG

Autumnwatch, BBC2, 2006

In the annals of 'They said it couldn't be done', the live transmissions from the remote Scottish Island of Rum, for the BBC *Autumnwatch* programme in 2006, must rate pretty high.

First, a bit of background. Rum is a small diamond-shaped Island off the west coast of Scotland, about nine miles long and nine miles wide. There is one small village, Kinloch, which is home to the entire human population of around twenty hardy souls. Simply getting to the island is a bit hit-and-miss at the best of times: if the sea is too rough the ferry stays moored up in Mallaig harbour on the mainland.

To get enough equipment across to the island to transmit live television pictures would be a significant challenge. Usually, for a 'live OB' (outside broadcast) we roll up in a series of huge trucks needing hard standing, lavatories close at hand, location catering, masseuses – you get the picture. Inside the trucks is a mountain of electronic paraphernalia; on top are the great erectable satellite dishes needed to send images up into space and thence into our homes. There will be a sound-recording area, miles of cables coalescing into the camera truck, editing facilities, an entire mobile studio with feeds from cameras, vision mixers, directors, sound supervisors – all cocooned in warm air-conditioned comfort.

There was no 'hard standing' on Rum. There is a very small jetty which welcomes cyclists, walkers and small boats. You need special permission to take a car to Rum. And if you did get a car there, there's not really anywhere to drive it. The only proper road goes no further than the village. On my first recce, after a long, bumpy four-and-a-half mile drive by Land Rover down a crumbling dirt track, I discovered a small number of slightly lopsided wooden huts standing forlornly surrounded by a bog were where we would need to be. Not promising.

Why go to Rum? Sometimes it's helpful to write a list of the pros and cons. Let's see...

Pros

1. Every Autumn the red deer stags on Rum fight it out for the right to mate with the females (hinds). This is known as the rut, and is one of the most dramatic natural spectacles we have in the UK. When a pair of huge red deer stags close for battle, roaring and truly formidable, it's heart-stopping.

2. In 2006, by a miracle of cosmic coincidence, the peak of the red deer rut on Rum perfectly coincided with our two-week BBC2 *Autumnwatch* transmission.

   But here is the best bit...

3. The red deer on Rum have been continuously studied since 1957 – it's one of the longest-running mammalian studies in the world, and that made it a dream for TV, because the researchers on Rum, especially the brilliant Ali Morris, know every animal intimately. They know their mothers, fathers, grandparents; they know precisely how brave or cowardly

the stags are likely to be during the rut – who the serious contenders are going to be in any given year; they can also instantly recognise individual stags and hinds. (I never worked out how Ali did this – all the hinds looked exactly the same.) This meant Ali could sit with our cameramen, Pete and Jamie, and tell them exactly who was who and what they were likely to do. This sort of insight is extremely rare in natural history television and by enabling the producer (me) to know exactly who to concentrate on, gives an unprecedented opportunity to tell a really good story. By knowing their past performances – the brave ones, the cowards, the old guys, this year's young thrusters – it also allowed us to imbue the deer with genuine character.

So far all good, but…

Cons

1. There was absolutely no way we could land even one of our usual live OB pantechnicons. The jetty on Rum was way too small.

2. The deer rut on Rum mainly happens in quite a small area – the so called 'rutting greens' in Kilmory Bay, an expanse of lush grass near the sea with fabulous views across turquoise waters to the isle of Skye. But the 'rutting greens' are almost an hour away from Kinloch, down a really challenging dirt track. Even if we had been able to get our trucks on the island there was absolutely no way we could get them to where they needed to be.

3. There was nowhere obvious to house our team of cameramen, video editors, director, vision mixer, sound men, technical boffins, etc. The only buildings near the rutting greens were some huts that used to be a laundry, and a creaky, leaky barn.

Luckily we had a secret weapon. Step forward Mr John Roberts, our engineering manager, a man who doesn't know the meaning of the word 'impossible'. John is one of those glorious people you occasionally meet who say, 'The answer's yes – now what's the question?'

Er, well, John: the question is, can we actually transmit live TV from the red deer rutting greens on Rum for two weeks? It's almost completely inaccessible.

OK. Are there any buildings down at these greens?

Three wooden huts and a sort of barn.

Are they waterproof?

Bits of them probably are… Let's get a Land Rover and go and have a look.

He had taken the challenge.

Act One: The Set-Up

In a London warehouse, an eighteen-ton Outside Broadcast truck was parked forlornly. It was going nowhere. The satellite dish that used to sit proudly on its roof was gone. Inside was a scene of apparent devastation. Where there used to be rank upon rank of complex electronics there was now empty space. Disconnected wires hung limp from bare conduits. It had been disembowelled. The long hand, and flying spanners, of John Roberts had been at work. If the OB trucks themselves could not go to Rum, reckoned John, then perhaps their contents, taken to bits, could.

Hundreds of miles north, a long convoy of battered Land Rovers and makeshift trailers was bumping along a dirt road. Balanced precariously on the trailers was around £3 million-worth of delicate electronic equipment – an eye-wateringly expensive kit of parts, which, if correctly assembled, should allow

34

us to create live television. On top of one trailer was the satellite dish. It was an inspiring sight. Some of the road had been washed away by recent rain, and the convoy had to stop periodically to make running repairs. Electronics engineers with two brains and soft white hands were humping the biggest boulders they could manage across the tussocky bog and dropping them into water-filled holes in the road to allow the convoy to continue. Everyone was mucking in.

For ten months of the year male and female red deer – the stags and hinds – lead largely separate lives. The hinds live in one herd, and the stags in another. Most of the time, surprisingly – especially if you have ever witnessed the explosive violence of the rut – the stags are quite content to live side by side, completely at ease in one another's company. But then, in late summer, probably triggered by a change in the length of the day, the stags' testosterone levels begin to soar, in fact to over a thousand times the 'resting' level. Now they feed furiously and put on weight, their necks expand as the muscles become huge, their voices change to a deep-throated roar – even their urine changes consistency, taking on a characteristic rutting odour. To make themselves attractive to the hinds the stags find a damp spot in which to roll about and wallow, covering themselves in their own urine and ejaculate, and decorating their antlers with urine-soaked vegetation. Other stags, alongside whom they grazed peacefully just weeks before, now become their mortal enemies, to be attacked and impaled at any opportunity. Like half-crazed, pumped-up body builders, red deer stags arrive at the rut a boiling mass of hormonal fury.

From the stag's point of view the whole objective of the rut is to try and gather up a large group of hinds to whom he has exclusive access, by fighting off every other challenger. For the hind the objective is to mate with the best stag and, despite appearances, it is actually down to the hind as to who she chooses. As we were to discover, it's not always the obvious choice.

Trying to keep control of the group of hinds and fight off all-comers is utterly exhausting for the stags, who will not feed during the rut, and may lose up to 20 per cent of their body weight. The stags must try to be with the hinds every second of the day because, and here's the crucial fact, the hinds will only come into season for a matter of hours – just a few hours in the entire year. To have any chance of mating successfully the stag must be on hand at that time. If the hind wanders off during the few hours she's fertile he may lose his chance, and all the battling will count for nothing.

It makes me exhausted just thinking about it.

As John Roberts' team started to assemble the delicate kit of parts, we noticed some of the huts were covered in deep gouges and bits of shattered wood. Sometimes, explained Ali, the deer expert, the pumped-up stags will attack anything they find – wooden posts, particularly annoying tussocks of grass, buildings, possibly passing Outside Broadcast technicians – so we needed to be careful. Sure enough, assembly was halted a number of times and we all took cover when a stag wandered amongst us to see what we were up to, and if we were hiding any particularly attractive hinds. We hid inside the huts until he stopped bellowing and moved away.

The inside of the old barn was like a set from *Dr Who*, a weird mix of the old and new. Amongst old fishing nets, sacks and broken timber now flickered rows of glowing lights in stacked grey electronic assemblies. Just outside, held down with an assortment of rocks, the great satellite dish pointed up into space. 'I'd not linger too close to that if I were you,' said John Roberts. 'Not if you are still considering contributing to the human gene pool.'

'Sorry?'

'We're about to test the link to the satellite, and that's a fairly powerful microwave beam you're walking in front of.'

Hummm...click click...'A bit to the right...Back...hold it...That's it. We're connected to the satellite – we're in business, Martin.'

What actually happens to get a signal from somewhere like Rum, or indeed any of our *Springwatch* or *Autumnwatch* locations, is pretty unbelievable. You might have noticed there is a slight delay between the main studio and a remote reporter – you see it a lot on the news. The delay can be quite short or it can be painfully significant: if you watch *Springwatch* or *Autumnwatch* you'll notice we very rarely try to chat to a remote presenter – it's called a two-way – as the delay is hard to handle. You know how difficult it is if there's even a tiny delay on a phone call? It's like that, or worse.

The delay is because the signal from the 'remote' – in this case the rutting greens on a small island off the west coast of Scotland – goes up to a geostationary satellite in space. To be geostationary, i.e. rotating at exactly the same speed as planet Earth, the satellite must be high up in space. (Little known facts: the first geostationary satellite used for television broadcasting was the Relay 1 satellite, which broadcast television from the United States to Japan on 22 November 1963. This was soon followed by Syncom 3, launched in 1964 and used to transmit the summer Olympics that same year.) The satellite we used was 27,500 miles up, and the signal takes about 0.26 of a second to reach it and then get back to Earth. There is also a small processing delay of between 0.3 and 0.9 of a second. The signal then goes to BBC Television Centre, across to Network, to Distribution, to Network Transmission, from where the signal is sent to all the transmission masts around the country and then, finally, exhausted, into your telly. This means there can be up to a two-second delay from a remote outside broadcast. Actually, never mind the two-second delay: when you think about it, it's a miracle it gets there at all.

So we now had the capability to broadcast – but how about our stars, the red deer themselves? Would we have anything to show the great British public? It looked as if we might. Things were starting to hot up on the rutting greens: there were large groups of hinds and, one by one, roaring out their challenge from high points around us, magnificent stags had started to appear. From all over the island the big hitters were drawn inexorably to the rutting greens. The great gathering had begun.

Ali Donald took us through the contenders as each appeared. 'See him over there, the one with the really huge antlers? He's Clatter95, he's fourteen, too old to rut really, but he might have a go. And over there, the one with just one antler? He's Porcha97, he's really sneaky, and a serial killer – he's already killed two other stags. Now that magnificent one there, you have to keep an eye on him: he's one of our most successful stags ever – he's Tanya94…'

'Whoa, whoa – hang on, Ali. "Tanya94"? You can't call that great testosterone- fuelled powerhouse "Tanya"!'

Ali (testily): 'Why not? That's his name…'

The scientists on Rum name the stags after their mothers and the date they were born, hence Tanya94 – but I just couldn't see the *Autumnwatch* audience going along with this. A vast, majestic, all-too-obviously-male stag called Tanya? It would be confusing to have all the stags bearing apparently random female names – the scientists' naming system would require constant explanation. We needed to give them individual names that were instantly memorable, and perhaps more redolent of majesty and combat.

After some slightly tense discussion Ali, against all her academic principles, relented. We went Roman-stroke-gladiatorial: Tanya94 became Caesar, Clatter95 became Maximus, and the strange-looking single-antlered killer stag Porcha became Brutus.

Interestingly, the hinds are named in the same way, after their mothers, until they gave birth for the first time, normally at the age of three, when they get their own name – to pass on to their calves. These names followed themes: one year it was Indian currys, so Masala, Jeera and Tikka; another year, cheeses – Mozzarella, Cheddar, Gorgonzola, etc. The human population of Rum, all twenty-two of them, were invited to offer their own suggestions for each year's deer-naming theme.

Act Two: The First Week of Transmission

There were twenty of us in the *Autumnwatch* team on Rum, doubling the population of the island at a stroke. Some of us were billeted out in the homes of the islanders, and some of us were staying in Kinloch castle. Yes, there's a castle on Rum.

In 1888 a textile tycoon from Lancashire, John Bullough, bought the island of Rum for £35,000. In 1891 his son George inherited the island, and began a series of modest improvements. First, with the help of 300 imported workmen, and stone brought over from Annan, he built a castle which cost £250,000, a not-insignificant sum in 1900, and equivalent to well over £25 million today. Kinloch castle had its own electricity supply, air-conditioning, a telephone system, and a ballroom laid out in a rather curious way so that the band, hidden behind high windows, couldn't see what the dancers were getting up to. Oh, and for after the dance, a Jacuzzi. Having sorted out the accommodation, young George turned his attention outside. Boatload after boatload of topsoil was imported from Ayrshire to build the nine-hole golf course, the Japanese garden, the water gardens, the walled garden, and hothouses in which he grew figs, peaches, nectarines and grapes. If you went inside the hothouse for a peach you were in for a surprise, because you would find hummingbirds and birds of paradise flitting hither and thither, imported to brighten the place up. He had heated ponds built and populated them with turtles…and alligators. To look after the grounds he employed fourteen under-gardeners, paying them all a little extra to wear Bullough tweed kilts for that authentic Scottish look. Smokers were paid an extra twopence a day to help fend off the notorious Rum midges. George only visited his castle in the shooting season. One memorable year the alligators escaped, and a shooting party was got up to dispatch them.

As I sat up in bed at 1 a.m., typing out the script for the first day's show, I wondered what had happened to all this opulence? The castle, in which I was staying, was slowly falling down: the gardens and Jacuzzi were long gone, and all that seemed to remain from that wild spending spree were some stuffed and faded hummingbirds, a last reminder of the long-lost hothouses.

I had worked out a system for telling the unfolding story of the red deer rut. Every evening I would buttonhole Pete and Jamie, the wildlife cameramen, who had been out filming all day, and get their report on what had happened. Then I would go to my room and write a script pulling it all together. This would generally take me until around 1 or 2 a.m., at which point I would nod off, only to wake with a start and discover I had typed the letter 'd' some 800 times. At 8 the next morning I would run through my script with Simon King, the presenter, and then, while he went off to put his own stamp on it, I would have a second meeting to perform the story for the director, live cameramen and vision mixers, so we all knew what we were trying to achieve. I don't think I have ever in my life worked so hard for such a sustained period. But it was worth it, because the unfolding story was a cracker.

Who were going to be the key characters? Ali had told us to watch out in particular for the stag called Caesar. Caesar had first appeared back in 2000, and had successfully rutted every year since then. In 2004 he'd sired eight calves; last year, in 2005, he'd sired nine. Caesar was a perfect blend of fighter and gentleman, and the hinds loved him. Clearly, here was an obvious contender for this year's 'King of the Greens'. But though Caesar, Maximus and the serial killer Brutus were already on or near the greens, there was an exciting development. There was a new kid on the block.

This new stag was not particularly big, but exuded confidence and power. Ali knew nothing about him, which was not surprising, as there are well over a thousand deer roaming across the forty square miles on Rum, and she can only follow the deer living in her study area. The stag with no name had to have a name, so, because she generally gave unknown stags names with five letters, Ali called him Percy. This didn't fit with our Roman-gladiator theme at all, but somehow the name stuck. Percy came amongst the rut like an avenging angel, hurling all others to one side. In one memorable battle he literally lifted his opponent up off the ground and threw him into a river with a mighty splash. Percy was spectacular.

Ali could not be certain, but she estimated Percy was ten years old. Red deer stags will join the rut aged five or six, but have little chance of success until they are nine or ten. At the other end of the age spectrum, few stags are likely to have a successful rut beyond the age of twelve. Caesar, for all his impeccable track record, was now twelve, so he was getting on. How would he compete with this formidable newcomer?

For red deer, fighting is a dangerous business. The point of an antler, driven home by perhaps 200 kilograms of furious muscle, can easily rip open an exposed flank, or even drill directly through an opponent's skull into the brain. In fact, given the weapons they wield, and the stag's hormonal state, it's perhaps surprising the greens aren't littered with dead and dying stags. If it were a general free-for-all that would probably be the case, but nature has come up with a way of averting total devastation. There are rules in the rut, to which all adhere. Encounters between stags go through a number of clearly defined stages, each escalating the threat another notch, up to the point where they actually engage in battle.

First, there is roaring. The soundtrack to the rut is the more or less constant roaring of the stags. Research has shown that the quality of the roar is directly proportional to the size of the stag's chest and its overall health, and therefore a very good measure of just how fit and strong it is. The frequency is a measure of its stamina. Both the hinds and the other stags tune in and from it get a clear indication of a stag's fitness. Often the roar alone is enough to put off a possible challenger (as well as draw in misty-eyed hinds). If roaring doesn't clarify the situation, they will move on to stage two. Now the stags 'parallel-walk' – pacing along-side, almost close enough to touch, watching each other from the corner of their eyes, carefully assessing the other's prowess. Again, this is often enough for one stag to realise the other is too strong for him and back off. But! – if neither the roaring nor the parallel-walking establishes a clear winner, and if both stags still feel evenly matched, parallel-walking will turn, in the blink of an eye, into full-blooded battle. Any serious contenders in the rut must be willing to engage in battle in an instant: battle that may cost them their lives.

During our first week the clash of the titans took place, and we held our collective breaths as Percy and Caesar joined battle. Despite the older stag's experience it was Percy who had emerged victorious. He seemed unstoppable. Along with Caesar, Percy had seen off Maximus and a host of lesser contenders. He was also quite a gentleman with the ladies, a thing we noticed they seemed to appreciate. But Percy had not yet locked antlers with Brutus – and we hoped he'd never have to, because it was not actually possible to lock antlers with Brutus. Brutus only had one antler, and that made him exceptionally dangerous.

Since the spring the stags would have been re-growing new antlers, having shed the old ones in winter. It's an astonishing bit of biology. In a few months each stag will grow a massive pair of multi-branched weapons weighing up to 20 kilograms. Antlers can grow up to an inch a day. The growing antlers are covered in vascular 'velvet', which provides the nutrients for this extraordinarily rapid growth. At the start of September growth is complete, the velvet dries and is rubbed off, and the new antlers emerge, gleaming and dangerous. The exact shape of the antlers is unique to each individual, and they grow into this same shape every year. Deer hunters name stags depending on the number of 'points' they have on their antlers. Six points per antler (a total of twelve) makes the stag a Royal; seven an Imperial, and eight points per antler is a Monarch.

The branching of the antlers makes them look superb, but it's also a sort of safety mechanism. As the combatants whip around and engage, their branched antlers lock together. So long as they are head to head they cannot stab one another, and the fight becomes a titanic wrestling match. But if one stumbles, or turns away to flee, then the points of the antlers may be driven home with fatal effect. The reason we didn't want Percy to meet Brutus was because, with only a single antler, Brutus could not properly engage. Unable to lock together with his opponent, his one antler would slide right through and into the body. That was why Brutus – not in fact a particularly powerful or impressive animal – had managed to kill two other stags.

By now we all loved Percy (so much for scientific detachment), and hoped he would not be injured by a close encounter with Brutus. They hadn't met yet, but we still had a week to go.

Act Three: The Second and Last Week of Transmission

Well, the very thing we hoped would not happen, did happen. Brutus, the serial killer, and Percy, our hero, did meet in battle – but with unforeseen results.

We had reassembled after the weekend to discover a very happy island: our satellite technicians, the remarkable Mike 'Two Brains' Bass and Chris Cobb, had spent it sorting out the satellite televisions for, it appeared, the entire island, and now had a lifetime invitation to return at any time to enjoy the finest hospitality the islanders could offer. On Sunday night, back in the castle, cameraman Jamie was bursting with news: 'It's happened! It's happened! Percy and Brutus fought!'

My heart sank. 'Is Percy OK?'

'Well, it was a close thing, but, yes, he's fine – but Ali says his rut is over.'

What had happened? So far Percy had been the undoubted King of the Greens: he'd beaten off all comers and had amassed a huge harem of hinds. We'd seen him mate successfully on a number of occasions too: it was shaping up to be his year – until the moment Brutus appeared.

They roared, they parallel-walked, exactly as per the red deer rule book, and then engaged. There was a short period of pushing and shoving and then, suddenly, unbelievably, Percy, who up to that point had looked invincible, backed off, turned tail and ran away. It seemed impossible – Percy was much bigger, much more powerful than sneaky old Brutus!

It was only when we ran the film in slow motion that we could see what had actually happened. As they went head to head, one point of Brutus's antler had slid right past Percy's and started to drive in toward his skull. It was the same deadly thrust that had already killed two other stags, but because at that moment Percy was retreating, the point of Brutus's antler had not struck home with his full weight behind it. In slow motion you could see Percy wince: he had felt the point begin its deadly work. It had been an extremely close call. We'd been filming Percy for the past two weeks, and this was the first time we'd seen him back off any battle – the first and the last, at least for this year, because Percy had been deposed.

At first sight, losing your crown looks bad, but in reality it might have been the very best thing that could have happened to Percy. The winters on Rum are harsh, and it's essential that after the rut the exhausted combatants have time to build themselves back up again. It might be tempting for a stag to go on and on, but the longer they go on rutting, the less time there is to feed and prepare themselves for winter. Percy had been successful, we'd seen him mate many times, and by leaving now he would have time to recover. Better to leave uninjured and come back next year to rut once more.

So who would inherit Percy's crown and his hinds, many of whom had yet to come into season? Hang on! Who's this in the wings? None other than that wily old gentleman, Caesar. With hardly a bellow, Caesar saw off Brutus, and suddenly the old master was back in charge. Caesar was obviously a highly desirable mate for the hinds.

In this last week we witnessed a fascinating but shameful scene. Yosemite, an attractive young hind, was in the harem of a handsome young stag called Flash. It seemed a marriage made in heaven: two young deer coming together in the prime of life. But then, when Flash's back was turned, dealing with another domestic matter, we witnessed Yosemite wander off casually. The wander became quite purposeful: behind a wall, across a strip of grass, directly towards...Caesar – with whom she immediately stood and mated. With red deer, mating is all over in seconds: one mighty thrust is all it takes. Yosemite then tidied herself up, trotted back across the grassy strip, back behind the wall, and was once more feeding with Flash before he realised she was gone. Subsequent genetic analysis confirmed that Yosemite's calf was indeed fathered by Caesar. Shocking, really. So all this talk of harems, and the stags controlling the hinds, is nonsense. It's the hinds who make the final decision. After all, if they don't stand still – if they take even one pace forward at the crucial moment – the poor old stag is left looking awfully silly. Yosemite's obviously calculated cuckolding gave the men on the team pause for thought. It was our last night of transmission, and time to sum up. Who had been the top stag at this year's rut? When we added it up, in terms of matings we had actually observed, it turned out Percy and Caesar were neck and neck. As a decider, and by popular consent, because Percy had beaten Caesar in their only encounter, the award of King of the Greens 2006 went to Percy.

However, when the scientists did their proper genetic analysis it was a different story. By the end of their lives Percy had fathered twenty-nine calves, but Caesar turned out to be the most successful stag ever known on Rum, with forty-eight calves to his credit.

By the end of *Autumnwatch 2006* the nation had taken Percy, Caesar et al to their hearts. A few months later, our characters even got name-checked in the Scottish Parliament, during a debate called to try to stop a proposed cull of the deer on Rum, so I like to think our work may have contributed, in some small way, to the conservation of these magnificent red deer.

After the last transmission the weather turned nasty. For a while we thought we might be stranded, but an awfully nice man called Lachie said he could whisk us back to the mainland on his speedboat. It was quite an exposed sort of craft: you stood up and grasped a metal bar to absorb the bumps, and stop yourself being swept overboard. It was raining, too.

'Er, Mr Lachie...'

'Aye, it's just Lachie, Mar'n.'

'Won't we get most awfully wet going back?'

'No, no, no – I've got fully waterproof suits for the lot of ye.'

We all put on the orange immersion suits over our clothes. Then we took our places and hung on.

The instant we rounded the small jetty we each received around a gallon of salt water in our faces. It was immediately apparent that Lachie had been, well, not exactly lying, but definitely optimistic in calling his suits 'waterproof'. They were anything but. In seconds I had the ghastly feeling of ice-cold seawater penetrating my pants. I could see, through the blinding spray, others were enjoying the same experience. It was an agonising trip.

Back on the mainland, shivering on the harbour wall at Mallaig, we gingerly stripped off the 'waterproof' suits so that Lachie could go back for the next group of victims.

'Just look at you,' said John Roberts, surveying the great patches of icy wetness at our groins. 'The Incontinent Society of Mallaig!'

4

VAMPIRES!

Nightmares of Nature, first transmitted on

BBC1, 28 September 1995

'Wow – look at this! 308 people have been attacked by vampire bats in Brazil. What a story!'

'Hey, that would be perfect for your film, Martin. Do you think you could film a reconstruction of a vampire bat attack?'

'Yes, of course, I'm sure I could, no problem. Can I see the article?'

What on earth was I thinking?

In 1994 I was busy working on a series called *Nightmares of Nature* for BBC1. Back then, 'reconstructions' were all the rage, and in the series we staged real-life incidents involving humans and animals: people who had been attacked by crocodiles, (see the Val Plumwood story in chapter 8), survived shark attacks and been bitten by huge spiders – you can imagine the sort of thing. One of my programmes was called 'A Cry in the Dark', all about scary nocturnal animals, so a mass vampire bat attack would be a great reconstruction, if I could do it. But how?

Being a vampire bat is not easy. You have to get a meal of blood pretty much every day – certainly every other day – or else you starve. Living on nothing but blood is a highly specialised way of life, and vampire bats have adapted in some extraordinary ways to enable them to be vampires. For example, if a bat returns to the colony (which may number hundreds of individuals) having failed to feed, it will beg a meal from one of the others, who will generally regurgitate and share a small amount of blood. It's a sensible plan – after all, tomorrow night the tables might be turned. Vampire bats are unusually sociable in other ways too: they are the only bat species in the world known to adopt other baby bats if the mother is killed. Some of those specializations would turn out to make filming them remarkably difficult.

On *Nightmares* we always tried to let the victims narrate their own stories: it added authenticity, and gave you permission, as a viewer, to enjoy the reconstructions because, however awful things got, you knew everything would be OK in the end. So the first task was to find out exactly what had happened in Brazil. My co-producer Mary Colwell jumped on a plane and headed for the small village of Apora where the attacks had taken place. With a very helpful fixer she spent the best part of a day driving from Salvador to the village, stopping along the way to leave an envelope stuffed with cash in a nearby phone box. Apparently they had broken a little-known law, punishable with a substantial fine, but not payable directly to the policemen who had stopped them. It had to be left, er, over there in that phone box, and then you must drive off and not look back. Such are the esoteric joys of filming abroad.

Once at Apora, they found the small two-roomed house of Ivite Brito, who invited them in, and told Mary her story.

It had been a hot, airless night in June. Ivite was having a dream. In the dream her baby was crying, and she woke with a start to find that that part of her dream was true – the baby was indeed crying in the room next door. She threw off her sheet and, because there was no electricity, reached around in the dark for matches and the candle she kept beside the bed. The baby was really crying now so, cradling the candle she went into the other room. Strange: what a lot of mice there seemed to be scuttling around on the floor? It was hard to see them properly in the flickering light of the candle. Was that one in the cot, too? Ivite brought the candle close to the cot, and it jumped out. Now her candle was close to the bedclothes she could see both baby and bedclothes were covered in stains…What was it? Bringing the candle right down to the baby she saw, to her horror, the stains were red. It was blood. Had the baby cut herself on the cot? Ivite got a cloth and gently wiped the blood away as best she could. After a cuddle the little girl seemed comforted, and Ivite went back to her bed. But the baby continued to cry and grizzle on and off for the rest of the night.

It wasn't until the morning that Ivite saw the full extent of the injuries. Her baby had peculiar cuts on her legs, her arms, her nose, and even on the top of her head: small, regular cuts. Ivite had never seen anything like it – what could possibly have done this? She took her daughter to the doctors who, after careful examination, told her the baby had been attacked by vampire bats.

Over the next few weeks a total of 308 people in Apora were attacked in the same way, at night, usually on the lower limbs. Often the victims felt nothing during the night, but found the cuts continued to bleed for a long time after they woke. After a few weeks, as abruptly as they had begun, the attacks ended.

What happened in Apora was one of the most sustained attacks by vampire bats on humans that has ever been recorded. Most of the victims made a full recovery, but unfortunately three of them died from rabies, passed on by the bats.

Why had this happened?

No one is absolutely sure, but, just before the attacks started, there had been a big cattle round-up, and the animals were moved away. Since the bats could not find their usual hosts – the cattle – and were thus threatened with starvation, it seems they had turned their attention to the only other large mammals they could find: the human inhabitants of Apora.

But, here's an interesting question: why did Ivite think the animals in the baby's room were mice? Surely she would have seen the bats flying? Well, no – once again, vampire bats are not as other bats. Uniquely, they have developed powerful front limbs as part of their wings, to help them creep up on their prey. The bat will land some distance away from its victim – a sleeping cow for instance – then carefully close in, walking gently and precisely until it reaches its target. If it just flew right in and crash-landed on its intended victim the cow would certainly wake up, but by creeping in stealthily on its fore limbs the vampire bat remains unnoticed. Actually, a walking vampire bat is quite a spooky sight. The fore limbs are powerful but a little stilt-like, and the bat scuttles along jerkily, then stops, flicking its head around, mouth slightly open, as it uses an array of senses to find its prey. Using these front limbs vampire bats can also run, bounding along the ground surprisingly fast. When running they do look very like mice, especially in flickering candlelight. Personally, I love vampire bats, but, given their creepy appearance and the lurid folklore that surrounds them, they could do with a PR makeover.

But why hadn't the bats taken off when Ivite came in and disturbed them? Because then it would have been obvious what they were. There was a good reason for this too. A full meal for a vampire bat is around twenty grams of blood, yet the bat only weighs forty grams – so once it has drunk its fill it has become far too heavy to take off – just as you or I would find it hard going for a run if we took on half our total body weight in a single sitting. So vampire bats start to concentrate the blood they have drunk by absorbing the watery plasma through their stomach, transporting it to their kidneys and urinating, dumping the excess fluid as fast as they can until they are light enough to take off. A full feed takes around twenty minutes, but they start to urinate within two minutes of starting to drink. The actual take-off is helped by their powerful fore limbs, which allow them to leap off the ground into the air.

It is thought the urine they leave behind may also act as a scent marker, allowing the bat to return to a good food source – a cattle shed, for instance – night after night. Anyhow, the reason Ivite did not see the bats take off was because they couldn't: they were so laden with blood they were unable to fly, so they had no option but to scurry about – like mice.

While Mary was with Ivite she carefully filmed her both cooking supper and working around the house, to set the story up. She also filmed the room where the attack happened, and photographed its key features: the shuttered windows, the baby's cot, and for an agreed sum bought the baby's bedclothes from Ivite. She bought other bits of authentic Apora bric-a-brac, too, including a small oil lamp which, all these years later, I still have. All of this would be crucial in reconstructing the incident back in the UK. They only had one day to do this, and in the end, Mary tells me, Ivite was quite pleased to see them go, as she wanted to finish cooking for herself and the child – now an energetic three-year-old – before it got completely dark.

Thanks to Mary we now had an accurate account of Ivite's story, with which we could tell the whole drama of the Apora vampire bat attack.

In theory.

Because – how on earth was I going to film vampire bats drinking a baby's blood?

The first thing to do in any reconstruction like this is to draw a careful storyboard, shot by shot, just like a cartoon, of how you imagine the entire sequence unfolding: bats creeping around windows, pretty babies sleeping in cots, bats crawling along the bedclothes, culminating in the final shot – the significantly tricky one – a close-up of the vampire bat drinking the unfortunate baby's blood, all brilliant crimson, gleaming wetly on the bat's flicking tongue. It looked pretty good on paper.

Thanks to Mary I could already tick off some of the shots on my storyboard: Ivite's house; Ivite cooking; exteriors of the house. We now had all the reference we needed to create the cot, a perfect match for the real one in Brazil. Based on Mary's film and photographs, we could accurately replicate the room in Apora. We even had the actual bedding. Now I needed to find a sacrificial baby…This bit was not too difficult. We found a baby and helpful mum, popped the baby in the cot, and filmed it both asleep and wriggling around. Of course, the baby and the vampire bats would never actually meet, but it takes fairly elementary film-making to make it look as though they did. We filmed close-ups of the baby's limbs just sticking out of the bedclothes, irresistible to a passing vampire bat, and suddenly another section of my storyboard was in the bag. Now it was time for the artifice. If we managed to get a vampire bat walking, and especially feeding on blood in the cot, the particular spot subtly hidden by a fold in the cloth, anyone would believe that bat and baby were together, and the bat was drinking the baby's blood…

So now, finally, I came to the really difficult bit. How would we film the bats?

There seemed to be three possible ways forward:

1. Go back to South America, somewhere where there were known to be vampire bats, and set up some sort of attractive decoy for them.

2. Use specially commissioned model bats, and film them in subtle low light.

3. Find a captive colony of vampire bats that we could control, up to a point, to get the shots I needed, and especially the killer shot: bats feeding on blood.

Option one was far too uncertain and prohibitively expensive. Models? Let's face it, whatever we did would probably look really naff. The third seemed the best option, but where could we find such stunt vampire bats?

Believe it or not, pretty soon we found them. To my immense surprise, it turned out there was a thriving colony in Germany. They were in the Zoological Institute at the University of Bonn. I got on the phone. 'Hello, Professor Schmidt, my name is Martin Hughes-Games from the BBC. I believe you have a colony of vampire bats?"

'*Ja! Ja*, of course.'

'Er, professor, do you think, for a suitable fee, we might be able to come and film your bats?'

'Why, yes – why not?'

Did he think we could film the bats' fascinating method of locomotion using their fore limbs? Yes, indeed. He had the perfect bat for this work: an older female, a favourite of his.

Could we film the bats feeding?

'But of course! They are feeding every day in the laboratory.'

And, um, finally: did he think we might film them walking about in…in a baby's cot?

Long pause. Much more wary: 'Why? What sort of film is this?'

Here I had to tread very carefully. Professor Schmidt was very passionate about his vampire bats, and had to be convinced the film would not portray them in an unflattering light. I'm not sure how I managed it, but I did, and soon we were on a plane heading for Bonn, complete with cot, sheets, windows and a big box of Brazilian bric-a-brac.

You know, it wasn't until I started to write this chapter that I got to wondering: what exactly was a colony of vampire bats doing in Germany? At the time I was so focused on getting the story I didn't stop to think. The professor has now retired, but I tracked him down and asked if he could throw any light on the history of the colony. This was his response to my first email:

> In 1969 I was working for the FAO (Food and Agriculture
> Organisation of the UN) in Mexico about rabies transmission
> by vampire bats and about their ecology. When I returned to
> Germany at the beginning of 1970 I took about thirty vampire
> bats with me and established a colony at the Zoological Institute
> in Bonn.

Easy! Now Professor Schmidt could undertake some ground-breaking research in the comfort of his lab. Which is exactly what he did. The email went on:

> The bat colony developed very well and by offsprings, and about
> a dozen vampires from Colombia, the colony grew up to about
> sixty individuals.

But how on earth do you transport thirty vampire bats from Mexico to Germany? How do you feed sixty vampire bats? The professor's reply threw up so many more questions I had to email him once more and, after a few days, this was his response:

> To keep vampire bats is quite easy. You must feed them every night with defibrinated blood [defibrinated blood does not clot], regulate the temperature carefully (between 23° and 25° C), and control the social composition of the colony. I myself or one of my students went every two weeks to the slaughterhouse and sampled two buckets of cattle blood, that had to be defibrinated by beating the fresh blood. The blood was deep-frozen in daily portions. Every evening the vampires got the blood (20 ml per individual) in small bottles (normally used for the water supply for birds).
>
> To transport the bats from Mexico I built a box that had individual compartments for every bat. Of course, the vampires had to be fed shortly before departure. And as I was able to transport the bat cage in the cabin of the airplane, there was no problem with the temperature.
>
> Please excuse the many mistakes, but since my retirement I practice English very seldom.

I badly wanted to know more about the business of beating the fresh blood, and whether the other passengers on the plane, as they nodded off, heads thrown back and jugulars throbbing enticingly above their collars, knew what they were sharing the warm cabin with, but we will never know; I thought I had bothered the Professor enough. Clearly, he and his students knew what they were doing, as the colony had bred successfully and was still doing fine when Professor Schmidt retired in 2004, thirty-four years after he set it up. Apparently some of the descendants of the original Mexican vampire bats are still having their daily blood from modified bird-drinkers in Berlin Zoo.

So, now we come to the critical bit. Having read many of Professor Schmidt's research papers I now realise why it turned out to be so difficult.

The professor had been so convincing about the ease of filming that we had not come with much actual film – this was in the days of 16 mm film which came in rolls, each of which only lasted ten minutes, so you had to be pretty disciplined. But the way he had talked I thought it was going to be a doddle. Idiot!

We set up the filming with the help of the professor's assistant, Anya, a full-on Goth with black leather clothes, massive black boots and heavy black make-up including black lipstick. Despite her intimidating appearance Anya turned out to be our saviour.

OK: first shot off my storyboard, the bats creeping in through the shutters of the window. Using the reference from Brazil we had made a perfect replica. The bats were carefully placed behind the window, I said, 'Turnover' to Richard the cameraman, the camera ran, and sure enough the bats crept through. Tick. A great start.

Now, bats walking along in the cot. We set up the cot, the bedclothes and the dummy baby. Richard lit it beautifully, and we then brought on the bat. This was the professor's favourite – 'She is twenty-one years old,' he said in an admiring voice. Which was actually older than my researcher on the programme. 'She is a very good bat.' But the professor's affection for the bat, it transpired, was not reciprocated. As he put his hand down to urge her along the cot…'*Verdammt! Gott im Himmel!*' she nailed him.

A very neat divot was missing from his palm. Blood flowed freely around our set, adding verisimilitude. Vampire bats have remarkable teeth, unlike any other bat species. The upper and lower front teeth overlap. The teeth lack hard enamel and so, as the upper and lower teeth slide over one another, they self-sharpen. This means vampire bats' teeth are always phenomenally sharp – as the professor had just discovered.

A vampire bat will remove a very exact amount of flesh as it bites: precisely 7 mm long and 8 mm deep. Also – as you might expect – the saliva contains anti-coagulants and chemicals that stop cut blood vessels constricting, as they would normally do: this ensures the blood continues to flow freely after the first incision has been made. As the professor did his best to stem the flow we could see this system worked remarkably well.

Something was distracting the bat. She stood on her strange-looking fore limbs, twitching her head from side to side. Whatever she was sensing was putting her off walking. The camera ran, using up precious minutes of film, but still she did not walk. Eventually she must have acclimatised, because she did start to walk up the cot, investigating the bedclothes as she came – it really is a spooky thing to watch: the jerky walk, the hungry-looking sensing, involving flicking the head from side to side…We'd used an awful lot of film, but another key series of shots could be ticked on my storyboard.

Just one more shot to go: the close-up of her feeding on blood. Now, I knew she had to feed every day, so I assumed she would probably be fairly hungry. I rather fancied discovering for myself what it would feel like to be bitten by a vampire. All I had to do was carefully place the sacrificial finger near the bat where the baby's arm or leg might be, but hidden by the bedclothes. Thinking myself rather brave, I offered my finger as bait.

Would she bite? Would she fairy cakes. Not a glimmer of interest. She did look; she came close; but nothing more. What was going on?

At the time I didn't know, but having since read about Professor Schmidt's research I think I do now. Vampire bats have one quite exceptional and unique sense. Nerves in their brains which usually detect heat have subtly evolved, so that the temperature range they detect has decreased to around 30°c, the temperature of warm blood. The nerves have also become immensely more sensitive, making vampire bats unique among all the mammals on earth in having a highly sophisticated heat-sensing system. It is so sensitive that, to a vampire bat, a cow or human in the dark must appear to be a fantastic network of warm blood vessels, like some sort of glowing web. Using this sense the bat can decide where to make its 7 mm by 8 mm incision, ensuring it bites where the blood vessels are closest to the surface of the skin, and exactly where the blood will flow freely. How curious we must appear to a bat in the dark using its heat sense: a glowing network of fine lines. I think my pudgy finger, the skin callused and thickened by years of climbing, simply had the blood vessels buried too deep for the bat to bother.

At the time, however, it was just clear that the bat wouldn't bite me. Time for a re-think. The solution was obvious, of course, if we ignored my vanity in offering myself as bait. The bats were used to drinking out of the professor's small bird-drinkers – surely we could make up a secure stand and hide a blood-filled drinker in the bedclothes? If we showed a shot of the baby's leg sticking out of the bedclothes, immediately followed by a close-up of the bat drinking blood from the hidden drinker, the audience would be convinced they had seen the bat drinking the baby's blood. We were nearly there.

'Martin,' said Richard the cameraman. 'I don't want to worry you. We've only got 150 feet of film left.'

This was very serious. My initial over-confidence about how easy this would be to film had finally caught up with us. It had proved far more tricky, and we had used a lot of film. A full roll of 400 feet in the 16 mm camera we were using only lasts ten minutes – so 150 feet is under four minutes. And we still did not have the most important shot of all.

It was going to be close.

We set up the drinker and blood. Richard set up the shot – tweaked the lights.

'OK, I'm ready.'

The bat was gently placed on the cot. It walked purposefully towards the hidden blood. The camera ran…The bat continued…Still the film ran…The bat stopped. The film ran some more…The bat looked around, its face twitching. The film ran…

Again something was wrong.

'Cut! Cut!' I hissed. 'Cut.'

'100 foot,' said Richard. The bat was still.

Suddenly Anya the Goth said, 'It can hear us! It will not feed with all this noise of all of you.'

'But we weren't making any noise!' I was slightly aggrieved.

'No, no – it is the breathing. She can hear too much.'

Anya was absolutely right. Bats have highly specialised neurons that are exceptionally sensitive to the sounds of breathing – yet another very useful adaptation for closing in on their prey in the dark.

Impasse.

We couldn't hold our breaths until the blasted bat decided the coast was clear and started to drink.

'Music!' said Anya. '*Ja* – loud music! Then she cannot hear nothing else.'

And so it was to the accompaniment of Anya's shatteringly loud German death metal reverberating throughout the laboratory in the Institute for Zoology that the twenty-one-year-old vampire bat, now deaf to our breathing, crept up on the bedclothes and, after a short pause, at last, her tongue gleamed crimson as it flicked in and out. The camera rolled. The vampire bat was feeding, to all appearances, on the baby's blood.

There was a clacking noise. 'I'm out, said Richard. 'The magazine is empty.'

We had got our final shot.

5

THE HUNT FOR 'JAWS'

Incredible Animal Journeys,

transmitted on BBC1, 22 October 2006

'You keep your hands where the guerrillas can see them. No sudden movements; all smiles; very calm; nobody gets out of the car. If they ask you, we do what we are told, but without invitation we do not move.'

We'd already been held up by armed police in the USA, drenched and battered by a hurricane, slept the night in a bus stranded on a garage forecourt, and now, in Colombia, it seemed we were about to be kidnapped by the bloody FARC.

How did we ever get involved in all this?

It was all because of three young ospreys.

Many months earlier some idle office chat back at the BBC Natural History Unit had gone something like this…'Hey – do you think it would be possible to make a series where humans try to travel alongside migrating animals? You know – actually do the journey with them, to find out what they go through?'

'Maybe…You'd have to put satellite trackers on them to know where they were at any point. But – how would you know when to go? You can't just hang around with a film crew waiting for a whale or a caribou herd to set off – it would cost a fortune.'

'Yes, but if you had a good idea when they might go – from a scientist that had been studying them, say – it could work? What animals would you try to migrate with?'

'Well…Grey whales? Caribou? Birds, um…How about ospreys?'

'Yes, ospreys would be great. They do enormous migrations, don't they? Let me look it up…'

Thus was born the idea for the series *Incredible Animal Journeys*. Take a presenter and an adventurous film crew, and literally migrate with the animals, experiencing all the trials and tribulations of the journey for yourself. It had never been done before. The reason soon became obvious: it was almost impossibly difficult.

We started with ospreys.

The osprey is a large bird of prey, weighing in at around four and a half pounds, with a wingspan of very nearly six feet. Ospreys have a white breast and dark grey-black wings. Their face is split by a black 'Mask of Zorro' stripe, accentuating a pair of piercing gold eyes, all of which combine to give them a remarkably fierce appearance. They are specialist fish eaters. Ospreys nest in spring right across Northern Europe, then, almost as soon as they can fly, the youngsters embark on an immense migration south to Africa. American and Canadian ospreys hatch in spring, and they too head way down south for the winter. On their very first migration these young ospreys, with no previous training or experience, will fly thousands of miles to reach their final destination. How they do it is still a complete mystery.

We decided to try to travel with three American ospreys.

Ring-ring, ring-ring: click. 'Hello? Oh, hi Rob – how's it going?'

'Good news. We got all three satellite trackers on the chicks. We're good to go.'

We'd found our scientist for this journey. Rob Bierregaard has been studying ospreys practically all his life. Choosing his moment with knowledge born of nearly fifty years in the field, Rob had climbed up to three different osprey nests, selected a chick, and fitted each with a satellite tracker. These lightweight solar-powered trackers – an eye-watering £3,000 a pop – are worn like a small rucksack: two thin Teflon ribbons fit snugly around the osprey's body and are sewn together across the chest to secure the device on the bird's back. You need a licence to do this, and the weight, and the way the tracker is fitted, are strictly controlled by the licensing authority, to ensure they don't interfere with the bird's survival in any way.

Once the trackers were on we could, in theory, follow the chicks' every move, essential if we were genuinely going to go with them. Rob named the chicks Tasha, Bunga and Jaws – Jaws because he'd bitten Rob badly while he'd been trying to fit the tracker.

Where exactly were Tasha, Bunga and Jaws going to go? We couldn't be certain. They would fly right down the eastern seaboard of the USA for sure. Some migrating ospreys then stop in the Florida Keys, but others keep going south – Cuba? Maybe, perhaps further. Wherever – whatever – we were going with them.

The transmissions from the satellite trackers fitted to the birds were sent directly to Rob at his base in Charlotte, North Carolina. Rob would then pass them on to us – so our phone calls to him would control our every move throughout the migration.

To get us off the starting blocks we were waiting on a call from Rob to tell us when to come to the USA and set the whole operation in motion.

'Hi there. I think the chicks are showing *Zugunruhe*, Martin.'

'Oh...really? Yeah – *Zugunruhe*, is it? Er – does that mean we need to come over now?'

'It sure does.'

Zugunruhe? Another of those fascinating biological terms – German because it so perfectly describes the behaviour. *Zug*, to move or migrate, and *Unruhe*, meaning anxiety or restlessness. So when a migratory animal is getting close to actually going, it may show *Zugunruhe* or 'migratory restlessness'.

The young ospreys we were about to try and follow would already have had a pretty tough start in life. First, the eggs (generally two or three) don't all hatch together. This is a sort of insurance policy. There may be as much as five days' difference between the first chick hatching out and the last. If there is plenty of food, all well and good: everyone gets their share. If food is in short supply, then the first chick that hatches, being bigger, tends to lord it over the others and gets the lion's share. If there's just not enough food, the younger chicks will starve to death, but the older chick will still do OK. It's a logical if somewhat brutal system to ensure as many chicks as possible survive, depending on the amount of food the parents can find.

Let's assume all is well and there's heaps of food. The chicks gradually grow up, and now they have to learn to fly. To begin with, they 'helicopter', flying up off the nest just a few feet and flapping inexpertly, before thumping back down. Then again; and again; and probably again. If a sudden gust of wind blows them off the shallow nest, or they simply drift off course, helicoptering can sometimes end in disaster. The osprey expert Roy Dennis has seen chicks fall off the nest into undergrowth below, and not be strong enough to fly back up. Such chicks will quickly fall prey to foxes and other ground-based predators. So helicoptering is functional but can be fatal.

At around twelve weeks the parents desert the kids. The female osprey is the first to go, generally two weeks before the chicks will start their migration. This is a very sensible bit of behaviour, because now all the fish Dad catches can be fed to the chicks without the female taking her share, building the youngsters up for the challenge ahead. Eventually, when he's done all he can for his offspring, when the first chill winds of autumn rustle his feathers, Dad disappears too. One morning the young ospreys wake up, and both parents are gone.

Which was exactly the situation when we arrived in the USA on 9 September 2004. The parents had gone: we just had to wait for Jaws and Tasha to follow in their wingbeats.

Jaws and Tasha – what about Bunga?

'I'm afraid I have bad news about Bunga,' said Rob when we met. 'She went offline a few days ago and we just found the body. Looks like she was hit by a truck.'

We were devastated.

'Yeah, well, you know only around one in ten chicks actually survives this migration?'

One in ten was not good odds. We were down to two chicks, and the trip hadn't even started…'Oh! Look at this!' Jen, Rob's research assistant, was peering at the computer screen showing Jaws' and Tasha's most recent locations.

They were already miles from the nest site. We had been in the USA just three days – and despite being only three months old the chicks had begun their migration. Rob had got it exactly right.

'You better get going,' said Rob. 'They're heading for New York…'

Ospreys travel by finding thermals – natural updraughts of warm air – which lift them up to dizzying heights before they glide out, sometimes for huge distances, before catching the next thermal, which lifts them up once more. Using thermals in this way, like a chain of elevators, ospreys can cover great distances using a minimal amount of energy. A city generates a lot of heat, which in turn rises up into the sky as a column of warm air: a thermal. So migrating ospreys like big cities, but by the time we got to New York our young ospreys were long gone.

For the first few days, as we headed south, we were playing catch-up: Tasha and Jaws were streaking ahead, with us, in a small convoy of self-drive hire cars, desperately trying to follow.

'Look, what are we going to do? They are just getting away from us – we can't keep stopping every evening drinking beer and eating pizza – we have to keep going somehow to keep up…'

'Anyone got any ideas?'

'How about some sort of vehicle we can all sleep on? Some sort of tour bus, maybe?'

When it arrived, our tour bus showed signs of a hard life. Turned out it was generally used by heavy metal bands, or possibly support bands – not headliners. Carpeted from floor to ceiling in stain-friendly brown, it came complete with a functioning glitter ball in the living area. It was all very Seventies rock and roll. However, having the brown bus meant we could sleep on board and travel right through the night.

The following days passed in a blur of freeways, anonymous towns, pizza crusts and daily phone calls to Rob at mission control in Charlotte, North Carolina.

'Hi guys: Jaws is well ahead now. He's on a small lake in New Jersey, just past Cape May…'

'Hi – Rob here. Jaws has flown down Maryland into Virginia – right now he's by a lake on the Chesapeake…'

'Hi guys. Well, Tasha has overtaken you, but she's stopped at

Lake Mattamuskeet – that's in South Carolina. If you can get there you might get a signal from her…' (We never did.)

If you look at the last three conversations we had with Rob as we raced down the eastern seaboard, state by state, you'll notice something: very often, when we got a fix, the ospreys had stopped beside lakes. Then it dawned on us what they were doing.

Ospreys are highly specialised fish eaters – in fact, 99 per cent of their diet is fish. As these first-time migrants flew down the eastern seaboard of the USA they were constantly on the look-out for lakes to fish in, fuelling up at every opportunity along the way. They are exceptionally good hunters. An osprey's eyesight is so good it can spot a fish underwater from 70 metres up. It hovers for a split-second, then plummets down head-first, eyes locked on the target, tucking in its wings as it falls. At the very last moment it flips its great talons forward and hits the water feet first. Ospreys can catch fish up to a metre deep, and that means they sometimes completely disappear underwater, with a terrific splash, before a wet head reappears at the surface. Now you have to hold your breath: will the osprey be able to get airborne again with its catch? Sometimes there is a quite prolonged period of suspense as the bird gathers itself. Then, with a series of mighty wing beats, which shower water in all directions, it starts to haul itself out of the water. Slowly, slowly, bird and fish rise up, the osprey laboriously clawing its way back up into the sky.

Once airborne the osprey shakes itself vigorously, spraying the surrounding airspace with thousands of glittering water droplets. It then transfers the fish into a characteristic 'flying position', with the head pointing forward, tail to the rear, making a pleasingly streamlined package, as it looks for a convenient spot to land and feed.

Up to now, despite our very best efforts, we hadn't actually seen them in the flesh, but at least – via Rob – we had been receiving strong signals from the transmitters the migrating ospreys were carrying.

But then: 'Hi – er…I don't want to worry you, but I've lost contact with Jaws…And actually I haven't had a signal from Tasha either for a while…'

A few days before we had arrived in the USA a tropical depression had formed way out in the Atlantic. This depression moved west and began to strengthen. Soon it was re-classified as a tropical storm. It continued to strengthen – fast. The winds inside the storm were now measuring 125 mph, and it was reclassified again – as a hurricane. On 11 September Hurricane Ivan swept into the Caribbean, and crashed into Jamaica, causing widespread destruction. It then headed for Grand Cayman. The winds had now reached 165 mph: it was the tenth most intense Atlantic hurricane ever recorded. As Ivan headed west and we headed south, we were on collision course. Ivan and BBC film crew were due to meet somewhere in Florida.

We had pulled over into a garage forecourt. The rain sheeted down and the wind buffeted the bus. Outside in the dark, brave – perhaps foolish – drivers continued down the freeway, their lights throwing spangly red and white patterns across the streaming windows. We had had no fixes for either Tasha or Jaws for a number of days. In these appalling conditions even our cell phones had stopped working, so we couldn't contact Rob. It began to look like the end – and how on earth were the ospreys dealing with Hurricane Ivan? Could they possibly survive?

Although we had been filming every step of our own human 'migration' as we followed hard on the heels of Tasha and Jaws, thus far it had proved impossible to film our heroes themselves. It quickly became obvious they were moving so fast that filming any detailed natural history of the osprey was going to be impossible. I was going to have to film all the osprey behaviour with other ospreys and specialist cameramen. It would still work, but if poor Tasha and Jaws had succumbed to the violent weather, well, then our film really was over. A pall of gloom settled over the brown bus.

There was a telephone landline inside the garage booth; donning waterproofs we sploshed across. 'Hi Rob – what's the news? It's lashing it down here.'

'Yeah, hi. Still not gotten a signal from Jaws or Tasha for two days now.'

'Do you think they are dead, Rob?'

'Well, no – no, I don't think so. The satellite tags are solar-powered, remember, and the solar panels may not be getting enough sunlight to juice up their transmitters. Let's not give up just yet – they may just be hunkering down and riding out the storm.'

Next morning the sun rose in a pinky blue sky. Everything was drenched, but after days of relentless wind and rain, Hurricane Ivan had abated.

'Hi Rob – any news?'

'Well yes – I have some good news. Jaws has resurrected himself! And is sneaking up behind you, so his radio is in good shape. He's near you in Florida, on Lake Okeechobee – it's quite a strong fix, too. You could go and see if you can find him with your tracker?'

Then, unbelievably, more good news. Tasha had come back on-line, too.

As we reached the Florida Keys, after a 1300-mile sprint, Jaws, Tasha and the chasing film crew were neck-and-neck. But this was as far as we could go. We had reached the end of the USA. We had been on the road for fourteen days. We were exhausted.

'You know I wonder how Jaws and Tasha are feeling right now?'

'Tired, I reckon.'

But were they? Maybe this was a breeze for our young ospreys – catching thermals to get height, then gliding along, stocking up on fresh fish as they went…We assume migration is hard and demanding, but perhaps for some species it isn't at all…

The next day Rob had more news. 'Both the youngsters are hanging around the Florida Keys – they often do that: it's like they are building up courage to do the big jump. Some of them never go, and they'll stay on the Keys all winter – but I think Jaws and Tasha will go soon. They'll head for Cuba – but of course that's ninety miles over the sea, and they can't see land from where they are, so it's kind of a leap in the dark for them: instinct has to kick in pretty hard right now. I think you should try to get ahead – get to Cuba before the birds if you can, 'cause once they arrive they won't hang about. By the way, calls from Cuba to me here in North Carolina may not be so easy…'

Ah, Cuba! It might be a leap in the dark for the ospreys, but all they have to do is open their wings and fly. They don't have crazy human politics to contend with. You can't fly direct to Cuba from the USA. We tried to hire a boat to take us across, but there were no takers. Before long we were on our way to Mexico, from where we were allowed catch a flight to Havana, hoping and praying that Jaws and Tasha would stay put in Florida for a while.

Owing to an unfortunate experience at school with vodka, gin, rum, Dubonnet and advocaat just after finishing my O-levels, I have been a stranger to strong drink for most of my life. But after a successful day of travelling around Havana picking up some colour for the film, including the wonderful old Fifties American cars that throng the capital – which our brave and resourceful cameraman Sam Gracie filmed from a skateboard as he shot in and out of the cars – to the horror of our Cuban minder, our glamorous researcher Elizabeth White induced me to try something called a mojito. It contained Cuban rum, but didn't seem to taste of rum at all. Neither did the pina colada I had next, or the daiquiri after that, or even the Cuba libre. I tottered up to my room in the magnificent old Hotel National. The walls were moving about a bit, but I could see they were covered with black and white photos of Frank Sinatra, other members of the Rat Pack, and a host of dubious visitors from the old Mafiosi days. As I fell asleep I wondered if, in some secret suite in this very hotel, Castro himself was having a cocktail. No one knew where he lived, and it really seemed perfectly possible he could be in the hotel perhaps just a few doors away.

Next morning I peered blearily out of my window, across the cobalt blue sea. Somewhere over there was America. Would Tasha and Jaws make the jump? If they did come, how would they know what direction to fly in to make landfall on Cuba? Cuba was invisible from where they now were.

The actual trigger for migrating birds to set off is changing day length, but how they navigate is extremely difficult for us to comprehend, particularly because we don't have senses that are in any way similar to those the birds are using. Two migration experiments give an idea of just how good birds are at navigating around the planet. Some years ago two Manx shearwaters – small sea birds that only come ashore to nest – were caught at their nest sites on a small island off the coast of Wales. One was flown west, across the Atlantic, to Boston, Massachusetts. The other was flown east, to Venice in Italy. After they were released, both were back at the original nest site within fourteen days. They had unerringly found their way home, covering, in the case of the Boston bird, some 250 miles a day.

That's pretty impressive, but it takes a German scientist to do the job really thoroughly. In a classic scientific paper from 1980, 'Does pigeon homing depend on stimuli perceived during displacement?' Dr Hans Wallraff decided to take some homing pigeons to a really remote location and let them go. But to ensure his 'EPs' (experimental pigeons) didn't get any clues as to where he was taking them, he did the following. First, he transported them in sixteen little pigeon-shaped coffins inside an airtight container, which was sealed and fed bottled air, so the pigeons couldn't smell anything. Lights were turned on and off randomly during transport, so there were no clues from light. Loud random noises were played 'according to a computer-made random programme' throughout the poor pigeons' journey. You might have thought that was enough, but Dr Wallraff hadn't finished – not by any means. The container containing the EPs was surrounded by magnetic coils which generated a constantly changing magnetic field, and – finally – the whole complex paraphernalia was mounted on a turntable that was spun in one direction, slowed, spun in the other direction at a different speed, and so on. So what happened after all this? The moment the birds were released they flew around in a circle a couple of times, as they always do – and simply flew straight home.

As you can see, birds have capabilities and senses we simply cannot comprehend. The current best guess is that they have an interacting system of three compasses: a sun compass; a magnetic compass, with which they can detect and orient themselves relative to the Earth's magnetic field; and a star compass – night-flying birds definitely use the stars to navigate by and locate themselves. It also looks as if some birds use smell to sniff their way home.

We thought we had been waiting for Tasha and Jaws to summon up the courage to come over, but in fact it was just that Rob had not been able to get through to us. When we did manage to contact him we discovered the birds were already in Cuba, and miles ahead of us.

Goodbye, Havana and hello, Lake Camaguey, which was where the satellite signals told us Tasha had stopped – yet another lake.

Camaguey was absolutely teeming with ospreys. Every dead tree sticking up out of the water had its own osprey. The lake echoed with their high-pitched, plaintive cries. We asked the fishermen about them. On the one hand, they liked them, because the ospreys led them to the fish shoals, but when we asked how successful the ospreys were they shrugged their shoulders and looked resigned: 'When the osprey goes fishing it's a catch for sure'. Not completely true, but not far off the mark. On average, one in four dives results in a fish, but some really skilful individual ospreys manage a 70 per cent success rate. And here's a statistic to make most fishermen weep: the average time an osprey takes from the start of hunting to actually having a fish in its talons is just twelve minutes.

As you might expect from such a specialist, the osprey has many subtle modifications for fishing including a 'reversible toe', which means it has two extremely sharp talons in front, and two behind, making it far more effective at holding a slippery fish. Even more ingeniously, the talons themselves have tiny backward-facing scales on them like a row of barbs, so they are fantastically grippy. As ospreys often completely submerge when they plunge into the water, they have closable nostrils, to stop water getting in. An osprey is a superbly modified fishing machine.

Later we climbed to the top of the mountain range that runs along the south of Cuba, up to Gran Piedra. It was exquisitely beautiful. At noon, almost like clockwork, clouds start to roll in, indicating thermals are building. Then, suddenly, emerging from the clouds as they caught the thermals, we saw ospreys: proper migrating ospreys. One after another they rose up, reached the top of the thermal, then started their long glide to the east, down the mountain range towards Guantanamo Bay in the distance. Some had a fish slung underneath, gripped in their talons, a 'packada-lunch', as our friendly Cuban ornithologist Freddie Sanyana called it.

That evening, as we approached Santiago de Cuba, three weeks into our trip, there was a tremendous storm, and we arrived in blinding rain. Our driver did not know the way, but we need not have worried, as waiting on bicycles, drenched to the skin, were some helpful local guides. A few friendly words were shouted above the noise of the rain drumming on the roof and we were off, whizzing down wet streets trying to keep up with our cycle guides. For a small sum they were very happy to show us the way, despite the weather.

We were nearing the southernmost tip of Cuba, as far as we could go. As we arrived at our hotel an almost unbelievable coincidence was about to be revealed. Bear in mind we had had to book this particular hotel many months before, taking a guess as to where both we and the ospreys would be. So, as we checked in, where were our ospreys? A call to Rob 2400 miles away in North Carolina revealed that Jaws was going to roost just 20 kilometres from where we were. 'Your arrival in Santiago de Cuba hours after Jaws was unbelievable,' Rob said to me in a recent email, 'given you'd planned the timing of the trip three months before. It made me wonder what coven Elizabeth your researcher was part of!'

We had managed to stay with our young ospreys as they made

their incredible journey, but although Jaws was snoozing literally just around the corner, we had still not managed to see either him or Tasha for ourselves. Plenty of other ospreys, yes, but 'our' ospreys, no. They had come to the tip of Cuba and were about to make the final, and most challenging, part of their journey. From Cuba Jaws and Tasha had to continue south, but that meant attempting to fly across the Caribbean, some 350 miles of open water, before they made landfall on South America. This was where young ospreys fell. What would happen?

'If we do get stopped by the FARC, just let me do the talking, OK. Remember: no sudden movements; do not get out of the vehicles unless you are told to…'

These fairly intimidating instructions were being issued by our brilliant – ex-army – fixer in Colombia, Jerry (short for Jeremy) McDermott. Jaws could have chosen somewhere a bit more user-friendly to end up, but, no: he had decided to go to Colombia, famous for cocaine, guerrillas and kidnapping.

It was now some weeks after we had left Cuba, and two things had happened. Tasha had gone off-line. She'd headed out across the Caribbean, turned left and, as Rob said, 'looks like she ended up in a stew pot in the Dominican Republic' – a very sad end to her short life. So we had lost Bunga and Tasha. But Jaws had made it, all the way to Colombia, where he had now stopped, his migration over.

We had to complete the story, so we were back on his trail to try to find out where he'd stopped, and see if we could actually film him at the end of his epic journey.

Soon we were driving beside the coast, heading north out of Barranquilla. This is cocaine-smuggling country – most of the cocaine that gets to North America is manufactured in Colombia, then shipped north by sea.

'Jeremy...'

'Yeah?'

'Some of these houses up here – they're quite small, but they often have enormous brand new speedboats in the yard? Look – there's another one: a red one, huge – it's got three engines...'

'They are very keen on water-skiing up here, Martin,' said Jerry in a droll voice.

We stayed in a small compound with a slightly suspicious family. 'No, don't take any photographs of the women, Martin,' Jerry warned. 'Keep smiling, be happy.' We slung hammocks across a single open room, just a roof and low walls, all seven of us close enough to touch. In fact, the beautifully-made hammocks were wondrously comfortable. Dogs barked, cockerels crowed. Someone snored. It was an adventure.

It took us two days to find Jaws, but find him we did. After his 2,886-mile journey he'd landed in a little chunk of osprey heaven. Right at the northern tip of Colombia the sandy desert turned into a vast green lagoon, with an enormous, shallow lake packed with fish of all kinds. It was spectacularly beautiful. We tracked him down with a directional aerial, and were rewarded by the sight of Jaws plunging into the water to fish. As the presenter Steve Leonard said, 'Jaws has led us a merry dance, but he's made it' – and we'd made it, too.

There was a remarkable coda to the story of Jaws. After we had made our film in 2004, Rob Bierregaard continued to receive positions from Jaws' satellite transmitter, but then the signals became intermittent and, because getting the data from the satellite people is expensive, Rob 'retired' Jaws' transmitter, and that should have been that. But it wasn't. Let's let Rob take up the story himself.

'In May of 2006, a friend called me from eastern North

Carolina. He asked if I had an osprey around there with a transmitter, because one had just flown in front of his car. (We haven't invented a word yet for how freaky that coincidence was.) I told him I didn't think so, and couldn't figure out what bird he had seen. About a week later, the satellite folks emailed to say that Jaws' radio was back on the air, and asked if I wanted to reactivate his ID. Which I did, of course.'

Jaws was back! He'd done what all young ospreys do, and spent a year at the southern end of his migration – in Colombia – before making the return journey. But by some sort of spooky miracle his iffy transmitter had come back on-line at just the perfect moment. He then stayed around Martha's Vineyard all spring, with the transmitter coming in and out all summer. It went down and then came back on again as he was flying back down through Cuba for the second time. It then stayed on, allowing Rob to track him all the way to Colombia, where he stopped around 50 miles away from his first destination. And then the transmitter switched off for good.

And yet, even then it still wasn't over! In 2011 Rob saw an osprey wearing a transmitter harness over Martha's Vineyard. None of his satellite-tagged ospreys were in the area. For that and various other reasons he is almost certain this was Jaws. If so, it means this remarkable bird will now have made the migration to Colombia and back six times – 36,000 miles. Me, I'd love to see him one more time.

Despite the fact we only managed to film Jaws right at the end of his epic journey, we did manage to include enough natural history footage of other ospreys to explain what was going on. It was a great story. The film was watched by over four million people on its first transmission, and has been repeated on both BBC1 and BBC2 a number of times since.

6

'THE BITE OF THE GIANT CENTIPEDE'

Nightmares of Nature, BBC1, 1995

Question. Is – as some authorities claim – the giant centipede's bite really the most agonising bite known to mankind? Hmm. The natural world is full of such questions: fastest, deadliest, most venomous – all puffed up with hyperbole. I mean, 'the most agonizing': how could you actually find out? Well, one afternoon back in 1994, it seemed I was about to contribute to the 'Giant centipede: just how agonizing' debate first-hand.

Have a look at the colour picture section in the middle of the book. There you'll find a picture of me sharing a bed with a real live giant centipede. These can grow up to twelve inches long and, as I can personally report, at this size they are surprisingly heavy. As it walked about on me it left strange, yellow, slightly sore 'zipper' marks along my body. It seems all the giant centipede's legs are mildly venomous, and as they grip, they inject. I knew the bite of the giant centipede was often reported to be agonizing, yet here I was, wearing only a pair of grey Marks and Sparks jockey shorts for protection, sharing my bed with a monster. What on earth was I thinking of?

We've already visited the 1994 *Nightmares of Nature* series in chapter 4. Then I was trying to film vampire bats; now I was trying to film another sequence for the same 'Cry in the Dark' programme. Just to reiterate, 'Cry in the Dark' was all about the most scary nocturnal creatures – you know: brown rats, vampire bats, man-eating big cats. Stuff like that, but also quite a few reasonably unsavoury, but undoubtedly fascinating, creepy-crawlies. Most of these are fairly small, but some are substantial. Imagine for a moment you're out digging the garden. There's a sudden movement in the soil: something fast, slightly intimidating, shiny chestnut-brown, perhaps an inch and a half long – a centipede. Now imagine that magnified, twice, three times. Turn up the dial: magnify that slightly intimidating garden centipede ten times. You're into *Scolopendria gigantia* territory: the giant centipede.

Giant centipedes are super-fast, aggressive and extremely venomous. They will happily hunt mammals, birds and reptiles, killing them with their toxic venom, which they inject using two large fangs. These are actually modified front legs, scientifically called forcipules, but I think fangs is way better. As well as dispatching prey, the fangs and venom also act as a superb defensive mechanism: one ingredient of the centipede's venom is specifically formulated to generate extreme pain – instantly. They say (well, in my well-thumbed 1976 *Guinness Book of Animal Facts and Feats* it does) the pain is so intense, victims have been known to plunge their bitten hand into boiling water as a counter-stimulant to the unbearable pain.

So what could be more unwelcome in your bed at night than a giant centipede? It does happen quite frequently, because the sheets on a bed make a very attractive place for a centipede to slide into. Centipedes, like many other invertebrates, like to feel something above and below their bodies: the scientific term is thigmokinesis, 'the inhibition of movement in response to contact stimuli'. If you think about it, that generally means they are hidden under something. Tucked between bed sheets is a very comfortable place for a centipede to hole up during the day, before coming out to hunt at night.

My best pal Jo (we've been friends since we were four) was bitten by a small-to medium-sized centipede the very first night he was on holiday in Greece. He went to bed a bit the worse for wear (retsina), and as he pushed his feet down between the sheets he felt something at the foot of the bed, and idly kicked out at it. The next moment, Jo was out of the bed shrieking like a small child, thinking someone had shoved a red-hot poker into his foot. Of the long tale of swellings, the agonising bus ride home, the very pretty girls who took sympathy, we need say no more – honestly, the fuss he made about it! Although the horror has grown with the telling there's no doubt the poor bloke was in terrible pain: his leg swelled up and was covered in a network of bulging purple veins. Now this, remember, was a small-to medium-sized centipede – not a proper giant centipede.

For 'A Cry in the Dark' I thought it would be stimulating for the audience to see a real live giant centipede crawling around over a real live person. Remarkably, I found the centipede. A wonderful man called Andy Rowell turned out to have a fabulous collection of extremely venomous animals in his neat house on a new housing estate near Milton Keynes. Would he, Andy, allow us to film with his centipede? With certain provisos, yes, he would. We would build a set, make it centipede-proof so it couldn't escape, get an actor to lie in the bed within the set, and encourage the centipede to crawl around all over him. The date was set, and I began to trawl around all the actors' agencies. There was initial interest, of course, but when the whole thing was explained, the number of possible takers for the part dwindled. In fact, it dwindled right down to … zero.

So there I was, on set in my pants, slipping between two thin sheets. Andy got out the big box and, very gingerly, with a long expanding metal hook, like they use for venomous snakes, started to try to get the animal out. It kept on falling off, and none of us could really see it, until at last, by now I suspect rather annoyed at being messed about with and prodded with a metal stick, the centipede emerged, to gasps of admiration from the crew. It really was a monster. I lay very still. Andy came over to me holding his metal hook with the centipede writhing about on the end, and gently laid the great ginger beast beside me on the bed, whispering encouragement… For the next few minutes the centipede rushed about investigating. It ran up my thigh, clinging on tightly through the sheets. It ran across the pillow past my face; it ran under my hand and flowed out between my fingers – I could feel the legs and cool body slipping through. Then, to my horror, it found a gap and came under the sheet, where I was, basically, naked, and coiled up near my groin. Out of sight, out of mind: the film crew relaxed, switched off the camera and, sipping coffee, began to chat amongst themselves.

'Er, Andy…' I said in a hoarse stage whisper – 'Andy!'

Eventually, after quite few takes, lens changes and re-positionings, we decided we had enough. The hook came back into play, and the giant centipede was lowered back into its box, writhing furiously, and the lid snapped shut before he – she? – could shoot out again. I had survived; I did not need to plunge any bits of me into boiling water. Actually, I had concluded by then, it was probably – possibly? – quite safe. Why would a centipede bite? – this was my logic. It's not going to waste valuable venom. There were only two reasons I could see why it might bite. First, if it thought I was food. I was too big to be food. Secondly, it would probably bite if it thought it was in danger and had to defend itself. I'd lain extremely still and tried hard not to move, except to pretend I was asleep (very poor acting). In the event, I was correct: no bites, but, although we had successfully got our film sequences for *Nightmares of Nature*, the lack of bites meant that, sadly, I was not able to contribute my own thoughts to the 'Most agonizing' debate. Could we ever answer that question? Turns out, we could.

Some years later, during the making of another series, *Ultimate Killers*, we needed to film the world's most venomous creatures, including scorpions. Yes, I know we're after the giant centipede, but stay with me... In 2000 we went to Texas, to Fort Sam Huston – Home of Army Medicine – to meet 'the toughest combat entomologist in the entire US army', world scorpion expert Major Scott Stockwell. Scott has got not one but two scorpions named after him, and he turned out to be one of the most remarkable men I ever met in all my years in TV.

Scott was teaching when we arrived, and his class was electrifying. Here was a room full of very green, very young wannabe army medical orderlies, there to learn about dangerous and venomous invertebrates the US military might encounter around the world. Scott produced a model scorpion from his pocket. 'This is what a typical scorpion looks like,' he barked. 'Who wants to hold it?'

Dubious looks. Even the model looked intimidating...

'Hey – c'mon! Would I give you guys a real live scorpion? C'mon!'

A brave soul (a girl) proffers a hand, on which Scot places the scorpion, which instantly raises its claws and scary-looking sting into a defensive position.

'*Aaaaaagh!*'

'Yes, indeed: I would give you a live scorpion!' yells Scott above the uproar, grinning hugely. 'You're holding an emperor scorpion, cadet – be careful with it, there!'

Class will not forget this lesson…After class it was our turn to film with Major Stockwell. Scott had a huge collection of different scorpions. We started with the less venomous ones and worked our way up. If you ever meet a scorpion on your travels here's an important tip: look at its claws! No, seriously. In general, different scorpions employ one of two different methods to subdue their prey. Either they use their front claws, or they inject venom with the intimidating-looking stinger at the tip of their tail. If the scorpion you're looking at has large claws, it means its venom will probably not be that potent. If, however, you find a scorpion with small, weedy claws, be careful: it will most probably be a species that relies on venom that may be extremely toxic. As a rule of thumb, *be wary of small-clawed scorpions*. The huge emperor scorpion Scott had just used in class has enormous claws, so is relatively safe, although those claws can nip.

For our filming, Scott followed the big but fairly harmless emperor with a squirming mass of much smaller scorpions, which he poured into the hands of our long-suffering presenter Steve Leonard. Now these all had small claws!

'Er…' says Steve, now armed with this important claw-knowledge.

'Yes,' says Scott, 'these will hurt. But don't worry: I estimate you only have perhaps a…50 per cent chance of being stung!'

Steve is reassured, but only for a moment as he realises what Scott has just said.

'That's 50/50!'

In the event – only slightly disappointingly – Steve is not stung at all.

As we were filming Steve, Scott was handling a death stalker. Now, this scorpion is a very serious proposition, and because of its exceptionally toxic venom is generally considered to be the most dangerous scorpion in the world. To our horror, the death stalker suddenly plunged its lethal-looking stinger into Scott's hand. Steve immediately stopped talking to camera. 'Scott – did that scorpion just sting you?'

'It sure did, Steve.'

'Are you not in terrible pain?'

'Yes. It feels like being hit extremely hard with a hammer. It is indeed extraordinarily painful, but I have trained my mind to control it.'

'But, Scott – that's a death stalker, the most deadly scorpion in the world! Aren't you in serious danger?'

'You know what, Steve? I'm not. Although this scorpion does kill quite a number of people each year, they are generally, sadly, either young children or old people. A big healthy person like you, or me in my size-ten combat boots – well, we'll get a lot of pain, but we ain't goin' to die…'

It turned out Scott had got stung, generally on purpose, by nearly every scorpion in his extensive collection, and many other venomous creatures besides. He considered documenting the effects of their venom on humans an important part of his research, and he used himself, usually his hand, as a test bed for this work. This is not what scientists normally do. He was once in South Korea, Scott told me: 'I was teaching my "envenomation" lesson. The audience was all civilian Korean men. As I am going through the slides of various arthropod bites and stings, the leader of all these men, a certain Mr Im, raises his hand and asks, "Mmm… These all you hand?" To which I responded affirmatively. Then he says, "You very stupid guy!"'

I would say very brave guy – with an extremely inquiring mind.

So we were in the presence of a man who had been stung by most of the most painful venomous creatures on Earth. If only he had been impaled by a giant centipede! Then he would be in a unique position to answer, once and for all, the main question.

And of course, he had.

The first time I met Scott was on the reconnaissance before the actual filming. We were chatting away, just getting to know one another, in his office, which was stacked high with translucent boxes containing some of the most venomous creatures in the world. I mentioned my experience of lying in bed with a giant centipede, and my abject failure to tempt it to bite me.

'Just a moment, Martin.' Scott got out a large box, opened it, put his hand in and drew out a vast giant centipede, which, finding itself thus manhandled, instantly drove its huge fangs into his hand and proceeded to pump in venom. I fumbled with a small video camera to try to film this awesome event as it happened, but got so flustered I managed to take just a single frame of the centipede hanging off Scott's hand.

'Jesus, Scott!' I yelled. 'Shall I call an ambulance?'

'No, no, Martin – keep calm. Just keep talking and keep distracting me – I've wanted to test out the effect of the centipede's venom for some time, and your visit has given me the motivation. Jus' don't stop talking…'

'But – but – it's the most painful bite known to man!'

'It's remarkably painful, yes,' said Scott. 'Shall we go for lunch?'

Scott drove me, one-handed, to the restaurant, while the other hand started to swell like a rubber glove being blown up. Every now and then he calmly stopped to take a photograph of the damage and the inflating hand. It was utterly amazing.

'Are you not in agony, Scott?' I asked wonderingly.

'Yes, but I can control it, and I know I'm not going to die, so I can remain calm. What would you like to drink?' he said, perusing the menu.

Scott's jokey claim to be the 'toughest combat entomologist in the US army' was surely true. And, of course, it now allows us to answer the first, somewhat hypothetical, question we started this whole piece with. Is the giant centipede's really, truly, absolutely the most agonising bite known to man?

Just before we go to Scott's answer, there is another contender who might claim to be able to answer the question. In 1990 an American entomologist, Justin O. Schmidt, published a paper attempting to compare and quantify, on a scale of 1 to 5, the pain caused by the stings of seventy-eight different species of insect. This is the so-called Schmidt Sting Pain Index. He did this by allowing himself to be stung by hundreds of different insects and describing the effect. The sting of the acacia ant, therefore – 1.8 on the scale – was 'a rare piercing, elevated sort of pain, as though someone has fired a staple into your cheek'. The bald-faced hornet (rating 2 on the scale)? 'Rich, hearty, slightly crunchy – similar to getting your hand mashed in a revolving door.' The paper wasp (3) was 'caustic and burning. Distinctly bitter aftertaste. Like spilling a beaker of hydrochloric acid on a paper cut.' Dr Schmidt ended up putting the bullet ant as the most painful, at 4 on the scale, describing the feeling as 'pure, intense, brilliant pain. Like fire-walking over flaming charcoal with a three-inch rusty nail in your heel.'

A brave effort, but Dr Schmidt only got himself stung by insects, and not scorpions or giant centipedes, so despite this honourable attempt the last word has got to go to the extraordinary Major Scott Stockwell. Scott has left the army now, but I managed to reach him by email in his well-earned retirement. This is how he describes his most extreme experiences.

> I was stung by a scorpion (*Hottentotta alticola*, I think) in Afghanistan, that put me out of commission for the better part of a day. I had been stung twice before with 'normal' results – nothing I couldn't handle. But this time, I couldn't just shrug off the pain, which was not just in my hand, but up my arm and into my chest. My face was numb. I was sweating and shaking. I took to my hammock, as I just could not stand to walk about any more. One of the hospital nurses heard about it from somebody and came in to check on me every so often. There wasn't anything they could do, really. I finally fell asleep. When I woke up a few hours later, I was dehydrated, but much improved.
>
> That was my worst experience with a scorpion. But for me, the centipede was the worst. It has become the standard by which I judge pain, that centipede sting being a 10 on a scale of 1 to 10. I was actually stung twice by the centipede you saw. Two weeks later, a student allowed it to escape, and I once again grabbed it carelessly and was stung on the back of my right hand. That sting was every bit as excruciatingly painful as the first. The pain was one I've never experienced with other beasts. It was as if I'd sprained every tendon in my hand and wrist all at once. At one point I awoke from a restless sleep and, feeling the pain in my hand, I was afraid to look at it for fear that it would look the way it felt – like it had been jammed into a meat grinder. I fully expected to see my fingers all bent in different directions from the bloody stump of my hand.

Even today, well over a decade later, Scott tells me, the centipede bites still flare up every now and then – he doesn't know what triggers it.

I would like to suggest, despite Dr Schmidt's honourable attempts, that no one else on Planet Earth has been stung by so many deadly creatures so regularly and so often as Major Scott Stockwell. What is more, he has been nailed not once but twice by a giant centipede. This gives Scott the authority to deliver the final arbitration. For once, in a world full of hyperbole and non-sense, we can cut away the hype and say – direct from the man who knows – that the giant centipede bite is indeed the most painful bite known to mankind.

7

ON THE ROOF OF THE WORLD

'Wild Goose Chase', *Incredible Animal Journeys*,

BBC1, 2006

I have a cabinet at home containing most of my collection of knives. It's a good cabinet, with top-lights and a nice finish. Each knife tells a story, and one of them – scruffy, with an old bit of multi-coloured climbing sling ('tat' in climber-speak) tied on it – sits there, battered and intriguing. This is a knife I bartered for and bought off a man at 5200 metres up on the Tibetan plateau. If you open the sheath and sniff, there is still a distinctive smell. The smell is yak fat.

Outside my tent the wind is furious. The fabric walls flap violently, showering me and my sleeping bag with ice: it's actually my own breath, condensed and frozen. At first I couldn't understand what was wrong with my jaw, until the uncontrollable tremble simply became my teeth chattering. How odd, I mused dispassionately: so this isn't something people just say – 'It was so cold my teeth began to chatter.' It really happens. I am terribly tired, but it's impossible to sleep, and this is why: just as I'm about to drift off, my breathing slows, even stops, and my oxygen-starved brain goes into full alert and yells 'Breathe – *now!*' and I jerk awake, gasping down great lungfuls of air. This happens again and again; it's not much fun. But not surprising: up here there is far less oxygen than my body is used to. I'm also confused: it's very hard to remember where I have put anything, but now, thank goodness, I have a simple system. Head torch is always on the right side of my pillow; gloves are to the left with my notes, etc...But, hang on: is it head torch on the right, or the left? In fact, where is my blasted head torch?

I want to go for a pee, but the effort of getting up, putting on clothes and boots (currently inside the sleeping bag with me to stop them freezing), unzipping the tent, staggering out into the dark – the pee is just not going to happen. I start to nod off...everything slows...then – *breathe!* Drift off, and then – breathe! So it goes on. This is known as 'periodic breathing', and if you go above 5000 metres you can enjoy it, too.

Eventually a dim bluey-greyness inside the tent tells me dawn is coming. It is time to rise and shine. I struggle out of the sleeping bag. On top of my tent is a thermometer: it reads -22°C. I peer around at a fantastic landscape of vast mountain peaks soaring up from the snowfields, up, up into a crystal sky. Then the edges of the mountains turn gold, kissed by the rising sun. This is glorious! Quick, says my befuddled brain – you must film it! Where is Doug? Needn't have worried: a small, powerful figure, hidden amongst serious cold weather gear, his ruddy face just visible through a fur hood, beams at me over the camera. Extreme cameraman Doug Allen is already on the case. 'Mornin', Mart – how ye doin?' His is a broad Scottish brogue. 'Have you had any breakfast yet? The boys are warming a brew.'

Tea! Yes, I must have tea!

We are over 5000 metres up on the Tibetan plateau, camping, waiting for a bunch of birds to fly overhead, which they might do, or they might not: we have no way of knowing when, or indeed, if, they will at all.

It is shocking how effortlessly anecdote can become fact. Here are some actual statements about a remarkable bird, the bar-headed goose. The first is quoted from an article in *Scientific American*, 5 November 2011: 'Climbers struggling the last few steps to the peak of Makalu in the Himalayas have long marvelled at the sight of bar-headed geese flying high above to their winter refuge in India. The birds cruise at an altitude of 29,500 feet, nearly as high as a commercial aircraft.' And this from the respected scientific journal *Molecular Biology and Evolution*: 'Bar-headed geese fly at up to 9000 m (29,500 feet) elevation during their migration over the Himalayas.' And more, from an authoritative climber's blog: 'Bar-headed geese have been observed flying at over 30,000 feet'.

Oh, really? However hard you try, you will not find any verifiable evidence to back up these claims. They, and a host of other such statements, all spring, it turns out, from just one single anecdote, which appeared in *Scientific American* in 1961 in a paper by Lawrence W. Swan . This is what Swan actually wrote:

> The British explorer George Lowe, who has spent as much time as anyone at mountain altitudes above 23,000 feet, has told me of watching from the slopes of Everest while a flock of bar-headed geese (*Eulabeia indica*) flew in echelon directly over the summit. On an April night from a camp at 15,000 feet on Barun Glacier, I myself have heard the distant honking of these birds flying miles above me, unseen against the stars over Makalu, on their way to the lakes of Tibet.

So Swan himself did not see anything – it was night-time. He says he heard the honking 'flying miles above me over Makalu'.

If Swan was on the Barun glacier he was 6 kilometres from Makalu. I'm not sure it's possible to hear birds honking from 6 kilometres off – and it was dark, so the suggestion the geese he could hear were over Makalu is somewhat hard to credit. George Lowe might have been above 23,000 feet on many occasions, but Swan doesn't tell us where he was when he thought he saw the geese flying directly over the summit. Do bar-headed geese go over the top? Really? For the series I was producing, *Incredible Animal Journeys*, we had come to Tibet to try to find out.

What had been known for many years was that bar-headed geese definitely migrate across the Himalayas each year, flying north to Tibet in spring, then back south to lowland India and Nepal in winter. Whichever way they did it – right over the top, or along the passes between the peaks – bar-headed geese are still the highest trans-montane migrants in the world. They perform the world's steepest migratory flight north in springtime, from sea level over the highest mountain range on earth – so how do they do it? If we attempted such a feat, climbing so fast to such extreme altitude, it would surely kill us.

I think this particular programme, 'Wild Goose Chase', prob-ably required more forward planning than any other show I ever made in all my thirty-plus years. If we were going to genuinely follow bar-headed geese from the Tibetan plateau over the top of the Himalaya, we had to fit individuals with satellite trackers. Now, it would be impossible to find them to fit trackers to once they were hidden away on a remote lake somewhere in the vast-ness of the Tibetan plateau. Also, the Chinese authorities took a dim view of people rushing around Tibet with satellite-tracking technology. So we had to think ahead – way ahead. A full ten months before the actual film trip, we got together with two fantastic scientists, John Takekawa and Salim Javed, to fit radio tracking devices to two bar-headed geese in Nepal, in their winter feeding grounds.

We fitted the trackers on 6 March 2005. Later that month (on the 13th and 28th, to be exact) the two birds left Nepal and flew, in a single day, right over the Himalaya up to their summer quarters on the plateau. Under normal circumstances they would now be completely lost, but thanks to the satellite trackers we had regular updates from John Takekawa, now back at his field station in California, telling us almost precisely where our geese – which, inevitably, we had named Tenzing and Hillary – were hiding out. Hiding out is a pretty good description of the birds' behaviour. The bar-headed geese fly up to extremely remote lakes high on the Tibetan plateau to breed. There they are pretty safe from many predators, who would struggle at such altitude, but additionally, in the short summer the plateau explodes with vegetation: a green bonanza to feed the geese and their fast-growing chicks, and further protect them from sight.

This was where Hillary and Tensing were now and, if we got the timing right, we hoped to be in exactly the right place to have an aerial rendezvous with them when they made the big jump back south as the extreme Tibetan winter began to bite. We knew from the northward migration that both birds had flown close to the 8013-metre peak Shishapangma, so, speculating that this would be their route back south, our ultimate objective was Shishapangma advanced base camp. Even if our birds did not pass by we should be able to watch others on migration, and see for ourselves if they went 'over the top', as Swan had suggested, or if they actually flew along the passes, keeping closer to the ground.

But we could not go directly to base camp. If we did, we would probably die of altitude sickness. We had to acclimatise. So our first stop was the forbidden city of Lhasa.

At 3490 metres (11,450 feet), Lhasa is one of the highest cities in the world, and you can get altitude sickness just going shopping. We had a strict regime of acclimatisation worked out, which involved spending our first three nights in Lhasa before going any higher.

It was dark. Flickering light spilled out from the flaming *stupas* – large, chimney-shaped structures filled with blazing juniper branches and incense, which sent scented smoke billowing across Barkor Square. In the gloom came a strange sound, a gentle rhythmic hissing and quiet muttering. Now the great golden statues on top of the Jokhang temple could be seen silhouetted against a lightening sky of pink and turquoise, spattered with grey-white cloud. Somewhere a drum was beating, small bells rang and there was distant chanting. Still the soft hissing continued…What was it? Now, at last, I could begin to see. All around were dozens and dozens of pilgrims, prostrating themselves on the hard flagstones in front of the temple. They knelt down onto their knees, put their hands down, and slid forward until their entire bodies were flat on the ground; then back up onto their knees, stand up, and repeat – again and again and again. The hissing was coming from the pieces of cardboard they held in their hands, which allowed them to slip forward on flagstones polished smooth by generations of worshippers. Everywhere you looked it was the same: old and young, women and men, prostrating themselves towards the temple as the sun rose. It was almost silent except for the gentle hiss of cardboard against stone. It was profoundly moving to witness. To my surprise tears welled up and rolled down my cheeks.

Being in Lhasa was, as our programme researcher Giles Badger so aptly put it, 'like living in a picture book'. The Tibetan pilgrims, all processing clockwise around the temples or the Dalai

Lama's former palace, the Potala, were fantastically exotic, different groups distinguished by clothing and jewellery. Many wore brilliant pieces of turquoise, contrasting beautifully with orange coral in a profusion of necklaces, hair clips and other decorations. Rouged cheeks and pigtails gave the younger girls a doll-like appearance. Older pilgrims had fantastically lined faces, etched into a thousand creases by hard work under harsh sun and cutting winds. As they walked, in a seemingly endless stream, many carried spinning prayer wheels embossed with the sacred mantra *Om mani padme hum*, which was also being muttered quietly by the passing pilgrims. Gleaming copper and brass prayer wheels, some absolutely enormous, are kept spinning so as to keep offering up prayers. In fact, *Om mani padme hum*, the six-syllable mantra at the heart of Tibetan Buddhism, is very difficult to translate: *mani* is jewel, *padme* is lotus, but the sentence isn't amenable to simple translation word for word, and its true meaning is the subject of endless discussion by scholars. It is more the rhythm and sound of the words themselves, it seems, that is precious.

After three days of acclimatisation it was time to leave Lhasa, and head for the lake on which we knew Tenzing was, and from there on to our base-camp rendezvous point.

Our journey was not on any tourist routes. To add to our difficulty, we had to try to keep to our acclimatization plan, by not sleeping more than 300 metres higher than the night before. Guided by Migmar, our excellent fixer, we piled into our first potential overnight. The rooms were utterly disgusting: filthy, stained sheets in the dormitories, excrement all around the buildings, pools of mud and effluent. We moved on, finally ending up in some sort of barracks. There was still excrement all around the building, but the beds, in a large dorm, were less filthy.

At 3 a.m. there was a terrible shouting. I peeped outside: people with guns were rushing about. We quickly locked the doors, and not a moment too soon. There was a sudden hammering and screaming. I honestly expected gunfire but, mercifully, none came. I have no idea what was going on, but it was extremely unnerving. From then on, we determined to be masters of our own destiny, and camp out each night.

Next morning, we went into the village for breakfast, watched by fascinated locals who crowded into the small room to peer at us. Unlike the banshee in the night, they seemed friendly enough. When we walked outside to get back into the vehicles, the local butcher had just dispatched a yak beside the road and, surrounded by pools of gore and innards that poured steam into the freezing morning air, he was haggling with a group of women. Clutching his cleaver, bespattered with blood, the butcher hacked off bits of the unfortunate animal as each negotiation reached a satisfactory conclusion. The purchases were stuffed, still steaming, into brightly coloured plastic bags. The gutter beside our cars ran with blood.

As we left the village to continue up towards our goose Tensing's lake, we noticed clouds rolling in, and pretty soon it began to snow. Things were about to get more difficult. But not as difficult as things were getting for our second film unit down in the French Alps.

Right at the start of the project I realised we would need a variety of pictures of bar-headed geese: flying high over mountains; close-ups; wide shots; mountains passing underneath, etc. The audience would expect to see such images. The chance of us filming all these shots in the Himalayas was zero – you can't pay a cameraman to hang around the Tibetan plateau (which stretches some 2500 kilometres east to west) on the off-chance a goose might fly past close enough to get all the shots you'd need – ridiculous. No: I had to think of another way.

The bar-headed goose is actually quite a popular ornamental bird, and eggs from domestic birds are reasonably easy to get hold of. It was time to call bird specialist Lloyd Buck, whose name has already appeared in these chronicles. Lloyd and his partner Rose are genius at solving this kind of problem. 'Yeah, I think we might be able to help. Let me talk it through with Rose.'

The first step would be to try and get the bar-headed geese to temporarily 'imprint' on Rose. My father used to do this with our backyard chickens – it's a fascinating bit of behaviour. Once you see the egg starting to hatch, if you pick it up and allow the chick to emerge in your hand – so that the first thing it sees is you – it will, at least for a while, 'imprint' on you, and follow you everywhere you go.

Rose collected the goose chicks when they were just one day old from a trusted friend in Hampshire, and now she did something very few people would have the dedication and stamina to undertake. She lived with the chicks twenty-three hours a day for four weeks, getting one hour off a day to go and have a shower. At night Rose and the chicks slept together in a small hut at the bottom of the garden. Being with goose chicks is not a good way to get a restful night's sleep. Rose was in a sleeping bag, but because they wanted to be as close to her face and voice (the bits they liked best) as they possibly could, each night she ended up wearing a warm, fidgeting mass of eight goose chicks around her neck like a downy ruff – which woke up every half-hour and nibbled at her eyelashes. By the end of an exhausting four weeks Rose and the bar-headed geese chicks were inseparable. It was time for the next stage.

We needed mountains, big enough to stand in for the

Himalayas, but within driving distance of the UK where Rose lived. The Alps seemed to fit the bill – if seen from above Mont Blanc would surely pass muster for a Himalayan peak. All we had to do was get the geese flying up there, and film it.

One summer's day, a white van containing eight noisy geese, Rose and the rest of the bird team, set off for the French Alps. Twenty-four hours later they arrived in the little town of Cipières. The first thing Rose did was let the geese out to stretch their wings, which they did. How lovely they looked in the sky! So good to see them flying free happily after such an arduous journey, higher and higher – such a great sight – higher and…Gosh, I can hardly see them…and…Now I can't see them – help! Scramble!

They managed to find six of the eight, and eventually, after a frantic search and inquiries in broken French, were led down to a honking woodshed by a slightly aggrieved farmer's wife, who clearly felt her supper had simply dropped out of the sky. All eight were reunited.

So all our ducks, or in this case, geese, were starting to line up. There were the eight imprinted bar-headed geese; there were the mountains – now to film the birds. And that's when things started to get seriously difficult. After much careful discussion of altitude and flight-speed, Lloyd and Rose had worked out that the best way to film the geese was from a paramotor – which, if you have never seen one, is a paraglider with the addition of a petrol engine, that attaches to the pilot and effectively turns the whole affair into a sort of small, noisy aeroplane. Very early on, Lloyd had contacted Bob Drury, a champion paraglider who also happened to be living in the French Alps, to see if he would help with the project. Bob had agreed: now came the crucial question.

'Bob,' says Lloyd. 'How fast can you go on your paramotor?'

'Well, 50 at least,' says Bob.

'That's great,' says Lloyd. 'We probably need to fly at around 40, so we've got a bit of leeway.'

But there had been a critical misunderstanding. Bob had meant 50 kph: Lloyd thought he had meant 50 mph, and 50 kph was only 31 mph. This would turn out to be a crucial error.

But they didn't know that yet, and as the team prepared to get airborne with the geese, it all seemed to be going wonderfully well. Thoughts were already turning to going home early, mission accomplished. Poor saps!

Meanwhile, back in Tibet, the snow continued to fall. We were trying to get up to the lake Tenzing was on, called Namtso, but the snow was making the roads extremely treacherous with super-slippy, melty slush. Our progress slowed, until finally our little convoy of Land Cruisers and equipment truck slithered to a stop. As evening fell we set up our camp beside the road, hoping the chill of the night would make the snow freeze hard enough to allow us to drive on and get to Namtso. As we tucked into noodles (again) in the mess tent it stopped snowing, and the sky cleared to reveal a vast starscape. The night was so inky black, the sky so clear, it was as if the stars were in 3-D – uncountable numbers, in the vast sweep of the Milky Way, which was truly milky. Presenter Steve Leonard and I lay on the rocky ground together in our sleeping bags staring up into the fantastic scene, conversation faltering, before slipping into an awed silence. Eventually the increasing cold drove us back into our tents.

The chill of the night did freeze the snow, and we made it right up to the high pass overlooking the lake. The pass itself, the Laken Pass, was 5190 metres above sea level, the highest we had been so far. We were all puffing and panting, but in better shape than others we found up there. Here's an extract from our cameraman Doug Allen's diary: 'A few vehicles stuck on the far side, folk puking, daft Polish folk who had hiked up the previous day, spent the night in the toilet at the top, suffering mightily from altitude sickness.' From the top of the pass we could see the lake, a startling cobalt blue, contrasting with the lighter blue of the clear sky above, both separated by the dazzling white of fresh snow. A lot of fresh snow. Meaning it was completely out of the question to try to drive down to the lake, as we would never make it back up to the pass. Stranded vehicles littered the road already. It was frustrating: there was the lake just ahead, we knew Tenzing was still on it, but now we had no way of getting there.

'Geese! Geese!' roared Steve, pointing up into the clear blue sky. Sure enough, there they were – four geese in a line, heading south, migrating bar-heads, way, way up in the sky. How high? It was extremely hard to judge, but there they were, the focus of our quest – could one of them have been Tenzing? Maybe; they were too far up for us to see any detail like a satellite collar. But then, as we watched, the geese seemed to falter: they were struggling with a strong headwind. Eventually, all four turned around, and began to glide back down to the lake. Conditions would have to be exactly right for bar-headed geese like Hillary and Tenzing to make the big jump.

For centuries Namtso ('Heavenly Lake') has been a place of pilgrimage for deeply spiritual Tibetans. There are five islands on the lake, and in past times the most devout pilgrims used to walk across the surface of the frozen lake at the end of winter, carrying provisions with them. They would then set up a simple camp on their chosen island. When spring came, the ice would melt, leaving the pilgrims completely cut-off, praying, meditating and contemplating life until the water froze over again the following winter. Rather sadly, the Chinese authorities have banned this practice.

We could not get to Namtso, so we had to give up on the idea of filming our birds on the lake where they had been all summer. However, all was not lost. It was now time to head for our final destination in Tibet, base camp of Shishapangma, to attempt to rendezvous with the birds as they made their way back south off the Tibetan plateau. We packed up the convoy and hit the road once more, hoping the birds would sit tight until we made it to base camp.

Meanwhile, back in the Alps, as the team struggled to film bar-headed geese in flight, things had unravelled somewhat. The 50 kph/50 mph misunderstanding quickly rendered Bob's original paramotor useless. It was way too slow for the geese to fly alongside. It turned out the geese's preferred flying speed was almost exactly 43 mph: at 30 mph they just stalled. An urgent search had uncovered a much faster racing paramotor which would do the job, but it then became apparent Bob, although a paragliding champion, did not have a licence to fly tandem with Rose. And if Rose was not on board the geese would not think of following the paramotor, which they already regarded with deep suspicion. All thoughts of an early return home began to recede. Somehow the geese must be encouraged to see Bob as their new best friend, and Rose had to come up with a way of transferring her hard-won authority over her nervous consorts to Bob. Bob was a genius paraglider, but had little experience of getting geese to love him.

An intense charm offensive swung into operation. First, Rose had to find some special treat the geese adored which Bob could give them. Many treats were tried, but the most popular turned out to be…lettuce. Bob and Rose would sit with the geese, and Bob would offer them delicious bits of lettuce. At a carefully chosen moment, Rose would slowly slip away, leaving Bob alone with the geese. Gradually this tactic began to work: the geese started to think Bob was really not too bad, and was certainly an excellent lettuce-vendor. Before long Bob was sitting on the ground, in the seat of the paramotor, engine idling, dispensing lettuce to suspicious but greedy geese surrounding him. From this it was but a short hop into the air. The plan was working! The geese would follow Bob, but only for around 200 metres before becoming frightened and peeling off to try to find Rose, who had to take to hiding in the van. It took eight days' hard work to get Bob accepted as leader and trusted friend of geese. Another week had gone by. They also lost five days to bad weather. However, the geese were now willing to follow the racing paramotor. A camera was rigged for Bob to operate himself once they had reached serious height. It seemed as if, at last, they were nearly there. Five weeks after they had first arrived in France Bob took off, and the geese followed, higher and higher. Rose came out from her hiding place in the van and the ground crew held their collective breath. Was this going to be it at last?

Back in Tibet we had got as far as our vehicles could go. We were now in the shadow of Shishapangma, the fourteenth-highest mountain in the world. Time to make camp. The slightest effort – shovelling small lumps of snow to pitch a tent, for instance – required enormous effort and many periods of rest. If you lost your breath it took an age to get it back. We were camping at over 5000 metres, and at this height there was less than half the amount of oxygen per breath than at sea level.

By now all of us were feeling pretty rough. You have a number of problems at altitude. It takes something like two weeks for the body to start to produce more red blood cells in response to the lack of oxygen. Before then you simply pee a lot, which has the effect of concentrating your blood to start to achieve a better oxygen-carrying capacity. This is no real problem. However, you are very breathless, again normal, but you can't help worrying that the breathlessness might in fact be due to your lungs filling up with fluid – pulmonary oedema – which is a much more serious effect of altitude. And then you have a headache pretty much all the time. Once again you are asking yourself: is this just a normal headache, or is it cerebal oedema – fluid leaking into my brain – which can be an extremely serious consequence of being at altitude. The view is nice, but it's very uncomfortable being at altitude, and the effects vary hugely from individual to individual.

Using the satellite phone to get the latest updates from John Takekawa on the other side of the world in California, we discovered Tenzing and Hillary were still on the lakes, so, feeling a little bit sorry for ourselves, we settled down to wait for the yaks to arrive, to help us carry our kit up to advanced base camp.

Meanwhile, in the cable-car leading to the top of the Aiguille du Midi (next door to Mont Blanc), tourists and mountaineers were surprised to discover they were sharing the gondola with two large noisy Carry-Pet boxes and a group of harassed Englishers. The boxes clearly contained a large number of birds, as evidenced by the racket coming from within. Being French, the tourists assumed the birds were destined for the kitchen of the café on the viewing terrace.

There had been a further hitch. Although the birds had now accepted Bob as the leader, it transpired their loyalty only extended so far – 400 feet, to be precise. They would go no higher. But we had to get shots of birds apparently flying high over the Himalayas. Then someone on the team had a stroke of pure genius. If the birds would not come to the mountain, then the mountain must come to the birds. They would carry the reluctant geese up to the highest point in the Alps reached by cable-car. Then, when Bob flew by in the paramotor, they would encourage the geese to follow him.

Two cable-car journeys and a ride in a lift brought them to the top of the Aiguille du Midi 3842 metres up. Gasping for breath, the team had arrived at the lift-off point. This was properly high at last – but would the birds, currently walking about on the small terrace outside the café, honking, actually take off? The team arrived at the top at 9 a.m. – now where was Bob?

In fact, Bob was having carburettor and fuel problems way down in the valley, but eventually, at nearly midday, the team heard a faint droning coming from – where? Somewhere amongst the towering peaks surrounding them – it was hard to know where it was coming from – the droning got louder, and suddenly – there he was! A bright blue and yellow wing – Bob on the borrowed paramotor, nearly 4000 metres up, heading towards them. Magnificent! Here he comes! The birds looked up…He was right by them now, and started to circle. Bob the lettuce-giver shouted to the geese, who took absolutely no notice and settled down comfortably to preen themselves. Bob circled – still the geese refused to go. To the bemusement of tourists, Rose and her assistant Lee began to run about flapping their arms, shouting 'Take off! Take off!'

Bob circled again, and at last the geese got the message – that was their lettuce-providing friend Bob out there in the noisy thing! They flapped their wings furiously, ran across the terrace and took off, just making it over the lip surrounding the platform, and flew out towards Bob.

Now, at last, all the specialised metabolic and physical adaptations of these extraordinary birds for flying at extreme height kicked in. They flapped hard, they flew strongly, their complex lungs inhaled deeply, drawing oxygen from the thin air with exceptional efficiency. Flapping furiously, they took up their position in a line stretching back from the paramotor's port side. Bob reached out and hit the camera's record button. The camera ran; the birds flew. Bob had no way of knowing exactly what he was filming, but at last, after seven weeks, it had all come together. The geese flew round and round – in fact, now they couldn't be stopped.

Suddenly the engine sputtered and fell silent. Bob was out of fuel. Gently the paramotor slipped away, losing height, and began its long glide down to earth. The geese, loyalties split, watched it go, and continued to circle, looking back at Rose, their original love, but they did not seem to fancy landing on the platform. Eventually they too broke off, and flew gracefully away from the Aiguille du Midi, all the way down to the comfort of the white van 12,000 feet down in the valley. Which was where, later that day, Rose found them, looking quite pleased with themselves.

When the producer I had asked to go down to help organise this shoot saw the resulting pictures, he burst into tears. They had got it. Now a very senior executive in the BBC, he recently told me this was the hardest shoot he'd ever been involved with. That one flyby was the only chance they had; the paramotor had developed a misfire; various other things had started to come apart at the seams – but never mind: after seven weeks of unremitting effort, endless setbacks, they had got the pictures of bar-headed geese flying high over mountains.

So now, when you see those pictures (which are used almost every time someone makes a film about the Himalayas), you know what went into getting those few precious shots, and you also know (*Shhh!*) that, despite whatever the commentary might say, they are not flying over the Himalayas at all. That's the Alps beneath them. But it was the only way to get those images.

Of course, up amongst the Himalayas proper, we had no idea what was going on thousands of miles away in the Alps. We had issues of our own to grapple with. We had a serious problem. I had organised a group of yak to carry the gear up the final part of our journey from 5000 metres to Shishapangma advanced base camp at 5400 metres – a fair way – and the yak and their herders had arrived looking magnificent against the snow. The weather could not have been more perfect and, to top it all, we had discovered Tenzing had left Namtso, and was moving closer to where we were. It all seemed to be heading towards a perfect climax. Except Steve Leonard, our presenter, had a headache. We all had headaches, but this one looked considerably more ominous. Another extract from Doug's diary: 'Bonny dawn, but Steve not at all well with a bad headache – probably a migraine, but just may be cerebral oedema. Better safe than sorry, so he set off down to Zangmu'. The trouble with being on the Tibetan plateau is that it's just that: an enormous plateau, and it can take a very long time to get off it and down to lower, safer altitudes. Not only that: on the way down you may have to drive over passes considerably higher than your departure point. I simply could not take the chance that Steve might be suffering from something life-threatening. It was the end of our attempt to rendezvous with the geese from Base Camp. As Steve disappeared off looking reasonably ghastly, I did my first-ever 'piece to camera', trying to explain what was going on, wearing a ridiculous hat, and surrounded by yaks.

Despite my altitude-induced confusion I had just enough wit to haggle with the chief yak herder to purchase his yak-fat-smeared knife for my ever-expanding knife collection. I thought I had done quite well, until I saw exactly the same knives on sale in Kathmandu for a great deal less than I'd paid the wily herder. But at least mine is smeared with genuine yak fat, hugely increasing its provenance and re-sale value, possibly.

The rest of us left the dazzling white brilliance of Shishapangma with mixed feelings. It is a beautiful but harsh place. Doug Allen's diary one final time: 'Can't say I was overly sorry to leave. Dry, dusty, cold, high and dirty just about sums it up, though some of them vistas blow your head off. But the over-riding impression is of a tough place, you just never feel 100 per cent coz of the altitude and the fuzziness just becomes the dominant memory.'

Throughout all this we had kept in contact with John Takekawa to get updates on Tenzing and Hillary's positions. Although they had both moved closer to the edge of the mountains, neither had left the high Himalaya to go over the top to their winter homes on the lowlands to the south. I could not justify the spiralling costs of staying in Tibet any longer. We flew home on 10 November and, infuriatingly, on the 14th, just four days later, both Hillary and Tenzing made their move. We had been so close.

So we had failed – or had we? One of the main objectives of this trip was to gather some direct evidence to answer the question: did the bar-headed geese go over the top of the Himalayas, as widely claimed in all the apocryphal stories, or did they, in fact, conserve energy and stay low, using the passes instead? The Himalayan plateau may have defeated us frail humans, but we still had the electronics. Although by the time Hillary and Tenzing finally made their move the batteries on their satellite tags were starting to fail, they had recorded detailed information about the geese's height as they flew over the Himalayas. Getting this real data was in fact a world first, and a credit to the hard work of John Takekawa – who has never received proper credit. So, the 64,000-dollar question: what was the highest altitude John's tagged geese attained? Drum roll... It was 6100 metres – nowhere near the 8000 metres-plus required to go 'over the top of Everest'. Subsequent studies have confirmed John's results: the migrating geese usually peak at 6400 metres, although they spend 95 per cent of their time below 5784 metres. Of a test group of 91 tagged geese cited in a recent scientific paper, only one went above 6500 metres, hitting a maximum of 6540 metres. The 8000 metres stories are nonsense. I suspect you will still see this claim in respectable reports for many years to come, however: old nonsense dies hard. As Winston Churchill said so perceptively: 'A lie gets halfway around the world before the truth has a chance to get its pants on.'

Nevertheless, 6400 metres is still an immense height, and if we went up to this sort of altitude in a single day, as the geese do, we would surely die. So how do they do it? The big problem is getting enough oxygen to sustain flight at this altitude, especially as they have to flap harder in the thin air. At 6400 metres the geese will only have 46 per cent of the oxygen that they would have at sea level. Faced with these conditions, experiments have shown, the geese start to breathe more deeply and more efficiently. Their hearts are far more richly supplied with blood capillaries than lowland birds', and this increases the heart's ability to pump blood. But by far the most important change is a single mutation in the haemoglobin in the bar-headed goose's blood, that makes it far, far more efficient at transporting oxygen around the body, and to the flight muscles. Because of this single mutation, bar-headed geese can do what no other bird on Earth can do: climb up from sea level to enormous height, up across the highest mountain range on earth on to the Tibetan plateau, all in around eight hours. It used to be thought that bar-headed geese were helped in this migration by hitching a ride on powerful winds blowing across the mountains, but it turns out this is not the case. These astonishing birds do the migration entirely under their own steam.

Finally, you may be wondering what happened to the eight geese that performed such heroic feats (well, eventually) down in the Alps. All of them returned safely to the UK, none the worse for their adventures. For a time they lived in the lap of luxury at Lloyd and Rose's place, becoming more and more independent, and gradually got re-homed at exotic wildfowl locations around the country – but only with people Lloyd and Rose knew and trusted. Geese are long-lived – twenty years or more in captivity – so it's very possible these wonderful birds are still with us. I wonder if they would remember Rose, Bob or the paramotor if they met them today?

8

CROCODILE ATTACK

'Man-Eaters' *Nightmares of Nature*,

BBC1, 1995

'So, Maggie, we're going to strap you into the crocodile's jaws, get you to hold your breath, push you and the croc underwater, then I—'

'Sorry? Strap me in?'

'Yes…?'

'And then I have to hold my breath?'

'Yes, hold your breath…'

'Well, how long for?'

'Oh, not too long. Then, once we've pushed you right underwater, I grab the handles at the other end and death-roll you round and round in the croc's mouth whilst we film with the underwater camera, and then…then…Yes? What is it?'

'I want to talk to BBC Contracts back in England right now, please, Martin.'

Actresses! *Tcha!*

It was a rainy afternoon in Kakadu National Park up in the Northern territories of Australia. Val Plumwood was on holiday, and had borrowed a canoe to get some well-earned rest from the stresses of her work. She was wet but relaxed as she glided through the half-submerged paperbark trees and lush vegetation. Then, up ahead, Val noticed something protruding from the water…Oh, just a log…As she drifted towards it the log seemed to move slightly. With mounting excitement Val realised it was not a log at all, but a crocodile.

Being a great wildlife lover, Val was thrilled but she knew better than to approach the croc, so gently paddled away to avoid getting too close. Yet, as she paddled, she found the distance between her and the crocodile seemed to be narrowing. She watched the croc getting closer – and then it disappeared. Val looked around. It was as though it had never been there: not a ripple…She lifted the paddle to move on, when there was a sudden crash against the side of the canoe, then another. She dropped the paddle and hung on to the sides – this couldn't be happening? Crocs don't attack canoes? Another blow – it must be using its head to hit the sides…The canoe was still moving slowly forward, and directly in her path was an overhanging branch – perhaps she could grab it and get out of the canoe? She had to make a decision, and fast. The branch came overhead, she jumped – got it! For a moment Val hung on the branch, arms over, but body dangling.

With a shocking explosion the crocodile leapt up out of the water and slammed its jaws shut right between Val's legs, before dragging her off the branch and into the water. Now it began to death-roll her, twisting round and round, intent on drowning its prey. The power was enormous. Val hardly had time to think, to comprehend what was happening to her. Her breath was running out when – the croc let go. She was free? Fuelled by a massive surge of adrenalin, and not yet aware of the injuries she'd already sustained, Val struck out for a nearby shore. She made it – but her leg wasn't working properly? She hauled herself out of the water and tried to pull herself up the steep, muddy bank with her fingers – what was wrong with her leg? Then there was second explosion. She felt teeth sink into her leg, and she was dragged down the bank, back underwater – the death-rolling began again. Through the cloudy water Val could see nothing, just feel the immense power of the crocodile. So this was how it all ended ... She couldn't hold her breath much longer ... And then, again, it let her go.

It was a sickening game of cat and mouse. Once more Val tried to drag herself up the slippery bank, digging in her fingertips. Exhausted. Waiting for the final attack. She knew if the croc came again there was nothing she could do about it – it would be the end. But the final attack never came. She lay there panting, waiting – just the sounds of the birds in the trees and the breeze in the paperbarks ... Despite some very nasty injuries – the crocodile's teeth had pierced her body right through to her vagina – Val survived. She felt no vindictiveness towards the crocodile, and it's a very unusual attack.

As you might have guessed, if you have been following these chronicles so far, this story pertains to the *Nightmares of Nature* series, and this particular episode I was producing was headlined, 'Man-Eaters'. Val Plumwood was one of the very few people who had survived a serious saltwater crocodile attack, and I wanted to re-construct her story to start the film. I needed to record an interview with Val, so that her voice could drive the film sequence. Which was why I'd come to Australia to meet her. Here's how the meeting went ...

Dazed from multiple flights, I'd just unlocked a padlocked gate, as instructed by Val, and was driving my hire car through towering rain forest. It was lush, damp and very beautiful. Five kilometres later I pulled up at a large, single-roomed 'eco house'.

Knocked on the door, and there was Val herself. Not terrifically friendly, somehow?

Our meeting got off to a frosty start with her opening salvo.

'I'm not really happy about having a man come here to interview me.'

'Er – why is that?'

'Men are responsible for appalling abuses of women worldwide. Could you go and get your researcher, Jan, to come instead?'

That would be rather difficult, I explained, as I had just come around 12,000 miles in order to have this meeting.

'Well, OK,' said Val. Having reloaded for a second broadside: 'But I want $1,600 dollars to talk to you, and an absolute veto over how you reconstruct my story.'

This was something that hadn't come up during our long-distance phone calls. Things weren't going tremendously well…OK, OK: tiptoe, eggshells, eggshells…

I put away my recording equipment. 'Well, I'll, er…I suppose I'd better book myself into a motel tonight, and I'll run this past the BBC lawyers, and hopefully come back tomorrow?'

'OK,' she said, clearly teetering on the edge of 'Don't bother'.

By now it was dark. As I prepared to go – pretty downhearted – there was a curious noise outside on Val's verandah.

'Hang on,' she said, grabbing a carrot from the sideboard. 'Stay there – just sit still and, whatever happens, don't do anything. Just watch, OK?'

The sounds were getting louder. Something big was coming towards the door. There was a crash, and a large, bizarre animal rolled in, unlike anything I had ever seen before. A quarter bear, a quarter badger, part koala, and part Sherman tank…'What that?' I blurted – overjoyed by this sensational entrance.

'It's my wombat,' said Val.

And so it was. Val had found the wombat as a baby, after its mother had been killed in a collision with a car. She'd successfully nursed it, and it had lived in the house until it had become a feisty teenager. Even Val's formidable personality could not cow a teenage wombat, whose favourite method of play was to bite Val's ankles. Other wombats love this sort of thing apparently – biting one another's legs is meat and drink to wombats – they're designed for it – but Val wasn't, and it made her bleed. So now the wombat roamed free in the rainforest, returning as it pleased for a square meal, and to be de-ticked and de-leeched by its surrogate mum. I was utterly entranced. I suspect Val noticed how genuine my reaction was: as I left I thought I detected a slight thaw.

I checked into a motel, then, and sent faxes. Back then, we producers all thought the BBC lawyers were notoriously spineless, though to be fair we really couldn't hand over the programme's editorial to Val. Sure enough, next morning I came down to breakfast to the predictable response: 'Do not under any circumstances proceed on these terms', etc. I pronged a moody forkful and got ready to call Val, not expecting much. But to my surprise, she was much more friendly that morning.

'Look – give me half the money now, and the other half when I agree to the story, because that way it will motivate me to be reasonable. After all, it's your film.' This was a curious line of reasoning, but, hey, I wasn't complaining – we were on!

Which was just as well. I already had a full-sized crocodile model in a crate on its way to Australia, and the film crew were booked and about to fly. I shot back to Plumwood towers, recorded the interview with this fascinating, angry woman, and made the flight for Darwin with minutes to spare.

A saltwater crocodile is not the sharpest tool in the box.

A three-and-a-half-metre-long croc has a brain somewhere between an almond and a walnut in size. Around .05 per cent of its body weight. But why do you need a big brain? We humans are so brain-ist. Once nature hits on a really effective design it tends to stick with it: the basic crocodile layout is fantastically effective, and has not changed significantly for some 80 million years. Saltwater crocodiles are described as 'hyper-carnivorous apex ambush predators', which means if the opportunity arises they will have a go at practically anything. An adult male crocodile can take prey up to a ton or more, and there's not much point in fighting back: not only does the croc have the strongest jaws of any animal alive today; its body is also armour-plated with a suit of bony plates, or scutes, just under the skin all along its back and tail. Crocodile and alligator skulls are so thick that once, when I was filming a 'gator hunter in Florida he accidentally shot himself – on camera – because part of the bullet ricocheted back off the 'gator's skull into the fleshy part of his leg. In 2011 a croc was recorded taking an adult tiger, for goodness' sake – a very respectable, well-armed predator in its own right.

The problem is that a saltwater crocodile has a tendency to treat any human in its territory as just another prey item. Given its size and speed, survival from a direct predatory attack is unlikely. A saltie can swim at 15 to 18 mph – three times faster than even a fit human – and despite its lazy appearance it can outrun you on land. An adult saltwater crocodile is truly formidable. Nevertheless, in Australia, with an estimated croc population of 100,000 to 200,000, there are just one or two fatal attacks on humans per year, often involving alcohol. To be honest, I'm amazed there aren't more – a testament, perhaps, to effective educational programmes.

So Val was on board, up to a point, but how was I going to

reconstruct her story? I drove to a Thai restaurant for supper – the Thai food in Darwin was fantastic – and got to work on my storyboard. As I may have mentioned before, a storyboard is a sort of cartoon. I'm very fortunate that I have always been able to see the story I'm trying to tell unfolding as a series of pictures in my head – I can quickly write a sequential list of the images as they flow into my imagination, e.g. 'wide shot of Val in canoe in paperbark swamp; close-up of paddle; close-up of her face looking around; detail of something in the distance, etc.' I could mentally rerun Val's story as she told it, and add the pictures. This shot list could then be turned into a storyboard, where each image is drawn like a cartoon. By looking at the storyboard you can generally see if the film you are trying to make is going to work for a viewer, and for the director it's also a really useful checklist to make sure you are getting all the shots you need to create the final sequence.

This ability to create a vivid picture-story in my head has its downside, though, because I can't switch it off. Driving on a motorway I can suddenly see, with terrible clarity, that red car on the other side of the road hitting another; close-up of driver's face; car flying up into the air; top shot looking down as it goes over the central reservation; next shot my POV (point of view) as, having cleared the central reservation, it flies towards me, filling the picture – and smashes directly through the windscreen; or in a nightclub I see the top shot of me trying to dance; a close-up of my sweaty face; detail of my out-of-time hips; wide shot of dance floor with expert dancers all around as I flail away – all in a series of vivid, painful images…Which I why I don't dance, and drive quite carefully on a motorway.

Anyhow, there I was, going through my storyboard, frame by frame, and checking I had organised everything we would need for each set-up. Suddenly I had a thought. I had rented one of the new-fangled 'portable phones' for this trip (this was 1994) – quite a large grey thing, with a pull-up aerial and a flip-top. But, I wondered, could this device call beyond Darwin, where I was – could it, for instance, call abroad? I put down my beer and tapped out the numbers: zero, zero, 44, the international code for the UK, then my home number. To my amazement it rang…Hello? Hello, love! I was speaking to my wife, in real time, on the other side of the world. I was about to go to bed, and she was about to go into work. This was my first-ever international mobile call, and even as we spoke to each other the entire planet seemed to shrink. I will never forget my astonishment at being able to do this.

Soon the film crew arrived, and on a hot, sunny morning we were all gathered together on location in Berry Springs wildlife park for our first day's filming. We must have presented an slightly unusual sight: the film crew in a variety of different swimwear; our – brilliant – actress Maggie Miles (contract now all sorted) in 'normal' clothes ready to play the part of Val Plumwood, and half a huge, and extremely life-like, saltwater crocodile, with a pair of handlebars sticking out of the back end.

Something suddenly struck me.

'So,' I said to the park ranger, 'there are obviously no crocs in here right now, are there?' We were standing beside a large waterhole.

'Woah, woah, mate! I dunno about that, mate! There could be – there's crocs everywhere here, mate.'

'But not here – where we're about to get in the water and film – are there?'

'Might be. It's a big hole – there could be a big old boy down there.'

'Really?'

'Mate, these salties move around all the time. One could have slipped in there last night, no worries.'

'?!'

'It's pretty unlikely there's a croc down there, mate – but, honestly, you can never be 100 per cent sure unless you have a look.'

So it was that I crept gingerly into the warmish water, wearing a mask and snorkel, to peer into the gloomy depths. Was there anything down there that looked like a bloody great crocodile? Not as far as I could see...We set up guards every night thereafter, scanning the darkness with torches looking for croc eyeshine. Despite this, every morning before we started filming there was a slight frisson – could a saltie have crept in overnight and be just waiting for us in the water?

Soon we were opening the model croc's great jaws and fitting Maggie in, her legs either side of the croc's head. Its snout came up to her stomach. Once she was firmly wedged, we strapped her in with a belt threaded through the underside of the croc's jaws. I took up my position at the other end of the model, holding the handlebar with which I could 'death-roll' both croc and Maggie once they were underwater. Richard, our superb cameraman, had the camera safe in its underwater housing. Ready? OK, nodded Richard, and he submerged himself. OK, Maggie? Nod, deep breath. *Huhhhh!* Shove her under! *Blub blub blub*, I start to roll.... And roll.... How long can she hold her breath, I wonder? Bit more rolling...One more...And up.

Gasp!

'Great!' says Richard. 'It looks fantastic. Let's do it again, but I'll get the camera a bit closer.'

'OK – are you ready, Maggie?'

'Well, yes, I suppose…'

'Deep breath, then, and under we go.' That marvellous actress certainly earned every dollar of her fee.

Eventually Richard is satisfied. Shot 23 on the storyboard is in the can. It takes us many days' hard work to film all forty different shots needed to tell the whole story.

Why did the crocodile attack Val? We already know that a crocodile, having a very broad 'prey image', will try to eat pretty much anything if it seems like a meal. But a boat? It's more likely this was a territorial attack. Most crocodile species are fairly social, happy to share basking-spots with others – sometimes they even work together to dismember large prey – but saltwater crocs seem to be more territorial, large males driving rival males out of their territory while at the same time welcoming females. There is a rude but droll comparison of salties with certain Aussie blokes: 'big mouth, small brain, lots of girlfriends'. Around a half of all crocodile attacks on humans are thought to be territorial. During a territorial attack crocs will go for anything, including boats, paddles, oil drums, lilos – all sorts of random non-living objects that happen to be in the area. Territorial attacks are less likely to end in death for any humans who get involved. So it could have been a male territorial attack – something the ardent feminist Val might have found deeply distasteful, that would chime with her anti-male philosophy (although she clearly stated she did not hold any animosity towards the crocodile). But there is another possibility, one I think more likely, and which would have caused Val a bit of bother. Having done a bit of digging, I think it's most likely to have been a female croc that attacked her. Why's that?

Crocodiles don't perhaps have many endearing features, but there is one trait we can all admire. The females are exceptionally good mothers. They lay eggs, generally forty to sixty, in a clutch in a carefully made-up mound of mud and rotting vegetation. But, having laid the eggs, the mother doesn't just clear off – not a bit of it. For 80 to 100 days she will guard the nest. When the eggs start to hatch – she can tell by the yelping coming from inside – she will sometimes pick them up and roll them gently around in her mouth to help them out. If danger threatens the youngsters (around 25 cm at hatching, and 70 g), Mum is on hand, and will pick them all up so they can shelter inside her mouth. She stays with her young for several months. Surprising, perhaps, for such a 'primitive' animal. But, and here's the rub, female crocodiles can be very aggressive around the nest. Val Plumwood was attacked in February: saltwater crocodiles lay eggs between November and March. I think it's very possible Val was attacked by a female guarding her nest site, another mum. The croc did not seem all that big, Val told me, and females are much smaller than the males. If it was a territorial female, an attack on her canoe would fit the picture, too.

Despite the close attentions of the mother, only around 1 per cent of hatchling crocodiles survive into adulthood, but if they do they can live a long time – 70 years, perhaps even 100. During their long lives saltwater crocodiles will roam far and wide, even, as their name suggests, travelling long distances in saltwater. Twenty salties were tagged in one research project, and eight of them took to the open ocean. One travelled 590 kilometres in 25 days, just cruising, allowing himself to be carried along by the current. Some saltwater crocodiles spend so long at sea they grow barnacles on their skin.

The filming was going well. I had been able to tick off many of the frames from my storyboard. Now we were on to number 17, the bit where Val (Maggie) leaps from the canoe to grab an overhanging branch. We had filmed Maggie actually doing the leap, but we needed her POV as she jumped, so cameraman Richard got into the canoe ready to make the camera 'leap' up as he passed under the branch. As he was getting ready I went for a quick wee. This was a slightly unnerving experience. On day one I had noticed something fascinating. If I went off into the undergrowth, which was carpeted with a layer of dry leaves, and stood still to relieve myself, I gradually became aware the ground all around me was on the move. Everywhere I looked, small creatures were looping their way directly towards where I stood. As I got my eye in, I realised there were dozens of them, brown, about 3 or 4 cm long – what on earth? Leeches, all homing in on me – fascinating. How on earth did they sense I was standing there? Was it the heat of my body, my movement? The urine? Whatever it was, they approached from all sides over leaves, twigs, even along branches of nearby trees. I don't mind a leech – innocuous things, really – the smaller ones, anyway. Many's the time I have pulled off a boot to discover a blood-soaked sock beneath and the remains of a leech. How they find us and then wriggle into the smallest places amazes me. It was exciting to see the small brown army homing in and then making sure I was able to exit just as the vanguard reached my boots. I always got away, but the same cannot be said for my good friend Phil Chapman.

Phil was filming in Borneo and found himself wading waist-deep in a swamp. He was actually wearing a fairly loose-fitting boiler suit at the time. Suddenly he felt a sharp pain in his willy. He got on to high ground and dropped his trousers to investigate. At the tip of his penis, he saw to his horror, the end of a leech disappearing up his urethra.

'I grabbed hold of it,' he told me.

'But how did you do that, Phil – they are so slippy and hard to hold onto?'

'Believe me, I held on,' he said with feeling. 'I was using my fingernails to grip the back end, but of course I couldn't actually pull it out because the head end was still firmly attached inside.' What could he do?

Suddenly inspiration struck. Fortuitously, Phil had a small can of DEET anti-mosquito spray with him. Using his free hand, he managed to extricate it from his pocket and push off the lid.

Very, very carefully he started to spray the neat DEET onto the tail end of the leech – the little bit that he could still see. This was a high-risk strategy, because DEET stings like fury on sensitive skin, but luckily 'the DEET hurt the leech just – only just – a bit more than it hurt me,' said Phil 'and eventually it let go.'

He then managed to extract the animal, which turned out to be a tiger leech. In fact, he was very lucky it was a tiger leech because they hurt when they attach to suck blood, unlike other leeches, whose bite is painless. The pain of the bite had alerted Phil to what was going on. There are other cases where the leech has continued to work its way into the bladder of the unfortunate victim, died in there, and caused serious medical problems. After this incident, us adventurous types would wear a condom if wading through tiger leech territory, or at least wrap our parts in clingfilm. This was known, after Phil, as being 'Chapmanised'.

Richard was ready to film the leap from the canoe, and I stood by on the shore as he did the shot to grab the front of the canoe. It was a fairly wobbly canoe, but Richard assured me it would be all right. After a few takes he was still not satisfied he'd got the sense of upward movement quite right. 'Just once more...'

The canoe came towards me; Richard leapt; the canoe wobbled;

Richard hung for a moment, poised, a look of horror on his face – and then over he went. I watched the £25,000 camera and its £12,000 lens descend towards the water as if in slow motion. Richard held his arm up as he fell in, like the Lady of the Lake brandishing Excalibur, but the waterhole was too deep. As the waters closed over Richard and the camera I could see the red 'On' light still flashing. Then it stopped. This was bad.

That, I thought, would be the end of our shoot for the time being. Expensive having an entire film crew in Darwin with nothing to do while a camera is sent off to – where? Sydney? – for repairs. I feared for my budget. By some sort of miracle, however, Maggie had a boyfriend who had a professional film camera. So the next day we were back in business.

It was a very good shoot, and the sequence was powerful. I never did find out what Val thought of it and now I never will, because she died in 2008. Despite our bumpy meetings I have great respect for this forceful and highly articulate woman. And I will certainly never forget the explosive and thrilling entrance of Val's wombat.

While researching this chapter I came across the strangest thing. Val herself may be gone, but her canoe is not. The actual canoe Val was in that day has been preserved for posterity: it was found, refurbished, and then purchased by the National Museum of Australia in Canberra, where it is now on display. That's a bit weird, isn't it?

9

BIRD STRIKE

Steve Leonard's Extreme Animals,

BBC1, first transmitted 2002

It had been a largely uneventful flight so far – some turbulence, but otherwise completely normal. In the warmth of the cockpit the pilot was a little drowsy. The engines droned. Suddenly there was a loud bang. The pilot jerked up in his seat, spilling his coffee, instantly wide awake. What the hell was that? Something was seriously wrong with one of the engines: there was a lot of vibration, and the instruments were going haywire. He tried to look out: there was nothing obvious, but he had to act fast – the vibration was getting worse. There was no option: he flicked switches, the engine shut down, and the vibration subsided. He studied his altimeter carefully: 37,000 feet – high enough for a long glide if the number two engine shut down, too. 'Come in, Abidjan; come in, Abidjan – I have a problem…' But happily, the second engine did not falter, and he was soon landing. It was 29 November 1973, off the Côte D'Ivoire – the west coast of Africa. The incident was just about to enter the record books.

Once the plane was safely down, the ground crew went to investigate. The engine was heavily damaged. To their immense surprise they saw there had clearly been a bird strike. They carefully gathered the remains of the bird: five full feathers and fifteen partial feathers. But what bird could possibly have been flying at 37,000 feet?

The feathers were sent to the US, to the legendary forensic ornithologist Roxie C. Laybourne. Roxie Laybourne had pioneered the technique of using the microscopic structures of plumulaceous (downy) feathers to identify different bird species. She had identified bird remains from literally thousands of aircraft-bird collisions. In this case there was no room for doubt: Roxie identified the feathers as being from a vulture, and specifically a Ruppell's griffon vulture. She wrote up her findings in a short paper, published in December 1974, simply and prosaically entitled, 'Collision between a vulture and an aircraft at an altitude of 37,000 feet'. This is the highest recorded altitude of any bird – nothing else has come close – but, as the temperature at 37,000 feet is a blood-freezing -50° C and there is practically no oxygen, what on earth was Griff the vulture doing up there?

On Thursday, 18 October 2001, I set off for India, on a film trip that would, I hoped, throw light on this mystery.

We had come to film HGVs. Not Heavy Goods Vehicles like the gaudily painted 'Horn, please' lorries that infest the highways and byways of India. No, we had come to film another HGV: the Himalayan griffon vulture, also one of the highest flying birds on Earth, and a close relation to Griff the record-breaker.

We were heading for the Indian Himalayas, and a place called Manali, in the company of world champion paraglider Robbie Whittall, and his good mate Bob Drury – Rob 'n' Bob. Why Manali? Because not only is Manali famous amongst paragliders as a superb launch site: it's also a great place to find Himalayan griffon vultures. And why paragliders? Because paragliding is about as close as you can get to flying like a vulture. In fact, it's an almost perfect match. The skills needed for Rob to become a world champion exactly mirrored the skills a world-record-breaking vulture – indeed, any vulture – would need to employ. The fact is, griffon vultures are so big and heavy they are incapable of sustained flapping flight, so our record-breaker could not possibly have flapped his way into the record books. So then, how did he do it?

Until fairly recently, when their numbers crashed due to side effects from the drug Diclofenac used in cattle farming, vultures used to be a ubiquitous feature of the Indian landscape, an essential part of the food chain. They may not be particularly beautiful-looking birds, but they are perfectly designed for their essential role as garbage operatives. Vultures – for all your worldwide waste-disposal solutions. Worldwide? Yes. There are two different groups of vultures: sixteen different species in Europe and Asia (Old World vultures); and seven species in the Americas (New World vultures).

I remember once being outside the city of Jodhpur in Rajasthan. Every day, any animals that had died in the area were picked up by members of an Untouchable caste, the Chamar. Only the Chamar were allowed to touch the dead bodies of sacred cows, buffalos or camels. These bodies were taken outside the city to a huge dump, a magnet for hundreds and hundreds of scavengers, who performed the essential job of cleaning the place up. There were pigs and jackals, packs of semi-wild dogs and, if you looked carefully, the ground was littered with black and white quills. Porcupines were sneaking out under the cover of darkness to share in the feast.

There was a whole community of scavengers at the dump, but most impressive of all were the vultures. Every day a host of different species would pour in, darkening the sky. There were Indian long-billed vultures, white-backed vultures, king vultures and Egyptian vultures. There seemed to be a clear hierarchy, and different vultures had different jobs to do. The Egyptian vultures were key: they alone were strong enough to rip open the tough hide of the dead animals. Once the Egyptian vultures had made the first incisions, the others piled in – a screeching, squabbling, scratching, bad-tempered mass. Occasionally one of the really huge vultures, a gigantic cinereous, would make an appearance, sweeping in and scattering his lesser brethren. Even the dogs would stand back respectfully.

Once satiated, there would be a line, in strict single-file, of stuffed vultures, walking slightly unsteadily up to the highest point in the area to launch their bloated bodies into the air and, with luck, sweep upwards and away. If disturbed, a vulture will sick up all its meal, not as an active defence-mechanism, like the corrosive projectile vomit of fulmars, which I have had the dubious pleasure of experiencing for myself, but as a way of lightening themselves to enable them to take off. The area around the carcass dump was littered with vultures standing torpid and sleepy, wings akimbo, in the hot Indian sun, already digesting their meals before making the trek up to the take-off point.

But here's a fascinating thing. Most of the carcasses at the Jodhpur dump were fairly fresh, but that is not always the case, and vultures will happily eat putrefying flesh that few other animals could stomach. Some of the animals vultures eat will have died precisely because of viral or bacterial infection, and so their bodies would be stuffed with pathogens (infectious agents). How can vultures do this without becoming extremely sick? Warm, festering dead flesh will quickly become a perfect substrate for some of the most deadly toxins known to man – how about anthrax, produced by the bacterium *bacillus anthracis*, or, most potent of all, botulinum, a fantastically powerful neurotoxin produced by *clostridium botulinum*, which specifically grows on festering meat products. Just 75 nanogrammes – a billionth of a gram – of botulinum toxin is enough to kill you or me. Yet vultures will happily gobble down great beakfuls of botulinum, anthrax and a host of other nasties, and come to no harm at all. How come?

It's partly down to their digestive systems, which have the ability to kill any virus or bacteria they ingest, functioning in effect as a sterilising process. But also, their immune system produces antibodies specifically designed to deal with the toxins that bacteria like *clostridium botulinum* produce. Vultures are a form of purification, therefore, because, despite the rotting, disease-ridden carcasses they eat, their droppings, and the pellets they cough up, are 'clean', and carry no disease at all. Vultures do nothing less than stop the spread of disease, because all the pathogens they take on board when they eat are destroyed. Even their urine is a disinfectant. Vultures urinate down their legs, which serves both to cool them as it evaporates, and kills any bugs they may have picked up wandering around amongst rotting carcasses.

Anyhow, back to our paragliding with Rob 'n' Bob.

The town of Manali is in the state of Himachal Pradesh, which stretches up into the Himalayas themselves. It's a favourite destination for Indians who want to see and touch snow. Manali was a hill station in the time of the Raj (the more famous Shimla is just down the road), and back then the Brits introduced two things: apples and – can you believe it – trout. The apple trees are still here and provide a useful income for many of the locals – we passed the Himcoop Juice Bar, 'selling 100 per cent apple juice since 1972'. And how on earth did the, presumably keen,

British fishermen transport trout from England to the streams of Himachal Pradesh? On a recent trip to India I met a man who had just been to a café in Manali called the Lazy Dog where he had been served – yes! – fresh trout. After all these years, the fish are still there.

We drove through Manali's mysterious and ill-lit streets, buzzing with Indian nightlife, bare bulbs revealing huts filled with delicious-looking vegetables, people being shaved by the light of a single lamp, shops piled high with metal boxes, tyre fitters wielding torches flashing blue in the darkness. In Manali market we stopped off at a *dhabba*. Very often, your driver will try to take you to a tourist café along the road – I suspect they get a few rupees from the proprietor for doing so – but I have generally found them to be relentlessly horrible. No, dear traveller: what you want is a *dhabba*. Inside this *dhabba* we stood beside the chef and watched. Unsettlingly, plump mice rushed about in full view, but don't worry. A good *dhabba* is one of the wonders of India.

Dhabba simply means 'box' in Hindi, and a roadside *dhabba* is a box or hut where food is cooked. There is a big clay oven. At the bottom is a wood fire, tended by a small grubby boy; there is a hole at the top. Over the hole goes the pan, a bit like a wok. Into the pan oil is spooned, then chopped onion, garlic, ginger, chillies, tomatoes and spices. This sizzles enticingly. Once underway, pre-prepared *dhal* (cooked lentils) is added, and more delicious spices. From another pot, a vegetable curry is heated on a second oven. Bread (*roti*) is spun into discs and stuck to the side of the oven. The resulting meal is generally mouthwateringly delicious.

A little tip for budding TV producers: *dhabbas* are also very good for programme budgets. You can make a film crew extremely happy and content for less than a pound a head, which

I call a bargain. (They don't need to know how much it cost, do they?) And this may surprise you: in over twenty trips to India I have never once had a bad tummy (although I am vegetarian, which helps).

On and on we went in our Jeeps, heading ever higher. It was getting very cold. We were right up in the northernmost tip of India. After a jarring drive up a dirt road we arrived, in the dark, at our camp site, perched on the side of a mountain. Next morning, we emerged from our tents to see where we were. The mountains were all around us, delicate water-colour shades of purple, mauve and dove grey in layers, one behind the other, receding into the misty distance, touched by the first light of dawn. It was extraordinarily beautiful.

What an experience – an expedition to the foothills of the mighty Himalayas, set up to paraglide thousands of feet up with a world champion, and interact with one of the world's most spectacular birds: I recently asked our presenter Steve Leonard what he remembered most about this trip. He didn't hesitate. 'Pancakes! They only had a single gas ring at the camp, but in the morning they gave us pancakes – delicious stacks of pancakes, with honey. The pancakes were just fantastic – I had eight one morning....'

Rob and Bob took us up to the launch site at the top of a hill. The town of Manali is already up at 2050 metres: here we were at 2460 metres – high enough to make us slightly befuddled, but the altitude would make taking off much easier. Himalayan griffon vultures rarely go below 1200 metres: they need a height buffer to help them take off, just as we did.

There were some unexpected surprises. First, we found ourselves at the Bijli Mahadev temple, dedicated to lord Shiva. Inside was a shattered stone *lingam* (a penis-shaped symbol of the energy and potentiality of lord Shiva himself, found in innumerable temples throughout India). This *lingam* was held together by butter, and the whole thing was, so we were told, regularly smashed apart by lightning strikes. There was a pole outside to help conduct the lightning into the temple to smash the *lingam* over and over again. It was supposed to happen once a year, and it was the priest's job to stick the *lingam* back together.

The next surprise was the gaunt, dreadlocked, very well-spoken young man (with a slightly eccentric green-eyed girl-friend) who was also preparing to paraglide. He turned out to be Sir William Mallinson, Fifth Baronet of Walthamstow, Eton and Balliol College, Oxford (D. Phil. in Sanskrit Studies), and an expert paraglider. These well-spoken lords get everywhere. The final surprise was just how vertiginous the blasted hill was. You ran along an increasingly steep, flattish area, which simply fell away into a valley a long, long, long way below. Rob and Bob had chosen well.

A modern paraglider is a single fabric wing. Two layers of extremely strong material are stitched together in such a way as to create a series of inflatable 'cells' all along the wing. The leading edge is open, and the incoming air inflates the cells, giving the wing an aerodynamic shape. The bit I don't much like is the suspension lines: tiny, thin, weedy-looking threads that attach the wing to the pilot.

'You're not that comfortable, are you?' said Rob, as he kindly took me up for a tandem flight.

'Er...'

'Want to do some big turns?'

'Well, umm...'

'Thought not. Shall we go back?'

I later heard, over the radio, our demure researcher Jessica begging Rob to go faster, and turn harder, until she squealed with delight. The suspension lines look scarily thin, but they are actually fantastically strong. A 0.66 millimetre line made of Dyneema or a Kevlar-Aramid mix has a breaking strain of 56 kilograms, and there are dozens of them. I needn't have worried.

So, here we were, all ready to unravel the mystery of the record-breaking griffon vulture: a perfect launch site, a world paragliding champion and, hopefully not far away, some real live Himalayan griffon vultures. Time to fly!

But our first attempt did not go according to plan.

We rigged cameras all over the paraglider that Steve and Bob were to use. Cameras looking down on them; cameras filming them close up; and one on the end of a long pole looking back at them. It would be quite tricky running and achieving a smooth take-off with all this gear added to the rig – especially the pole sticking out the front – but Bob was happy to give it a go. It's an ungainly business trying to take off on a tandem paraglider at the best of times: two people running across the ground, trying to coordinate their running as the wing comes up with a crack behind them. Add in poles with cameras, cameras on the lines, cameras looking back at them, sound gear…Bob and Steve struggled together; they ran, awkwardly, faster and faster; the wing came up; they were close to the edge – and they were up. And then – they were going down…

I stood next to Rob as he watched his friend try to fly. Rob began to mutter. 'Bob, you had better find a thermal…Bob, you had better find a thermal soon…Bob, if you don't find a thermal you will be walking…' Pause. 'Bob – you are walking.'

Bob had not found a thermal. Now the almost perfect analogy between vultures and paragliders became clear. To remain aloft, both initially open their wings and launch into a glide. Now they need to find lift to help them gain height. There are two ways of finding lift: you can use updraughts along rising slopes – the faces of mountains, hills, even sand dunes will do. This is known as slope-soaring or ridge lift. The second way to get lift is to use thermals – as we saw the ospreys do in chapter 5. These can provide a paraglider or a vulture with some dramatic uplift. To obtain the maximum benefit, you must try to find the 'core' of the thermal where the uplift is strongest; that's why you sometimes see vultures – and many other birds, for that matter – 'kettling', or flying in fairly tight circles in the air as they try to stay in the core of a thermal and gain maximum lift. Once they reach the top of a thermal they can simply glide out, covering the ground while looking for the next thermal to lift them up again. In this way, paragliders and vultures can travel very long distances and gain some serious height. The current world record for flying the maximum distance in a paraglider is 502.9 km, by Nevil Hulett, on 14 December 2008. That's quite a way, and you can bet vultures, with skills evolved over millions of years, could easily beat that record if they put their mind to it.

But thermals are invisible – so how do you find them? That's a highly skilled, almost intuitive business. Top paragliders like Bob and Rob will do exactly as the vultures do: look for tiny signs – dust devils, insects being carried aloft, leaves flying about, the behaviour of other birds, of course. Wind is pulled in underneath a rising thermal, and that current can give away its presence. It's a subtle game. Both vultures and paragliders are very interested in other flying objects, living or inanimate, to help them find that crucial lift.

Bob and Steve made their way back up to the launch site – running. 'Bob's as fit as fury!' gasped Steve. Once they'd got their breath back it was time to try again. As the sun warmed the landscape more thermals were likely to appear. Could they find one and hitch a ride? Another ungainly run, the wing up, off the edge…

Paraglider pilots rely on a 'vario' – a variometer – to help them find and stay in thermals. The vario bleeps, increasing in pitch and tempo during an ascent – you need this because, although you can initially feel the lift from a thermal, once you are climbing steadily, the human body cannot detect the movement. The vario also drones if you are descending: a thoroughly depressing sound – a drone that gets deeper as the rate of descent increases. This time the subtle genius of Bob Drury had found a thermal, and the vario was soon bleeping away happily, confirming he was on to a winner. The tandem wing was sweeping Bob and Steve higher and higher above the purplish mountains, and then, as if by magic, from nowhere one, two, three, half a dozen vast birds appeared. Himalayan griffon vultures – the real thing! Steve and Bob were about to share their thermal with HGVs. Slightly worrying, as the vultures occasionally attack the paraglider wings – no one is quite sure why. Soon paraglider and vultures were all circling together, rising up into the hazy blue sky.

I had written a simple piece for Steve to say to the camera on the end of the pole. It was not that tricky, but the altitude had befuddled him. 'The vultures use different currents of air like an invisible heavens – no, no. Again – sorry. Vultures use different currents of air like an invisible stairway to heaven as they – no, I forgot the climbing from airflow to airflow bit. I'll try again. The vulture uses…'

And so it went on.

It took Steve no less than 42 takes to get the one sentence out – a record for any production I have ever been on – and every time Steve fluffed, poor Bob had to fly around in a circle to get the perfect mountain-filled backdrop again. He was very patient. You can actually see the whole thing on YouTube if you fancy ('Flying with Vultures', *Extreme Animals*, BBC Wildlife).

There's an obvious question. Why do vultures have to fly so high at all?

Apart from places like that carcass dump outside Jodhpur, vultures can't predict where an animal is going to collapse and die – so to find food, they get up to great height, then use their exceptional eyesight both to look for a carcass themselves, and scan the sky for other vultures – who may be very far off – in case they are flying towards a carcass that they have spotted. This is why vultures suddenly seem to appear, often in great numbers, 'as if from nowhere'.

I'm often asked, 'Can birds smell?' and the answer is a resounding yes. Not all birds, but some have a much better sense of smell than we do. There is a special part of the brain called the olfactory bulb, which is dedicated to the sense of smell, and a number of birds have a well-developed olfactory bulb. There's more evidence, too. Interestingly, there is a clear split between the Old World vultures, who 'hunt' using sight alone, and the New World vultures of North and South America, who use both sight and smell to find their prey. That New World turkey vultures have an excellent sense of smell was discovered almost by accident. In California, maintenance teams looking out for leaks in gas pipelines could always tell where they were because large flocks of turkey vultures had gathered nearby. It turned out the vultures were fantastically sensitive to the smell of mercaptan, a smelly gas added to the odourless gas in the pipes to help humans detect leaks. Mercaptan is the chemical primarily responsible for the smell of bad breath and farts and – here's the killer fact – it is also produced by the bodies of recently dead animals like cows and deer. It's calculated that turkey vultures are around a million times more sensitive to the smell of mercaptan than we humans.

Whether they are New or Old World vultures, whether they are using sight or smell, it generally means they have to get high to find food, surveying the land far below with their extraordinary senses. But 37,000 feet? 'I've seen them at 22,000, 23,000 feet,' said Bob. Flying with Bob and Rob at Manali had shown us how vultures are able to get up to enormous heights in order to find food, but what Bob had actually observed was still 15,000 feet short of the world record. How could we explain the extra altitude the record-breaking vulture had attained when it was sucked into the aeroplane engine?

For the final answer we have to introduce one more paraglider. On 14 February 2007, Ewa Wisnierska-Cieslewicz, a multiple world champion, was warming up for the paragliding world championships in Australia. She and a Chinese paraglider, He Zhongpin, were in the air, looking for thermals, when, to their horror, they suddenly found themselves accelerating upwards at a fantastic rate. Her ground crew monitored exactly what happened next. Ewa started off at 2500 feet, but within 15 minutes she was up to an astonishing 32,612 feet. On the way up to this extraordinary height she became unconscious – not surprising, as there's just not enough oxygen up there. Ewa was a victim of what is known as 'cloud suck' – extremely violent acceleration upwards when a thermal is bubbling up underneath towering cumulus clouds.

After a long period of silence, Ewa's shocked ground crew suddenly heard the radio crackle into life. 'I can't do anything,' Ewa mumbled. 'It's raining and hailing, I'm still climbing, I'm lost…'

Ewa had regained consciousness. By a miracle, her paraglider wing was unscathed and, after a three-and-a-half-hour flight, she landed, covered in ice, with frostbite. Sadly, in the same 'cloud suck' incident her fellow paraglider, He Zhongpin, was killed. His body was found 75 kilometres from where he had taken off. Ewa was unbelievably lucky to survive.

So, finally, we have an answer to the mystery. This is what happened. Griff the record-breaking Ruppell's griffon vulture was out hunting, looking for thermals, as all heavyweight vultures are obliged to do. He got caught in a 'cloud suck' incident under a huge cumulo-nimbus cloud, which shot the unfortunate bird up to 37,000 feet where, by a fantastically unlucky coincidence, he was sucked into the engine of an aeroplane. It just wasn't his day.

10

ROLLING CARS UP THE TOP END

Nightmares of Nature, BBC 1995

Could you roll a car? Any idea how to do it? Do you sort of twiddle the steering wheel in a funny way – perhaps going around a corner? Ever wondered how they do it in action movies? Cars are forever rolling over onto their roof, or off the road down an embankment. If you watch carefully, you will notice there is nearly always something immediately in front of them that hides the car just before they do the roll – another car, a lorry, a big bush…There's a reason for this, as you'll see.

In fact, there are any number of ways of rolling a car. A method that's quite often employed, at least in Australia, is the 'spider roll'. For this, of course, you need a spider – and the right sort of spider, too.

Australia is particularly blessed with spiders. There are around 10,000 different species. Most of these are completely innocuous, but a few are potentially dangerous. To be a threat to us, a spider needs fangs capable of penetrating human skin, and a venom that has a serious effect. There's the infamous redback, responsible for more bites needing anti-venom than any other creature in Australia – that includes snakes (though a redback hasn't actually killed anyone since 1956, when anti-venom was first produced). A particular favourite of mine, because it's somehow so, well, so Australian, is the Sydney funnel web spider which is found in an approximate 100-mile radius of Sydney. First of all it's big and brash, a spider that, unlike the vast majority of spiders, tends to react vigorously and aggressively towards a threat. 'Oo are you lookin' at, mate?' it seems to say as it comes towards you, fangs bared and front legs in threat posture. If it bites, the Sydney funnel web really means it, more often than not injecting a full dose of its very toxic venom, whereas other potentially dangerous spiders often deliver a warning 'dry' bite, without injecting any venom at all.

Spider venom is fascinating. It's really intended to paralyse and kill the spider's prey, but it can be devastating to us too. The detailed chemical composition varies enormously from species to species, but spider venom tends to fall into two distinct categories: either neurotoxic or necrotic. Neurotoxins, as you might expect, affect the nervous system, often causing massive over-stimulation, either by initiating the release of neurotransmitters, or by opening up transmission channels in the neurons themselves. A minuscule amount can cause your nervous system to go into complete meltdown, disrupting the basic body functions, causing muscle cramps, seizures, respiratory failure and comas. The necrotic part of spider venom causes necrosis – i.e. tissue death, creating rotting gangrenous lesions around the bite that may grow to ten inches across. These necrotic lesions can be extremely difficult to get rid of.

This is all very interesting, but actually, when it comes to rolling cars, Australia's venomous spiders are pretty useless. What you need is a huntsman. This is a huge spider – up to 160 millimetres across. Despite its size the huntsman is not dangerous: if you get bitten it just stings a bit.

However, a huntsman can be extremely dangerous if you suddenly find it in your car, and this is a fairly common event, because huntsmen love to rest under car sun visors. Huntsmen like to feel something above and below them – it makes them feel secure – and the gap between the sun visor and the roof of the car is perfect: exactly the right size, nice and snug, for a huntsman to squeeze itself underneath. When you flip the sun visor down and a heavily built six-inch spider drops on to your lap, you may well forget all about the business of driving while you desperately try to find where on earth the bloody great spider has landed. And – good lord! – what's that on my leg? *Aggghh!* You look up to see a lorry coming towards you, desperately twist the steering wheel and…. *Voilà!* Roll the car!

That is exactly what happened to Janine Dean, and, despite what her husband had to say when he saw the car afterwards, I can't really blame her.

Janine rolled the family car naturally, expertly and without any special training, but when I came to reconstruct her experience for the BBC *Nightmares of Nature* series, I had to do it a more conventional way – it's not that difficult really. Just in case you ever have to do it yourself, here's how.

Fly to Australia. They are pretty 'can-do' up the Top End (that's the Northern Territory: I went to Darwin). Ask at the local police station if they mind if you roll a car on the slip road around the main police station, as it's pretty quiet. 'No worries, mate,' they will say. 'So long as you tidy up after.' Call ambulance, tow truck and road-sweeping van.

Hire a car. In this case a Holden Commodore (Holden – made in Australia), in white. Hire company very happy so far. I suggest you don't go into too much detail about what you intend to do with their vehicle. Now you have to find someone to actually drive and roll the car. Janine herself was disinclined to have another go, so you will need to find yourself a stunt woman. I found Polly, and her stunt organiser Rocky. Receive plans from Rocky for a steel safety cage to be built inside the car so the whole thing doesn't cave in when it hits the ground. This bit is very important. Steel cage to be built by Holtie, expert metalworker, and drummer with a local 'mutant country thrash metal' band.

Me: 'What's the music sound like, Holtie, mate?'

'Loike rain battering on a hot tin roof mixed in with wheel nuts being over-tightened, mate.'

You may have spotted the flaw in all this. Yes, the hire car. We had to have the hire car to do all the driving shots in order to set up the story, but we also needed to roll the car, and you can't really roll a hire car. Despite the story only requiring the car to roll over on to its roof, I think Hertz Australia might take a dim view if the car was returned in subtly different form from how it went out. So, I went to a secondhand car place, Marshall's Motors, to meet the salesman, Scab. I'm not making this up. In a 'special deal', for $1,800 dollars Scab sold me a surprisingly low-mileage 1979 Holden Commodore – the same model as the hire car we were currently using for the driving shots, only a lot older. If you ever meet Scab you might think him, as I did, a bit 'sharky', but the car ran at least. Take car straight to AANT (Automobile Association of the Northern Territory) for inspection to see if it's going to kill anyone even before we put the steel cage in. There is one tiny problem. The Scab stunt car is livid yellow, and the hire car it's got to match for the rest of the filming is white. Drive car to the local paint shop. Do a deal.

Buy yourself a genuine Aussie Akubra hat – you'll get sunstroke standing around.

Have a beer.

Draw breath.

Whilst the stunt car is being repainted and the cage being built you could go and do a bit of sightseeing. Maybe go up to a croc farm, or hire a canoe and go for a day out in Kakadu National Park – it's a fantastic place, the Top End. Me, I had to film all the other shots with the spider in the hire car. But how was I to get hold of a really big huntsman spider?

Eventually a local spider expert, Jenny Webber, came to my rescue, though not until the very day of the shoot. At the very last moment I get a call: she's got a spider, we're in with a chance – it's a monster! So: how do you get the huge, lightning fast, reasonably venomous six-inch spider to go where you want it to go, rather than where *it* wants to go?

Two key shots were needed: first, the spider crawls up the actress's leg. The actress we were working with, Maggie Miles – whom we'd also worked with on the croc attack reconstruction in chapter 8 – although brilliant in every respect, takes one look at the spider and goes wobbly. It's not going to happen with Maggie. She really, really wants to help, but she just can't. I have a brainwave. Jenny Webber is clearly completely unfazed by the spider: if she dresses up in Maggie's green dress, could her leg stand in for Maggie's leg? A quick strip at the side of the road, and Jenny is in the hot seat. Moments later, the huntsman is creeping across the floor of the car, delicately up her calf, and on to her bare knee, where it sits looking suitably menacing. Perfect.

Finally, the really tricky bit. We have to film the spider crawling under the sun visor, to 'load' it, as it were. How do we entice the spider underneath, so the visor can then be flicked down and the spider fall out, as required by the story? Now my arcane knowledge of invertebrates comes into play. Many invertebrates – spiders, insects, centipedes, etc. – show very predictable behaviour patterns: give them a particular stimulus, and they will react in a clearly defined way. These are known as *taxis* and *kinesis* – fancy words for movement. The thing they are moving towards or away from becomes part of the description, so 'negative photo -taxis' means moving away from light. A more obscure one, as I mentioned in an earlier chapter, is *thigmokinesis*: 'inhibition of movement in response to physical stimulus'. In other words, an animal tends to move if its body has minimal contact with things around it. A wood louse with just its legs touching the ground will tend to walk, but as more of its body comes into contact with things – if it's gone under a bit of bark, or a stone, which is its touching its back – it slows and may stop. It's a simple and effective behaviour, because it means that when it stops the woodlouse is generally underneath something that protects it. Negative photo-taxis will have the same effect: the woodlouse will move into darkness, generally somewhere safer than being out in the light.

I suspected our huge huntsman would be both negatively photo-tactic and show thigmokinesis, and, blow me – it was, and it did! If I put a cup over it, it immediately stopped (dark) and bent its legs, so its body was in contact with the cup (thigmokinetic). And there it would stay. I carried it to the car. 'Turn over!' I cried to the cameraman.

The camera ran. I put the cup up to the roof, turned it the right way around, tapped it a bit, and the huge – I must be honest, it really was intimidating – spider emerged on to the roof of the car. We held our collective breath. What would it do? The huntsman paused. It was now in bright light, and close by was a dark place: the underneath of the sun visor. Slowly she began to move…directly towards, and then under the visor. *Yesss!* Feeling her body in contact with the visor below and the roof above, she stopped. Double *yesss!* A huge cheer went up. Sometimes a little arcane natural history knowledge can be very handy.

We did the driving shots in the wild and lovely Top End countryside. Now it was time to get back to the next challenge: rolling the car.

At Polly and Rocky's hotel, Polly was slouched on a sofa watching TV. She appeared to be completely bored, and her conversation was monosyllabic. This is how it went…Gushing producer-director: 'Have you done this sort of thing before, Polly?'

'Yeah.'

'I, er…hope it's always gone OK, ha-ha!'

'Nah.'

(Struggling): 'Have you worked with Rocky long, then?'

'Yeah.'

(Desperate): 'It must be a pretty exciting job you have, Polly!'

'Not really…Got any chips, Rock?'

Rocky was a lot more approachable. With him we checked:

1. Helmet, good

2. Holtie's in-car protective steel cage – good work

3. Holtie's pipe ramp

Ah, the pipe ramp: now we're getting to the nitty-gritty. If you want to roll a car you'll need a pipe ramp, and it is why you'll generally see something in front of the car just before it rolls over in movies, because you have to hide the ramp behind something.

For a regular, family-sized car you need a pipe ramp about twenty feet long. The whole thing is shaped like a long thin triangle gently sloping upwards. The 'pipe' makes up the top rail, which slopes from ground level up to about five feet high. Now, to secure it, you hammer steel pegs through the side pieces of the ramp, which extend out all the way along the bottom rail on the ground, directly into the road. Take it in turns: this is hard work. Once totally secured, your pipe ramp is ready.

Collect freshly painted Scab car with checked safety cage all fitted. Strap monosyllabic stunt lady Polly into seat.

'Straps not tight enuff Rock.'

The whole idea is you drive just one side of the car up the ramp, which therefore lifts that side up, and begins to turn the car over. The skill is to drive the car with exactly the right velocity to roll it over the correct amount. A slowish approach will roll the car on to its roof nice and smoothly. A faster approach will revolve the car completely, maybe back on to its wheels, and a really fast approach will send it cartwheeling over and over in complete mayhem. But first you test it. Polly drives one side of the car up on to the ramp to ensure it slides smoothly. Nice. She allows the car to slide gently off again backwards, then rolls it up again. Off. Gently. Good.

If you want to film the roll, fill the car with cameras shooting every angle you can think of. Also, sink small cameras into the road, and set three film crews beside markers you've placed in the road after calculating exactly where the car will gently roll over on to its roof.

Again, just to reiterate: the speed you hit the ramp is crucial. Too slow and the car just slides down again; too fast and things get totally out of control; just right – Goldilocks-style – and the car will roll nicely on to its roof.

Now you have to put something in front of the ramp to hide it from all the cameras. In my case this was easy, because it had been a large road train that Janine had looked up and seen just before she rolled her car. So I put a road train in front of the pipe ramp to hide it. If all went well, we would see the car approach the road train; disappear momentarily behind it – as it hit the hidden pipe ramp; then fly out to the side of the road train, already rolling over on to its roof.

'Ready? Steady? Roll the cameras!' I yell.

'Cameras running!'

'And...Action!'

I'm not sure if Polly is still working as a stunt woman. She was jolly good, but I wouldn't, perhaps, use her for this sort of thing again. That bored monosyllabic stuff fooled me completely. I'd heard the engine note of Scab's Holden each time she'd done her gentle slide-up practice runs, but now...The poor old engine screamed, smoke belched from the ancient exhaust, valves howled in protest. 'Er, Polly...*Polly – not too—*', I bawled. Should have saved my breath – it was far, far too late...With a mighty bound and a squeal of tyres the brakes came off, and the Holden shrieked down the road, slewing slightly from side to side. I held my breath. With a *whack* it hit the ramp, shot up into the air, rolled over, and over, smashed into the ground, and rolled once, twice, three times. Out of the corner of my eye I saw film crews – including the local TV channel – scattering in all directions. After the next roll the car hurtled over a dirt bank, and was lost to sight in a gigantic cloud of red Top End dust.

Obviously she'd killed herself.

I began to run.

Well before I got anywhere near the wreckage it was obvious Polly had not in fact killed herself. Her arm was thrust out of the smashed-in window giving the thumbs up, and there was a good deal of shouting going on. Nor was she monosyllabic any more. 'Yee-haa! Yee-haa!' I could hear her shrieking. 'Wow, that was something! All that shit was hoonin' in thru the screen when it blew out, yee-haa!' Rocky got Polly out and hugged her. 'I hit that ramp good – I hooned it! Yeah!'

By the time I ran over to Polly she was leaning against the wreckage, helmet in hand, chewing gum. 'Wow! How was THAT, Polly!'

'It was OK.'

'Are you all right?'

'Yeah.'

'You know it was only supposed to go, ha-ha, on to its roof, really?'

'Whatever.'

I gathered my ashen film crew, who in the final cut can be seen sprinting out of the way. No one was hurt. The ambulance left, patientless, and as the tow truck and road sweeper arrived we all went off to have a cold beer and listen to some mutant country thrash metal.

So that's how to roll a car. Simples!

11

IN POLAR BEAR COUNTRY

Incredible Animal Journeys, BBC2, 2006

On 21 August 2005, at precisely 15.29 and twelve seconds, my TV career was about to come to an abrupt end. More significantly, so were the lives of a number of my best friends. In the next few moments, as they sat in their small boat, it appeared they would be killed by thousands of tons of falling ice. If you look at the picture of the icefall in the middle of this book, you will understand. That tiny black speck at the bottom of the picture: that's the boat, containing a film crew and presenter. Above the speck is a towering cliff of ice which, if you look closely, is toppling, and will obviously crush boat and crew in the next few seconds.

I took that picture from another boat to record the end of all our hopes and dreams. The words of Jim Morrison's sorrowful song echoed through my mind; this was, indeed, *the end* . . .

Only, by some impossible miracle, it wasn't.

What were we all doing underneath that vast cliff of ice? How had we got here? How did we escape the icy the jaws of death, and what happened afterwards? To answer these questions, I'll have to wind the clock back four days.

It is 18 August 2005. The MV *Polarhav,* an ice-strengthened, solid-looking ex-fishing boat, was tied up at the harbour wall. A film crew could be seen struggling to help move a small mountain of supplies from the jetty on to the boat, then stow everything in the old fish-processing area, which was richly imbued with a heady aroma of diesel oil and very old fish. The day before, we had flown into Longyearbyen, the capital of Spitsbergen, the largest of a group of islands which together comprise the icy archipelago of Svalbard. Svalbard is way above the Arctic Circle and, as we humped another box of supplies on board, we were only 800 miles from the North Pole. Actually, we were all glad of the exercise because it was, as it says simply in my diary, '*V cold*'.

We had come here to hunt polar bears. Not with guns, of course, but with a camera. In fact, we had come to try to find just one polar bear. At first sight, this looks like quite a tall order, seeing as there are probably 3000 bears on Spitsbergen roaming across 15,000 square miles of snow, ice and jagged mountains. The name itself is from the Dutch: *spits*, pointed, and *bergen*, mountains.

But we had a secret weapon.

Let's wind the clock back still further. Four months earlier, a helicopter could be seen flying across the dazzling landscape. The team on board spotted a great shape running across the snow below them. The helicopter descended, and a gun was expertly loaded. As they got closer, they saw a much smaller shape alongside the big polar bear – a cub. The pilot skilfully manoeuvred alongside the running bear, and the scientist took aim. There was a *crack*. For a while the bear continued to run, but gradually her pace slowed. She stopped, peered angrily at the helicopter. She sat down. By the time the helicopter landed she was fast asleep, her cub at her side.

When she woke up, the cub was suckling. She reached out and curled a vast protective paw around him. Something was around her neck, which was annoying: she tried to use her other paw to get it off, but it wouldn't come away. Soon she would forget about it. The great polar bear rose groggily to her feet and shook her head. The noisy thing in the sky – gone, good. She put it to the back of her mind, because there was another feeling demanding all her attention: hunger. The polar bear hadn't fed for a very long time and she was starving. She shook her head once more: yes, she was hungry, very hungry, but she knew exactly what to do about that. Aurora, as we came to know her, started to walk purposefully across the snow towards the ice and the deep blue sea beyond, her little cub bounding along behind.

As Aurora walked, the electronic tag that had been fixed around her neck began to transmit her position. First, the signal went up to a satellite, then to a receiving station in France, and finally to the scientists at the Norwegian Polar Institute in Tromsø. As the data came in, a computer began to draw a trace of the polar bear's movements. Dr Jon Aars, leader of the project, peered at her route: she was following the edge of the ice sheet. Interesting…

Aurora was satellite-tagged in April, soon after she and her cub had emerged from their winter den under the snow. While adult males and non-pregnant females just keep going throughout the dark, frigid days of winter, during which the sun never rises above the horizon, pregnant female polar bears dig a den and slip into, well, it's not hibernation proper, more a sort of chilly torpor. Although their heart rate does slow, from a normal 46 bpm to about 27, the mother polar bear's body temperature remains normal, which makes it different from typical mammalian hibernation. Some time around Christmas, she will give birth to a tiny baby, or more usually twins. Mother and cub/s remain in the den until March or April, when the adult bear bashes a hole in the snow above the den and the little family emerge, blinking, into the bright light of the Arctic spring. Throughout the three months she has been underground, the female polar bear has lived off her reserves, while at the same time providing milk for her offspring, which will have grown to well over ten times their birth weight by the time they leave the den. When she emerges from underground, after such a prolonged fast, the female polar bear is extremely hungry.

It had been known for a long time that polar bears cover considerable distances as they hunt for food. But no one knew exactly how long these journeys were, or where they went during their travels. By attaching satellite trackers to individual bears, Dr Aars was going to find out. And because Dr Aars was able to track individual bears, it made a perfect story for one of my *Incredible Animal Journeys* programmes.

The idea was to follow in Aurora's footsteps, as far as possible re-tracing her journey: see where she had gone, and why she had gone there, and then, finally, we would try to catch up with her, to meet the star of the show face-to-face.

OK, you might be thinking, nice idea – but if Aurora was tagged in April, why on earth did you wait four months, until August, before filming her? Why not get on her trail right away and do the journey with her? A very good point. The fact is, we couldn't. During the winter the seas around Spitsbergen freeze solid. If you could somehow go up into space above the North Pole and watch as winter progressed, you would see the ice extending down from the top of the globe, a gleaming white cap, creeping down, engulfing any land masses, like Svalbard, that it meets on the way. In spring the sea ice will start to melt back, but it needs some warmth to do this, and up here, this close to the North Pole, warmth is in short supply. In Spitsbergen the sun disappears below the horizon on 26 October, and doesn't reappear until 16 February, when a tiny glowing edge just breaks the horizon. In the following days it quickly climbs above the horizon, and by 18 April the midnight sun period begins, meaning the sun never goes below the horizon: a very odd thing to experience if you are not used to it –as the sun does circuits in the sky above, your body clock goes into freefall. Though Aurora had been tagged in April, our Arctic expert Jason Roberts had calculated that we would have to wait until August before the sea ice had retreated far enough to allow us to get on Aurora's trail.

After a brief visit to the shops in Longyearbyen, for final supplies, Norwegian trinkets for the folks back home, and a breathtakingly expensive knife for my collection, it was time to depart. Already the satellite trackers Dr Aars had fitted had provided some remarkable revelations. Researchers had always known polar bears were long-distance travellers, but nothing like this: Aurora had travelled an astonishing 3500 miles since she had been tagged. She was averaging around 30 miles a day. The latest satellite fixes placed her way over on the east of the island. It was time for us to find out where she had been, and why she'd been there, before making our attempt at an actual rendezvous. Oh, and one other thing: when Aurora had been tagged she had her cub with her, but more than half of all polar bear cubs die in their first year, so as the *Polarhav*'s powerful engines gathered speed and we pulled away from the harbor wall, none of us knew if the little cub was still alive.

Polar bears are the largest bears in the world. They are extremely carnivorous: whereas other bears supplement their diet with some vegetable matter – so are classified as omnivores – polar bears live almost exclusively off freshly caught and killed seals. A fully-grown male polar bear or boar can stand ten feet high and weigh over 700 kilograms – that's ten average human males – making them the biggest land carnivores on earth. They are magnificent and formidable. I have never met a polar bear that has shown the slightest fear of me, or anyone I was with: they just seem to come right at you, posing testing questions like, what are you? Can I eat you? This makes going into their world, where they are the masters and we are just tourists, something to take very seriously.

You need to be very respectful and careful around any bears, of course, but if the worst does happen, note this: when a brown bear attacks a human it tends to maul you, then leave you alone; a polar bear attack is more likely to be predatory, and so is almost always fatal. Polar bears are extremely unpredictable, especially when they are hungry.

As well as considerations surrounding the bears, there were other safety issues to think about on this shoot. The average daily summer temperature in Spitsbergen is 5°C; the average daily winter temperature is -14°. It's cold. So is the sea up there. Whereas adult polar bears are comfortable spending literally days swimming in these waters, if we fell in, we would be insensible within minutes, and dead soon afterwards. However, we needn't have worried: our outstanding fixer Jason Roberts had thought of everything. The high-tech immersion suits he'd brought along would buy us time if we did fall in. We had enough supplies to feed a small army, and he'd also hired a very moody, somewhat difficult to please chef, Svein Arne, who, night after night, angrily produced dazzling culinary masterpieces – unexpected, but very welcome.

Polar bears are ambush hunters, and perhaps the most effective technique they employ to catch their favourite prey, seals, is to creep up on them when they are asleep. One of the seals' favourite places to score some snores is out of the water, on a bit of floating ice. Aurora, a very experienced bear, would know all this, and, as we could see from her track, after emerging from her den she had made a bee-line for the edge of the ice, where there would be lots of bits of floating ice, and thus sleepy seals for her to hunt. We really wanted to try to film bears hunting and feeding on seals, and although by the time we set off most of the floating sea ice had melted, there were other possibilities.

One of the best places to find blocks of floating ice in the Arctic summer is near the front of glaciers, where they meet the sea. Every now and then, chunks of ice fall off the front face as the advancing glacier grinds its inexorable way off the land and into the water. We moored the *Polarhav* in a fjord with a glacier at one end, lowered two smaller boats with the crane, and set off. The film crew were in one boat and, to give them space to get around, as well as providing a safety back-up, I hung back in another. From a distance, the glacier face looked impressive enough, but as the crew got closer, in their small boat with a spluttery, unreliable outboard motor, it became a vast, towering ice cliff, a dazzling mix of turquoise and electric blues. Snaking alongside the glaciers were moraines, grey rivers of crushed stone. Further back were brooding mountains whose jagged peaks were lost in a layer of mist. Immense geological forces were at work here, and we humans felt small and insignificant, lost in this primordial place.

Obviously, you have to be careful around the front of a glacier, but we had been assured this particular bit was absolutely bomb-proof – nothing was going to fall off. Something to do with the colour, I seem to recollect. The team in the filming boat started to look around, and our presenter Steve did a piece to camera right up by the ice face. The little outboard motor was too noisy, so they had to turn it off to do the filming. Noisy and a bit rubbish, because it kept cutting out…From my support boat I kept track of what was going on using our walkie-talkies, keeping quite far back so as to avoid getting in shot. As Steve said the last few lines, about how, one day, this entire face would give way, there was a sort of deep groaning noise, then a series of mighty percussive explosions and cracks. Jason struggled to start the outboard – mercifully it caught. He turned the throttle to flat-out, and aimed directly away from the ice.

At this point, right above my crew in their tiny boat, hundreds, or possibly thousands, of tons of ice suddenly gave away, and, seemingly in slow motion, the entire face began to collapse into the sea. I had my camera and took the picture. The date and time were recorded as I pressed the shutter, letting me know, to the second, the exact moment the fall began. As the ice hurtled downwards, and the little black speck continued to move away, agonisingly slowly, I could see that blocks of ice the size of cars and fridges were landing in the water – appallingly, *ahead* of the boat. One direct hit and it would all be over. I saw the headlines – IDIOT PRODUCER KILLS ENTIRE BBC CREW IN ARCTIC ICEFALL DISASTER – and myself in the dock trying to explain how this dreadful fiasco had happened.

Then the mountain of falling ice hit the sea. I naturally assumed this would produce a tidal wave, which would instantly swamp the boat, if it hadn't already been hit and sunk. To my surprise, the fall simply created a gigantic swell, that radiated out and gently lifted the film boat up. I now remembered to start breathing again. I had not killed them. They had survived, and, as the ice blocks crashed into the sea all around them, cameraman Sam Gracie had, with immense courage, continued to film throughout.

Then, of course – afterwards – we were all very jolly, and thought we had a tremendous sequence. After moments of extreme danger – if you survive – you are filled with a wild euphoria, an overwhelming sense of jubilation. 'Nothing in life is so exciting,' said Winston Churchill, 'as to be shot at without result.' The crew had definitely been shot at. That evening we did some maintenance on the outboard motor, and over an excellent supper decided we shouldn't go quite so close to the ice in future.

After the excitement of the previous day we were hungry to keep the adrenalin flowing – and a golden opportunity arose. We were still near the ice face of the glacier, still hoping to see and film polar bears hunting seals. All eyes were on the look-out for a bear's head just breaking the water's surface as it swam along, but this was proving to be extremely difficult, because the sea was littered with debris from the glacier. And then, suddenly…

'Oh, my goodness – what's that?' A vast, gory, amorphous lump, a mess of red and white and grey, was bobbing up and down beside the boat, oozing matter into the water.

'It's a seal carcass,' said Jason. 'Grab it before it sinks.'

'Grab it? Why?'

'You want to film polar bears, don't you? It's bait. Quick – get on with it!'

Four of us got out of our boat and on to the floating ice, and attempted to haul the gruesome remains out. In the water the carcass hadn't seemed that big, but it was very heavy indeed – we nearly gave up, even with four of us. But eventually we managed to drag the remains of the seal up on to the ice, leaking gore, and looking and smelling irresistibly appetising, or so we hoped, to a passing bear.

We backed off. Sure enough, to our delight, just as Jason had predicted, a large white head appeared, cruising amongst the shattered ice, paddling steadily towards our bait. We jumped into the small boat (the outboard motor running very sweetly that day), and slowly crept up. The bear sank his claws into the ice, and hauled himself out of the water in one smooth, fluid motion, then padded towards the carcass. It wasn't quite in the right place for him, so with a single paw he impaled it, and effortlessly carried it some distance across the ice before settling down for a snack. The same carcass four of us had nearly given up trying to move he'd lifted as if it were a toy. We slowly drifted in to get closer shots, cameraman Sam filming off the prow.

'Look!' I hissed. 'Another one.'

Sure enough, a much, much larger bear was swimming in. He too sunk his claws into the ice and began to haul himself up. This was potentially explosive, surely – what would happen? Would the huge adult attack the smaller bear? We expected fireworks, but we couldn't have been more wrong. Short of some perfunctory growling and pacing around, they soon settled down to the important business of opening up the carcass to find the best bits. They ended up almost nose to nose, eating peacefully together.

Sometimes you come across carcasses in the Arctic which appear to have been killed but not eaten – all the red muscle is left behind untouched. This seems inexplicable, until you discover that adult polar bears are mainly interested in eating the calorie-rich blubber of their seal prey, often completely ignoring the 'meat'. Younger bears, still with some growing to do, will feed on the protein-rich meat as well.

During the breeding season in spring, adult male bears, the boars, will fight for access to the females [sows] but, despite the fact that polar bears are basically solitary, when they meet they will sometimes play together for hours on end. Some adult males have well-developed and long-lasting friendships with other males, and adults have even been seen sleeping together, wrapped in a (warm) embrace.

Which all sounds rather endearing. However, it would have been a very different story if the smaller bear had been a cub. One of the grave dangers Aurora's cub would face was being killed by a large male polar bear. Small polar bear cubs are regularly killed by adult males, and as yet there is no credible explanation for this behavior. It may simply be hunger.

So intent were we on filming the amazing spectacle of the two bears feeding side by side that we were rather surprised when, with a soft bump, our boat banged against the ice floe, and we realised we could almost touch the biggest bear. If he wished, he could join us on the boat in an instant, and there really wasn't room. As we drew away, it was a relief to realise both bears were too intent upon their meal to give us any thought. This filming was going well. It was a jolly crew once again that sat down to yet another gourmet feast that evening, We'd survived monstrous ice falls, shared intimate moments with very big polar bears – what could possibly go wrong now?

The weather, that's what. Next morning the captain called a meeting. A powerful storm was blowing in from the southeast. Did we want to continue to try to follow Aurora's trail, in which case it was going to get extremely uncomfortable, and he could not guarantee he could find a safe anchorage? Or, did we want to go to a safe, sheltered area, drop anchor and wait for the storm to pass? Each day was costing me a small fortune but wise counsel prevailed: we sailed the *Polarhav* into the sheltered fjord, which we soon discovered we were sharing with a large number of walrus.

I had not encountered walrus before. It's exciting. You are going along quietly, minding your own business in a smallish boat, when suddenly perhaps twenty whiskery heads appear around you (they always go around in groups). Snorting and puffing, many with gigantic tusks, they look at you; you look at them; they snort, they puff; you grin; then, suddenly, they all turn and dive. There's a mass of swirls which coalesce and resolve into nothing where moments before a great – shoal? team? Actually the correct term is a herd of walrus – was bobbing about.

This was a superb filming opportunity. Someone thought it would be a great idea to get into the small, unstable canoes we had brought with us, to paddle up and get a closer look at the walrus we could see sitting here and there on floating lumps of ice known as 'pans'. In retrospect, this was not the most sensible plan. Steve Leonard and Jason Roberts paddled off together. When they got closer to the walrus we got a real sense of scale. When walrus bob up all together with just their heads showing you get no idea of what's underneath, but out of the water walruses are simply vast. A male can weigh more than 1700 kilograms. I know numbers like this are pretty meaningless, but that's the same size as an adult black rhino, or a medium-sized hippo: really huge. And aggressive: males can be extremely aggressive both towards each other and to intruders.

Jason and Steve paddled out of the water, sliding their canoes up on to a floating ice pan, and sat there together.

'You know, Steve – I wonder if the walrus might be territorial about some of these ice pans?'

Crunch.

With perfect timing, a huge whiskery head had appeared, and commenced to smash its tusks around at the rear of Steve's canoe, trying, as far as I could see, to impale it, and drag it and its occupant off 'his' ice pan. Happily, the tusks did not go through the canoe itself – he missed – and instead snagged the rudder wires, so although Steve and canoe shot backwards for a bit, the wires snapped, and the walrus slid back into the icy water, blowing hard. Not for long: soon he and a pal were back, and Jason was trying in vain to fend them off with the end of his paddle. All of a sudden, Steve and Jason were waving and shouting to us on the safety boat, urging us, if we did not mind, to pull our blasted fingers out and come and rescue them.

'I'd far rather come face-to-face with a polar bear than a walrus,' Jason told us over a sumptuous dinner with multiple sauces that evening. 'I reckon walrus are by far the most dangerous animals around here.'

Now he tells us.

Once the storm had abated, we continued to follow Aurora's trail, and soon we came across a bizarre sight: a ghost town, the fabled Pyramiden. Pyramiden is down a fjord on the west coast of Spitsbergen, and is a deeply spooky place. It is, or was, a Russian coal-mining town bought from Sweden, who first developed it, in 1927. Aurora had passed about 35 miles to the east of the town, but apparently polar bears were frequently encountered wandering down the main street, much to the discomfort of the inhabitants. We wandered through the echoing cultural centre, with its impressive colourful mosaics and surreal grand piano – the most northerly grand piano in the world. A huge black granite bust of Lenin dominated the square; children's swings squeaked in the chill wind, and their exercise books, even tiny shoes, still littered the school rooms. This was home to around 1000 people and a busy mining town, right up until day when a message came from the Motherland: 'Pack your bags. Your coal is no longer economic,' they were told. 'We are sending a boat to take everyone back to Russia.' A few days later, on 10 January 1998, the place was evacuated. And that was that.

We'd retraced key parts of Aurora's 3500-mile journey – seeing where she had fed on seals, raided a bird colony, crossed water, criss-crossed the melting ice. Now it was time to attempt the climax of our film: to actually meet the star of the show. We set sail for what we thought was Aurora's latest position. She had doubled back on herself, and after spending time in the north had travelled south and east, ending up inland on another island in the Svalbard archipelago, Edgeoya – the third largest, and situated to the east of Spitsbergen. As I stood at the front of the *Polarhav*, watching the bows slicing through the deep blue water, and admiring the fulmars gliding expertly and effortlessly past, hoping for an opportunistic titbit from the galley, everything looked set for a lovely climax.

But how often does that happen? Just when everything is looking rosy, up comes fate with a bit of lead piping and delivers a nasty clump to the back of the head. While we'd been busy filming we'd rather lost contact with the scientists in Tromsø, but now we received a deeply worrying message from them. Unless there was a fault with the tracker it appeared Aurora had stopped – dead. In fact, it now transpired, she, or at least the tracker, hadn't moved for ten days. What had happened? If a bear did not move for ten days there surely seemed to be only one grim conclusion.

We dropped anchor off the north coast of Edgeoya Island, and started to transfer all our filming gear into the smaller boats to get ashore. We needed to start early in the day because the map had shown it was going to be quite a walk: the signal from Aurora's collar was coming from a spot seven miles inland. After packing our rucksacks on the shore, laden with heavy tripods, lenses, batteries, etc., we began our hike. Already the nights were drawing in, and I had worked out there was just time to get there and back before it got dark. Edgeoya is uninhabited, desolate and, like so much of Svalbard, imbued with an untouched, primeval grandeur. We had to cross dangerous-looking snow bridges, sinking bogs and, agony of agonies, glacial melt-waters. With boots and socks off, trousers rolled up, the cold is fantastically intense – you have to shout and howl to keep going.

At last, after many hours, we found ourselves in a vast brown valley (the snow had all melted here), U-shaped and with enormous mountains rearing up either side. Once again we felt dwarfed by the enormity of the place. But where was Aurora? A white bear would stand out like, well, a very white thing in this uniformly brown environment that stretched for miles ahead of us. But there was nothing to be seen. We walked on, checking and cross-checking, until we were on the exact spot the transmissions were coming from: absolutely no sign of anything. We got out the satellite phone and called back to base in the UK. Could they check if the transmissions were still coming from this spot? Yes, they were. But we were right on top of them! What was going on?

There was a small click behind us. Our minder, the silent Stein-Roger Hammari, had carefully slid the bolt forward on his high-velocity rifle. We all turned, and there, just beside us, having been hidden in a shallow depression, a vast white head appeared, eyes locked on to us. Then, miraculously, a much smaller white head appeared just beside Mum. It was Aurora and her cub. For a moment we stared at her and she stared at us. Then, smoothly, calmly, the huge white bear rose up and, with deceptive speed, walked away from us, her cub bouncing along in tow. Aurora, a grand old lady of some eighteen years, now coming to the end of her life, had successfully given birth and, throughout the vast distance she had covered, she'd kept her baby safe and sound. Both mother and cub were perfectly OK, not dead as we had all secretly suspected. We were ecstatic. As we stood there watching them walk off into the distance, I suddenly remembered why we were all here. 'Camera!' I yelled. The next few minutes were a flurry of frantic activity as we tried to assemble tripod, tripod bowl, camera baseplate, camera, battery and finally connect up the huge telephoto lens I had been lugging in a rucksack for the last seven miles across difficult country. All this time mother and cub were moving away from us with surprising speed. At last the camera was ready and we turned over, just in time, to film Aurora and cub as they stopped, turned to us, sniffed the air, then walked on, cub gamboling around his mother. To the naked eye the bears were now just two white specks in the far distance and then – they were gone, swallowed up into that vast wasteland. We had made our rendezvous and, by the skin of our teeth, filmed a perfect finale to our programme.

Why had Aurora stopped for so long? It's an interesting bit of polar bear behaviour. Once the summer is at its height and the ice has melted, it becomes increasingly hard for polar bears to find seals to hunt. It would therefore be a waste of energy to keep up the remarkable pace that had characterised Aurora's movements over the past few months. Back then, she had followed the retreating ice sheet as it melted, in order to hunt seals along the way. Now, with the ice and seals gone, she had settled down to another period of torpor, partially shutting down her metabolism. We were sorry to have disturbed Aurora, but she would soon settle somewhere else, and continue to conserve as much energy as possible while she waited for the cold, the ice and the seals to return.

It was a long walk back to the *Polarhav* but, despite the blisters and the exhaustion, it was a very happy film crew that struggled back on board as darkness fell. Aurora was all right after all; her cub had survived and, what's more, there was a delicious smell coming from the galley. We had been at sea for nearly three weeks: it was time to go home.

Post script. When we did get home, we got another message from the scientists at the Norwegian Polar Institute. They had now analysed the samples they had taken from Aurora when they had fitted the satellite tracker. It turned out she was not eighteen, as they had first thought, but twenty-three – making her the oldest mother polar bear they had ever known. I wonder what happened to that grand old lady, whose life we had, briefly, been privileged to share. I hope that Aurora's cub is still out there, now a huge adult male in the prime of life, hunting seals on the Arctic ice.

12

SWIMMING WITH ELEPHANTS

Land of the Tiger, BBC2, 1996

Imagine you're submerged in the sea, looking upwards; shafts of sunlight pierce the clear blue water. But now, above you, what's this? One, two, perhaps three huge shapes heave into view. Elephants! Swimming elephants, magically suspended in space. What an image, and one I badly wanted to try and film for the *Land of the Tiger* series, which was all about Indian wildlife. I just couldn't get the swimming elephants out of my mind – and no one had ever filmed it before. What a coup it would be!

What follows is a step-by-step guide to ease you through the process of filming swimming elephants, should you ever need to do it yourself. You never know…First, to whet your appetite, here's the plus side – the sort of thing you might be lucky enough to experience along your way.

This is my actual diary entry for 1 April 1996:

I'm writing this by the ship's light anchored off Cinque Island. The hiss and suck of the waves hitting the seashore, the moon above – flashes of lightning on my left illuminating towering clouds over the main island. It's incredibly hot still. Today was a big day. I made my first scuba dive with Jason. Bit of a panic when my goggles began to fill with water on the bottom eight metres down – my efforts to clear them unsuccessful – became completely full – couldn't see anything. Bit panicky, but then 34 min. dive, barracuda, sea snakes, vast groupers, quintillions of brilliantly coloured fish. Inspiring. Then to Manta Bay off Passage Island. Rory (cameraman) just saying to me, 'I'm really hungry to film a good sequence today, really hungry', when suddenly the cry goes up 'Two manta rays'- fabulous Rory hurls on his kit and leaps in – two joined by two more, then another two! Cavort right over Rory for nearly 30 minutes, some stupendous shots, all of us buzzing. I get in and snorkel with one RIGHT BESIDE ME, VAST. Lovely.

Yes, as part of the trip to film swimming elephants I ended up in the water with six gigantic manta rays, with their six-metre 'wing span' the mantas (*manta* is Spanish for cloak) seemed to be playing with the swathes of bubbles left by breaking waves. They swept gracefully back and forth, disappearing and suddenly reappearing through the blankets of bubbles, seemingly totally unfazed by the humans around them – curious, even. They hardly seem to move their wingtips, yet, even with his biggest fins on, a highly experienced underwater cameraman like Rory McGuinness had no hope of keeping up with them. As the mantas swept over my head I could see the strange horns in front of their mouths, and the rows of gill slits running along underneath. Playing with manta rays in the boiling surf of exotic Cinque Island: a lifetime experience, and more importantly a wonderful sequence for your film, and all before we even get to the elephants... One of the best places to film swimming elephants are the Andaman and Nicobar islands, some 750 miles off the east coast of India, across the Bay of Bengal. A chance comment had led our assistant producer

Wendy Darke to discover something extraordinary. It seemed elephants were being used to haul timber out of the dense forests on the Andaman Islands, and every day, at 3 p.m precisely, the elephants downed tools and, so the story went, took to the sea for a refreshing dip. In fact, they were so good at swimming the *mahouts* (elephant handlers) simply 'swam' them from island to island as the work moved on.

It looked like we had found our swimming elephants. If you want to actually film swimming elephants you'll need a dive boat – ours was based in Thailand – an underwater film crew – ours were from Australia – and that's about it. Oh, and one other small thing. You will need permission, of course…I don't want to bore you but, because you want to film the elephants and I genuinely want to help, I'm going to give a tiny flavour of what you'll have to go through if you want to get permission to film on or around the islands of Andaman and Nicobar. In fact, forget Nicobar right now, because unless you are Indian, with some very powerful Indian friends, you are not going to get permission to go anywhere near Nicobar with a film camera.

If you want to get a permit to film in India at all, you have to apply to the Ministry of External Affairs, who consider your request, then send it to all the other departments they feel should be involved, and ask them to give permission. Before I got the boat and crew to Andaman I had spent ages in the UK sending off faxes and letters. Then, I recommend you do what I did: go to India in person – to Delhi, to the Ministry of External Affairs itself, up some stairs in Khan market, to help move things along.

I'll spare you every detail of my particular case: just to say I presented myself at the ministry on a Tuesday, and Rory, our cameraman, was due to fly from Sydney on the Thursday, two days later. The tickets for his flight had been bought but, despite us applying weeks before, he had not received his visa. Nina, my helpful contact in the Ministry, said the papers had been lost, but she thought she might be able to get something ready for Friday – perhaps. This was a disaster. By dint of a huge bunch of flowers, and a solemn promise from me we would not film until all the permits were through, Nina took a huge risk, and the visa was sent. Rory could catch his flight.

Nina had sent our application to film to the Ministry of Defence (MOD), but it had not come back. After many phone calls it turned out the MOD had received the application, but their response, when it was sent, had not got to Nina because the driver of the motorbike returning it had been diverted – to deliver invitations to an MOD cocktail party. Since the cocktail party the response had been lost. For me it was perversely useful to know where the BBC came in the pecking order: well below a cocktail party.

Now it's Thursday: I go to the Ministry of Home affairs (MHA), who may or may not issue the RAPs (Restricted Access Permits) we need. A gentleman sitting at a desk half hidden by vast heaps of folders and files explains he will give us the RAPs once he gets the OK from the MEA (Ministry of External Affairs), once they get the application back from the MOD once MI (Military Intelligence) have OKed it – and he isn't sure if the Forestry Department need to be involved as well. I'm due to fly out of Delhi to meet the team in Madras on Friday – er, tomorrow. The dive boat is already on its way from Thailand, and the camera team has left Australia and is actually in the air.

A crisis was approaching. In my diary it says, 'Ate 10 green chillies and 2 bottles of Kingfisher beer – worked until 12.30.'

Friday 22nd: I was booked on a flight to Madras to rendezvous with the whole team. Would I make the flight? There was no point in going if the permits were not in place.

I'm at the Ministry of External Affairs when it opens at 1000. A patient but slightly fed-up Nina tells me to go away and come back at 1700. I have a crisis meeting with my friend Toby, who is organising all our travel. Toby is clutching great fistfuls of tickets for us all; he looks grim. I'm clearly not going to make the flight I'm currently booked on. Toby goes off to change my flights to later ones – how late can we get? Wickedly, I return to Nina before the appointed hour – 1500, in fact. Nothing. Go away!

Back at 1645. 'Oh, come on!" says Nina. 'Look, it's nearly ready at the MOD – they will send a messenger.'

'No, *no*, Nina! Please not a messenger! May we go and get it ourselves?'

'Most irregular – but OK.'

At 1720 I am handed a small buff envelope by a man at the MOD. I rush back to MEA in a small noisy auto-rickshaw, risking life and limb in the madness of Delhi traffic. Nina inspects the contents of the small buff envelope: it appears we have been granted permission – for just two of the 572 Andaman islands, but it's a start!

At 1755 I walk out of the MEA clutching our permission document. We still need the RAPs (remember them?), but they should now be OK. I rush to the airport. The plane is delayed – such a surprise. It was to fly at 2010, but is now due to go at 2145. At last the flight goes. Not a comfy flight – diary again: 'Grim wait – have to be tough – on at last, next to dirty cross-legged barefoot old man, who farted mightily and smelt of wet washing' – but who cares? Small price to pay – I was in the air, and the crucial permission document was safe in my bag in the overhead locker.

Arrive at hotel at 01:30, stumble into my room to discover pile of notes under my door confirming the rest of the team all safely here. Don't bother to sleep, as we are going to leave in two hours to catch flight to Port Blair, the capital of Andaman, and make the rendezvous with the dive boat.

And that, dear reader, you will discover, is the easy bit. Over the permissions issues we had once on Andaman, I will draw a veil: you have suffered enough. It was – no, honestly – actually worse. To the customs official (no names) who made our lives so unbearable: I hope you get worms. And to Nita Bhali, the forceful Finance Minister who finally knocked some sense into the endlessly unhelpful men: thank you, madam.

For a while, waiting for more permissions, we were stuck in Port Blair. This place has had a chequered history. Shameful things went on in the jails that the British built to house political prisoners arrested after the Indian rebellion (Mutiny) in 1857. Such prisoners were often kept in appalling conditions. There is a zoo in the town, and the assistant producer Wendy Darke and I went to see if they might have any interesting animals we could film for the series. I had heard they had a Nicobar pigeon – a most fantastic-looking bird, like a pigeon, obviously, but covered in long greenish feathers that give the appearance of a badly-made but colourful cloak. Wendy and I hired a taxi and, after being driven at breakneck speed, thrown around as if inside a pinball machine, we got to the zoo.

It seemed deserted. There was no one at the little hut where you paid to get in. Wendy and I discussed our next move. Suddenly, a disembodied voice came from inside the hut. 'Yaars?'

Surely there was no one there?

'Helping?'

We peered cautiously over the counter. A sorrowful midget was looking up at us.

'Yaars?'

'Oh, er, hello, hi! We hear you have a Nicobar pigeon in the zoo?'

The midget considered this statement for a long time. Then he looked up again, and spoke in a hollow voice. 'Deeead!'

'I'm sorry?'

'Deeead,' he moaned.

This was sad news indeed, but just to be sure we had understood we went to look at the Nicobar pigeon exhibit ourselves. To our horror the pigeon was there, but – hanging upside down from its perch. As far as we could see it had been nailed there, through its feet. Quite an unusual way of exhibiting animals in a zoo, and certainly one that would not help us in our quest to film a live one.

Finally we got permission to leave Port Blair. We headed north towards Havelock Island, where the elephants were currently based. But, as with all things in the magical subcontinent of India, could we be sure the swimming actually, really happened – and if it did, could we make it happen for the camera?

Our elephants were operated by a dubious character. In fact, the whole logging operation appeared to be probably illegal, and very sad. It was run by – well, I'm not going to name him; let's call him Mr X. He was a smallish chappie, with a neat moustache and a scooter. Mr X was not what you might call a spiritual man. His main interest soon became clear: money. As far as I could see, it was his only interest. Soon I was riding pillion with Mr X as we shot about the dirt roads looking for a beach from which we could 'launch' the elephants. Mr X began to complain. 'Ah, I am having such troubles. I'm only making

£6,000 per month from stripping the rainforest, and I must pay £1,000 in bribes alone...'

'What – £1,000 in bribes every month?'

'Yes, yes, it is most expensive. I am going to move to another island to get more trees. My daughters are at English public school, the fees are very great...'

'But, Mr X – this is awful about the trees!'

'Yes, I know – and I have such school fees to pay.'

'No, no, I mean it's awful you are removing all the trees.' No reply.

'I am definitely going to move to another island where I can make more money.'

We looked at three different beaches, and chose one. The palm trees swayed gently in the breeze, and the pure white sand was lapped by a sparkling turquoise sea. It was spectacularly beautiful.

'Tomorrow morning at eight I will send elephants,' said Mr X as he dropped me off on the beach and I took the tender back to our dive boat.

The 27th March 1996 is a day I will never forget. It was to be a searing emotional bareback ride. Little did I know what upheavals the next few hours had in store for me. I was up on deck well before 8 a.m. scanning the edge of the forest – would they come? To my huge surprise they did, almost exactly on time. Out of the jungle not one, not two but three elephants appeared, one a little calf scampering along behind its mum. It was a lovely sight: the palms, the sea, the sand, the elephants...They walked down the beach, trunks swaying, the mahouts on top urging them on – this was fantastic. Upon arrival beside the boat, both mahouts immediately demanded 500 rupees to take a single step further, which I paid up immediately – joyfully, even.

We had two cameras: one a new-fangled – at the time – video

camera; the other a film camera, both with their own underwater housings. On our first attempt we got in the water – but the elephants did not. They didn't like it, and stood on the coral roaring furiously, with the *mahouts* on top, unsuccessfully urging them on. Perhaps the whole 'going for a swim at 3 p.m. prompt' was a journalists' fantasy? Second attempt; now the elephants go further in, and – they swim, it's true, but when we look at the video the water is full of dirt: it's too shallow. We need to get out deeper. Both the adults, mother and auntie, are very protective toward the calf and – how they can see us underwater I don't know – always keep their bodies between us and the calf.

This is the make-or-break attempt. The electronics on the film camera housing are playing up, but Rory says we can still do it if we start the camera on board, then go in immediately. With a full roll of film we should have ten minutes. The elephants come out; they are much bolder now, they are swimming in the clear blue deep water – it looks fantastic from above. We all dive in with the camera running. From underwater it looks stupendous: three huge elephants, suspended, floating in blue space, using their trunks as snorkels to breathe, all swimming beautifully along, now in a circle, now in a line astern. I'm on the surface wearing a mask. I watch Rory swim down deep to film looking up; I watch him get right up close (careful of those feet, Rory!); he films side-on; the camera is rock-steady, the water perfectly clear. This is as good as it's possible to get; this is my dream of swimming elephants coming true…Rory looks at his watch and gestures upwards – time up. The dive team come to the surface; we are all bobbing about, ecstatic. 'Just about perfect, mate,' says Rory, grinning. Even the greedy *mahouts* are smiling: they know it was good. We fin happily back to the boat, and the elephants head for the shore. Everyone is cock-a-hoop: we cheer at the mahouts; they cheer back. I go down to my cabin floating on air, in a haze of happiness. The camera assistant starts to take the underwater housing apart to remove the film magazine containing our precious footage.

Not long afterwards there is a knock on my cabin door. It's Rory. 'Mate, I don't want to beat about the bush – I've got some really bad news. The film broke as soon as we started to run the camera. The footage indicator hasn't moved. We didn't shoot a frame, mate. I'm really sorry.'

I leap upstairs, just in time to see the back end of the elephant disappearing into the greenery way up the beach. I shout and roar and shout again, all to no avail. It's hopeless: they're gone. Stung into furious action I leap into the small tender boat – I have to find Mr X. I rush to the shore – but it's no good. Mr X and his scooter are nowhere to be seen.

I returned to the dive boat a broken man. I had scaled the heights, and now we were plumbing the depths. We had been so near.

Rory was on the prow, waving at me. What's happened now, for goodness' sake?

'Mate, mate,' he said, 'I was wrong! Just after you went we checked the magazine properly. The film didn't break at all – the ruddy footage counter broke. The camera worked perfectly, mate – we got the lot!'

Euphoria.

We had our main sequence. But it's not every day you find yourself in such an exotic location, with a film crew. We had a few more days, so we set sail for Cinque Island, where there were sea eagles, deer, monkeys and other wildlife to film.

On the way we were approached by a huge pod of dolphins, who came over to play around the boat. We lay on our stomachs out over the bows, just feet away from them as they broke the surface, rolled left, rolled right, rode our bow wave – dozens of them, Rory trying to film this wonderful spectacle. As if this wasn't enough, flying fish began to break the surface, flicking out their hugely overdeveloped pectoral fins and gliding through the air way further than I ever dreamed possible. (Average distance of a flight is 50 metres.) A flying fish? What a fantastic piece of evolution – extraordinary if you think about it.

At night I went out on deck to escape the heat. I can't sleep at the best of times, so I'd wander around the silent boat for a bit, then lie in the mesh netting strung between the bows (the dive boat was a catamaran), and look up into the vast black dome studded with countless stars. Every now and then a shooting star would blaze across – make a wish, make a wish... As the water lapped gently against the hull it glowed with eerie blue bioluminescence. Try not to forget this, Martin: you won't come this way again.

When we arrived at Cinque Island we discovered there had been a new addition to the fauna. Incredibly, another film crew had come to Cinque to make a film about king cobras, and in so doing had managed to lose one of their stars. Yes, on this small island, along with the spotted deer, monitor lizards and a sea eagle, was a five-metre-long, exceptionally venomous king cobra which, if it saw us, would chase us from one end of the island to the other in order to kill us. Or so we were repeatedly assured. I have had the interesting experience of meeting a king cobra face-to-face – and I do mean face-to-face. A king cobra, when 'concerned', will rear the front third of its body up into the air. If it's a big one, this means it can literally look you in the eye, while showing you its fangs and hissing loudly. This is intimidating.

The king cobra's huge size means it can potentially deliver a massive dose of venom. I say potentially because it's thought over 50 per cent of king cobra bites are 'dry', i.e. don't actually inject any venom – so the bite is more a warning to back off. If they do inject venom you are in extremely serious trouble. King cobra venom is a complicated chemical mixture, but the main component is a neurotoxin that quickly gets to work on your nervous system. First you get pain, then blurred vision, vertigo and drowsiness, which briskly progresses to paralysis, respiratory failure, cardiovascular collapse, coma and death. This can happen in less than thirty minutes.

But it's not all bad! Perhaps this was a female. The female king cobra is an extremely good mother. She makes a nest of leaves and debris, then lays some twenty to forty eggs. She stays with the eggs, guarding them for up to ninety days. The exact time taken to hatch depends on the temperature. At the first signs of hatching, something fascinating happens. The mother, having been so dedicated for so long, immediately clears off. King cobras mainly eat other snakes, and you can see the mother's dilemma: eggs are one thing, but a whole mass of wriggling babies – the temptation! *Mmm*, my babies look so sweet – but also so delicious! If she stayed at the nest grappling with this awful conundrum, the 'bad' side of her character might get the upper hand, so as soon as she realises the eggs are about to hatch, she slips away, never to return.

Despite the dire warnings about the king cobra chasing us from one end of the island to the other, we were not that bothered, because it seems the stories about the king cobra's terrible temper and belligerent nature are highly exaggerated. Like most snakes, they would rather avoid confrontation than go looking for trouble. Slightly to our disappointment, we never saw the king snake.

We filmed the manta rays, as per my diary, fearsome-looking barracuda, and exotic, brightly-coloured sea snakes. All of a sudden our time was up. We had to return to port.

When we got into Port Blair there had been an awful incident. A forester had had a dispute with some tribals. He had been shot with arrows, and then had his throat cut. It was a reminder of just how remote and removed from our comfortable world of shopping malls and fancy cars these islands really are.

Part of the Andaman archipelago, not far off the west coast where we were moored up in Port Blair, is a small outcrop named North Sentinel Island. North Sentinel fascinates me. I would dearly have liked to have gone there to film but, as you will see, there was a very good reason why we couldn't. North Sentinel is almost square, and around eight kilometres by 8 kilometres. If you look at an aerial photograph you can see it's thickly forested – deep green, with typical Andaman beaches, white and sandy, all around. Sentinel is inhabited, but no-one knows for sure how many inhabitants there are. In 2001, the census of India tried to find out what the population was. They recorded thirty-nine individuals, but 'out of necessity this survey was conducted from a distance'.

It was a necessity because the Sentinelese have a history of attacking anyone who comes near their island home. There may be as few as forty Sentinelese, or as many as 500; no one knows. Very, very little is known about them, because the Sentinelese are one of the very last 'uncontacted' peoples on Earth. Every time the modern world and the Sentinelese have met, the outcome has been violent. Back in 1867, an Indian merchant ship, the *Nineveh*, was wrecked on one of the many reefs surrounding the island. The 106 survivors then had to fend off constant attacks, until they were saved by a Royal Navy rescue party. Much more recently, on 26 January 2006, two fishermen fishing illegally close to the shore in their boat were attacked by Sentinelese archers, and both were killed. A helicopter was sent in to try to retrieve the bodies, but was driven off by a hail of arrows. What on earth, I wonder, do the Sentinelese make of a helicopter? Or the vapour trails of passing aircraft, or passing container ships?

Where did they come from? How do they live? What is their world view? Completely fascinating questions, but we do not know and, probably best for them, we don't – not for a good while, anyhow. From the highest point in Port Blair you can look across the sea to North Sentinel, just 33 miles off shore. So close in distance, but unimaginably far off in time. The Andaman and Nicobar administration said in 2005 that they had no intention of interfering with the lifestyle or habitat of the Sentinelese, and are not interested in pursuing any further contact with them. This policy, backed up by the Sentinelese's own spears and arrows, should ensure they retain their privacy for the foreseeable future.

I left the dive boat. Flew to Madras, then caught a flight home. Last diary entry for the trip reads, 'Land, confused, clear customs, baggage, passports etc. in 25 mins. Drive home. Spy my lovely boys playing in the garden – bliss – cuddles. Wife out posting letters. Wife home, heaven all around. Dunno what time it is or anything, just stuffed full of love and happiness.' Was it really forty-eight hours ago I was lying on that net between the prows of the dive boat, staring up at the stars, whilst the luminescent sea lapped against the sides? *Really?*

13

NUNA BHALE – WALKING WITH A MAN-EATING TIGER

Wild and Dangerous, BBC2, 1998

Dhan Bahadur Tamang is a senior wildlife guide at Tiger Tops resort in Chitwan National Park in Nepal. Dhan started work at Tiger Tops aged thirteen. Back then he was the youngest employee; now, at nearly sixty years old, he is the oldest. Dhan has an infectious smile and a wicked sense of humour, and his knowledge of wildlife is encyclopedic. He has the marvellous ability to bring an unprepossessing cluster of scrapes and marks in the sand dramatically to life – 'Look, a tigress walked here, just three, maybe four hours ago, and here the rhino print – no, two rhino prints, mother and small baby! The tigress is following the rhino to try to kill the baby…' I recently went back to Nepal to catch up with Dhan, to remind myself of the story of one particular tiger, a marvellous animal whose path crossed Dhan's many times, and almost crossed my own.

Just as we did many years before, Dhan and I went out on an early morning elephant safari, through the dripping jungle, trees half-shrouded in mist. Ahead sits the mahout, his feet pushing behind the elephant's ears; I sit in a simple howdah, while behind me stands Dhan, his bare feet firmly planted on the elephant's rump, rolling with an effortless grace born of decades of experience. On elephant safari you cruise along like a great grey ship, suspended perhaps twelve feet above the jungle floor, sailing through the undergrowth, almost silent apart from the odd command from the mahout and the liquid calls of black-naped orioles, chatty squawks of babblers and parakeets. It's completely magical.

I first met Dhan in 1998, because back then he was involved in working out what to do with a man-eating tiger – a very special man-eating tiger called Nuna Bhale, perhaps the most famous tiger that ever walked the lush green jungles of Chitwan.

The story started one sunny afternoon in 1984.

If you want to, you can go on Jeep safari in the jungles of Chitwan, but this is somehow a bit isolating: it's too comfortable, and your thoughts stray to the delicious breakfast and hot *masala chai* waiting for you back at camp. No, the way to get focus is to go on foot safari. Now you are walking through the jungle using paths, called *dhondis*, that have been punched through the undergrowth by the very animals you have come to see, i.e. Indian rhino (short-tempered and massive), gaur (a sort of vast one-ton wild ox with formidable horns, also short-tempered), and, of course, patrolling tigers. I once asked Dhan what we did if we met a rhino in its dhondi, and he turned to me, eyes twinkling, and said simply, 'Run!' That was almost as much advice as I ever got, except he also suggested it would be good to climb a tree – not a kapok with lacerating thorns, or a rhino apple tree with its super-slippery bark, but another tree, 'Six foot 'igh for rhino – maybe seven foot if 'ee lift 'is head!'

Back on that hot afternoon in 1984, Dhan had a group of clients out on foot safari walking towards a creek, called in

Nepali *Nuna Kohla* ('Salt Creek'), where he knew a tigress was often to be found. Obviously, the most memorable high point of any walking safari is a face-to-face view of a tiger, and Dhan was determined to oblige. This day the clients did not get to meet the tigress – which, as it turned out, was probably just as well.

Dhan found pug marks (footprints) just where he expected them to be, but then he saw something else. Beside the tigress's were a set of much smaller tracks: a cub. Calmly, Dhan steered the clients away from Salty Creek: a lone tigress was one thing, but a tigress with a cub was a completely different proposition.

'What usually happens when you meet a tiger, Dhan?'

'Usually look at you, then move slowly away, then suddenly turn into the jungle.'

'Do you run away?'

'No, no – just move away slowly.'

'But don't turn your back, I suppose?'

'No, always keep looking at the tiger.'

'I suppose it's more dangerous if it's a tigress with cubs?'

'Yes, very bad. This is more dangerous.'

Tigresses are ferocious in protecting their young, and they need to be. The cubs are born blind and helpless in the den, with only the mother to look after them. There can be up to six cubs, but two or three are the norm. This particular tigress, named Dhaja Pothi, appeared to have just the one cub, and because it was found in the Salt (*Nuna*) Creek it was decided to call the cub Nuna. In Nepal, all female tigers are called Pothi, and all males Bhale. When he first saw the pug marks of the cub, it was only four or five months old, so Dhan had to wait to find out if it was male or female. Eventually it became apparent the little tiger was a male, so Dhan named the cub Nuna Bhale.

The cub grew up fast – by eleven months tiger cubs are pretty much fully grown. It quickly became obvious Nuna Bhale was an exceptional tiger: he just seemed to get bigger and bigger. Soon, the youngster was far larger than his mother, yet still she continued to look after him, offering her protection and teaching him how to hunt. Despite his size, it would be eighteen months before Nuna Bhale became completely independent, and even then, as with all tiger cubs, he would not finally break the bond with his mother for over two years.

The pattern of stripes is unique to each individual tiger, just, as the cliché goes, like a fingerprint, so it was easy for Dhan to recognise Nuna Bhale whenever he saw him. Also, the tiger had a large gap between two toes on his left front paw, so Dhan could also track his movements easily. Fairly soon the young tiger began to stray, which is normal but risky. Despite the mother's diligence only 50 per cent of tiger cubs survive beyond their second year, and the most dangerous time is when they start to try and carve out a territory for themselves.

All tigers need a territory in which to find food. Until fairly recently it was assumed that tigers were effectively solitary and each male carved out an exclusive territory for himself (male and female territories overlap). More recent observations have thrown doubt on this simplistic concept. Tigers have been seen together fairly often. On one memorable day researchers were lucky enough to find a mother tiger with her three cubs at a kill. This family was joined by two other adult females and an adult male, all relatives of the mother tigress. Then these seven were joined by another two, unrelated, tigers, making an astonishing total of nine tigers at one kill. There was very little growling, and generally the tigers displayed remarkably good table manners throughout. So perhaps adult tigers are not quite as solitary and intolerant of each other as used to be thought. However, there is one specific time when male tigers are completely intolerant of other males, which we will come to in a moment.

Young tigers like Nuna Bhale have to find some sort of territory for themselves. They have two options: find a game-rich area that has no other tigers around, or live quietly in someone else's territory, being submissive if the more dominant tiger turns up. So long as he showed proper respect and kept out of the way, the young Nuna would have been tolerated. Hidden away in the green depths of Chitwan, far from human eyes, Nuna Bhale grew up. Despite the poor odds, he survived.

By 1988 things began to change. Nuna Bhale was now four years old, and becoming sexually mature. The group of dominant male tigers in Chitwan were in for a surprise. Nuna Bhale stopped being quite so submissive; he began to flex his muscle. It must have been quite a shock to the resident dominant males as this huge youngster started to make his mark. First, he deposed the resident male in the western part of Chitwan where he had grown up. Now Nuna had some real territory. But he was not finished yet. Like some unstoppable imperialist power, Nuna Bhale's ambition grew: he wandered further and further, pressing his claim – north, south, and especially to the east, battling with and deposing male after male. By 1992 his territory was so huge it encompassed the territories of no less than six female tigers. He had fought his way to the top. None could stand up to Nuna Bhale: he was lord of a huge domain.

You might think being a tiger was a fairly easy way of life – after all, you are one of the strongest carnivores on Earth. A tiger was seen to kill an adult gaur, and drag its prey about 12 metres into some undergrowth. After the tiger had departed a group of thirteen men went to try to pull the gaur back out, but they were unable to move it, at all. A tiger is also formidably armed: it has the longest canines of any big cat – up to three inches long – and sharp retractable claws. On average, a male Bengal tiger at 488 lb easily outweighs a male lion at 400 lb, so, to answer the child's oft-asked question of who would win in a fight between a lion and a tiger: the tiger! A tiger can jump around 10 metres, or 33 feet, and its forelimbs are so powerful it can kill its prey with a single blow. Tigers are excellent swimmers, and can run at speeds up to 40 mph.

But...

No other land predator takes on such enormous prey relative to its own size. A tiger will regularly hunt animals four or five times bigger than itself. Its chosen method of attack requires a leap, a grab with its powerful forepaws, and a perfectly timed strike at the throat or the back of the neck with its jaws. All of which has to happen practically simultaneously. If it's a strangling bite, the tiger may have to hang on to a wildly thrashing creature many times its own size, for quite a time. Sometimes the tables are turned. There have been several well-documented cases of tigers being gored and trampled to death by gaur and wild buffalo.

A tiger relies on the surprise attack. It is not built for long-distance, high-speed chases. It needs to creep to within 10 to 20 metres of its intended victim before launching itself. The hunting tiger is constantly calculating and recalculating the odds of success: as soon as it thinks it's wasting energy, it gives up. Interestingly, the alarm calls many animals give out are probably not to warn others, but to say to the tiger, 'I've seen you, don't bother', because once a tiger has been seen and lost the element of surprise, the fleet-footed animals it prefers to hunt can generally escape. It's estimated that only one in twenty tiger hunts is successful. That's a lot of sometimes highly dangerous work for not much reward. A tiger may go for two weeks without food, and then balance that out by gorging itself when it does make a kill. One tiger was observed to eat 77 lb of meat at a single sitting. Altogether, a tiger's life is one long round of extremely dangerous hunting, and sometimes fighting, risking his or her life time after time.

For many years this was Nuna Bhale's world, and no other tiger could touch him. And with his dominance came the rewards. Nuna Bale had exclusive access to all the females in his territory. He began to father cubs – lots of cubs. Ultimately, he had more cubs that any other tiger ever recorded in Chitwan National Park: an astonishing total of fifty-five, of which, as far as Dhan and the other tiger researchers know, thirty-five reached 'dispersal' age, i.e. survived long enough to start forging their own territories. Nuna Bhale was on velvet. But, inevitably, it couldn't last.

One morning in 1997 Dhan was summoned urgently: a person had been attacked and killed by a wild animal. Could he please come and help identify what had been responsible?

Dhan has seen many deaths in Chitwan, and can tell hair-raising stories: bodies half-eaten; bodies dismembered by the feet of furious elephants; bodies dragged into caves, propped up staring out with sightless filmy eyes; 'bad smell' – many victims of accidental or intended attacks from animals. This makes him disconcertingly matter-of-fact about such things.

In this case it was fairly easy for him to interpret what had happened. A woman around forty years old had been collecting young fern shoots for food. As she bent over, she had been attacked and killed by a tiger. There were pug marks all around. The woman had been partially eaten – man-eating tigers generally eat the muscular part of the human thigh first. Dhan looked carefully at the pug marks. So, they asked him: could he tell which tiger was responsible? The front left paw had a characteristic gap between the toes. Dhan's heart sank. He knew exactly who this was.

'But now must be very careful,' he told me.

There were a number of reasons Dhan might want to be cautious at identifying Nuna Bhale right away. One was simple sentimentality: Nuna Bhale had been part of his life for many years, and he respected and admired the great tiger. Secondly, in Nepal they have an enlightened attitude towards tigers that attack humans. Many attacks on humans by tigers are nothing to do with man-eating. If a tiger is surprised, feels threatened or has cubs, it may attack — but with no intent of actually eating a human. We are the wrong shape and size for a normal tiger to see us as prey. Sambar, their number-one preferred food item, is a very large shaggy deer, and practically all the food on a tiger's menu, mainly different sorts of large ungulates, has all four of its feet on the ground. We humans are small, upright and bipedal. All wrong. It's sometimes said that the Nepalese give a tiger a 'first free meal', which may sound frivolous, even heartless, but is actually sound good sense. What it means is that the first attack is generally treated with caution, without the tiger being labelled a man-eater right away.

The third reason was biologically fascinating, fraught with moral ambiguity, and thus emotionally challenging. When I heard about it, I thought it would make an immensely interesting film for the TV series I was producing, *Wild and Dangerous*, which was why, in March 1998, I set off from the UK to Nepal on an urgent recce, to meet Dhan Badur and find out more about the man-eater. I soon found myself on a tiny airplane en route from Kathmandu to Meghauli, the closest airport to Tiger Tops.

Flying almost anywhere in Nepal is exciting. You are bumping along in a little aeroplane, looking out of the window, marvelling at the wonderful patterns of the terraces. These narrow terraces are made by farmers, and allow them to cultivate food right up to the tops of hills. Suddenly, a much bigger hill rears up, and you find yourself flying actually beneath the summit. Sometimes you can see people, huts, and buffalo dragging wooden ploughs, almost alongside you. The air turbulence caused around the hills does tend to make flights rather bumpy, and, there's no getting away from it, smaller airlines in Nepal do have a fairly worrying safety record. Something that was accentuated for me as we came in to land on a grass airstrip. At the far end of the runway was a smashed-up twin-engined aeroplane, with text-book bent-back propellers, between which someone had thoughtfully stretched a large banner that read: 'Welcome to Meghauli airport.'

Whenever a plane is due at Meghauli, an ancient air-raid warning siren is cranked up with a big handle – the signal for soldiers to chase small children and their goats off the runway where they have been grazing. The same children can be seen when an aeroplane is revving up to take off, leaning into the back-draught from the propellers at crazy angles, ragged shirts thrashing in the gale, before being spun off backwards like autumn leaves, shrieking with delight. Health and Safety would have conniptions.

By the time I was being whisked off to Tiger Tops in a Jeep, a complimentary mango juice inside me, plunging almost immediately into the deep green jungle, Nuna Bhale had killed and eaten four more people. Clearly that first attack was not an accident. Understandably, local people were now starting to demand that something should be done. What slightly undermined their case was that all the kills had taken place inside the official park, where, by law, no humans were supposed to go. Local people were allowed to collect fodder, wood and food from the buffer zone surrounding the park proper, but so far all the kills had taken place within its boundary. Nevertheless, things were coming to a head.

Yet still the authorities held back. Here was the moral ambiguity – a complex situation deeply rooted in tiger biology.

The reason Nuna Bhale continued to roam free, despite being a confirmed man-eater, was this. A resident dominant male provides essential protection for his cubs. If he is killed, or driven off his territory by a stronger incoming male, the new arrival will do his best to kill all the cubs in the territory he has just acquired. I know this sounds terrible, but it's simply biological necessity. The average reproductive life of a male tiger is just 2.8 years – 33 months. A female tiger will look after her cubs for about 18 months, and will not come into season during this time. The reproductive life of the male tiger is too short to allow this to happen. If he kills all the cubs, the female will come into season in a matter of weeks, giving him a chance to reproduce. So that is why a male coming into a new territory will kill all the cubs under a year old. It's a brutal reality of tiger life.

It turned out that two of the females in Nuna Bhale's territory had cubs: three each, and all under a year old. It was simple: if Nuna Bhale could be kept alive, he would continue to offer the cubs protection. If not, they would be killed. So Dhan and the park authorities were not just dealing with one man-eating tiger: they were also dealing with his six rapidly growing cubs as well. Every month Nuna Bhale stayed alive, healthy enough to protect his territory, the greater the chance of the cubs surviving. Every single tiger cub is important. At the start of the twentieth century there were estimated to be more than 100,000 tigers globally.

Today there are less than 3000, and they have lost 93 per cent of their historic range. There were just over 100 tigers in Chitwan, so losing seven would represent a significant loss.

So here was I, as part of my recce, walking in the territory of a man-eating tiger. It's slightly surreal – initially quite hard – to feel your life is actually in danger. The jungle seems – apart from the enthusiastic leeches – benign and full of beauty. It would be very different if you lived here, and relied upon the jungle for your living. Some famous man-eaters, like the Champwat tigress – 430 victims – have killed hundreds of people, attacking them in their fields during the day, taking them from their beds as they slept, paralysing whole regions in a reign of terror.

As we walked, there were signs of patrolling tiger – the fairly obvious footprints – but also more subtle signs. Dhan showed me deep gouges some twelve feet up a tree trunk, where a tiger had sharpened its claws. He invited me to sniff the urine scent mark at the base of the tree. Sharp, tangy. There were large scrapes in the ground made by the tiger's paws with either urine or scat at one end – more markers. To Dhan, evidence was everywhere. 'Look here!' He was pointing at the trunk of a tree. I could see nothing. 'More close!'

Oh, yes – perhaps a dozen tiny white hairs were stuck to the bark.

'Tiger has rubbed his cheeks here, leave a smell from 'is face.'

All these scent marks outlined individual tiger's territories, both male and female – a continually updated message board from which other tigers could gather information about the sex, size and strength of the locals, as well as the sexual condition of a female.

When a female tiger comes into season it's a dangerous time. While for much of the time male tigers seem to be surprisingly tolerant of other males in their territory, as soon as a tigress is in season everything changes. Fights between males become more common, and much more serious — sometimes fatal.

And then there is the whole process of mating itself. To a human observer, this seems fraught with extreme danger. A male tiger is usually considerably bigger than the female but, as the tiger expert Stephen Mills neatly puts it, 'even though he may weigh at least half as much again, she is still the second most dangerous animal in the jungle after him, and it pays to treat her with respect.' To avoid getting injured, a sensible male tiger will not push his luck with an unreceptive female. Tiger mating is usually more successful with experienced animals who know one another. Tigers need to mate frequently to stimulate the tigress's ovulation. If you are ever lucky enough to witness the event, this is what you can expect to see. Both tigers lie close to each other in some secluded spot, trying not to catch the other's eye. When the female is ready she will walk over to the male, crouch down, belly to the ground, and move her tail to one side. It is now fairly safe for him to make his move. The male mounts her and, grabbing her by the scruff of the neck, proceeds to thrust for around fifteen seconds. Then it's payback time: he'd better be ready to jump, because the second she senses he has finished, the female will often whip around and try to whack him in the face. This process will be repeated perhaps every quarter of an hour for two or three days. After fifty or sixty orgasms the exhausted male generally takes a hit from his beloved — but, as Dhan told me, 'Looks like fight but she keeps claws in'. Dhan has never seen a serious injury from a female attacking a male during mating.

We walked on; Dhan pointed. High up in a tree was a whole troupe of grey Hanuman langurs, a type of monkey, with their long elegant tails and striking black faces. They were plucking leaves. On the ground were a small herd of spotted deer. 'No tigers here now,' said Dhan.

Langurs and spotted deer are often seen together, creating a highly effective early-warning system. From their high vantage-point, eagle-eyed langurs can often see an approaching predator and send out volleys of alarm calls. When the langurs come down to the ground to feed, which they frequently do, the deer protect them with their superb sense of smell. If the deer smell danger, perhaps a tiger or leopard hidden in the grass, they let out a series of their *poup poup poup!* alarm calls, alerting the langurs. Up in the tree tops the langurs also provide the deer below with a steady shower of fresh green leaves, because they tend only to eat the stems. It's such an effective system. If neither langurs nor deer are alarming, you can be sure there is no predator in the area.

Sometimes tigers roar. Sadly, I have never heard this, but if the tiger roars far away, Dhan says, you can still feel it in your chest. 'If he is close, your heart goes up to throat, can hardly breathe, after, heart *bang bang bang!*' As the roar dies away it is immediately replaced by shrieking peacocks and deer alarm calls.

Now we were wading through a river. I was waist-deep, holding my rucksack above my head. 'Around the corner here,' said a forest guard in hushed tones, 'Nuna Bhale favourite resting place.'

'But – what do we do if he is there?'

'If it's our time to die, then we must go,' said the guard simply and sincerely. All very well for someone who believes they will be reincarnated right away; less reassuring for me. Our defensive armoury consisted of two bamboo sticks and a multi-function penknife, currently buried somewhere in the bottom of my rucksack. In midstream I hesitated. Up to now, any sense of any genuine threat from the man-eater had, if I'm honest, seemed remote. But now it hit me like a punch in the stomach. This was real, visceral. In my film-maker's mind I could see exactly what was about to happen. The huge tiger would be stretched out on a rock (wide shot); he would hear us, instantly raise his head (mid-shot) and fix me with terrifying eyes (close-up tiger's eyes and teeth); spring up – I could hear the snarl as he leapt – front legs splayed apart, directly towards me (my POV). I would see the teeth, smell his breath as he fell upon me (side view as tiger and producer crash back into water). 'Um—' But it was too late. We rounded the corner. There indeed was a huge stone upon which Nuna Bhale liked to sun himself. But, thankfully, of Nuna Bhale himself there was no sign.

My heart was thumping. This is the tiger's home; the tiger knows every nook and cranny. The tiger can hunt silently, and is fantastically well armed. The tiger has changed its opinion about what constitutes a good meal: no longer a tough sambar or spotted deer – no, a good snack can be provided by the soft pink human, slow to run away and terrifically easy to dispatch. Once a man-eater has made this mental adjustment, what was a friendly forest full of joyful birdsong becomes something infinitely more ominous.

Nuna Bhale was not waiting for me around any other corners, so I returned to the UK to make arrangements: book cameramen, flights, accommodation – all the mundane paraphernalia of a film shoot. Back in Nepal, unfortunately, events were about to overtake us all.

A small group of men had crossed, illegally, into the park to cut fodder. As they worked they heard a guttural noise and, before they had time to react, the tiger had attacked one of them. They yelled and shouted and managed to drive the tiger back, but it was too late for their friend. They half-carried, half-dragged the body through the jungle, across the river, back, eventually, to their village. Then, as is the custom, the body was cremated the evening of the same day. This was not the end. That night, under the cover of darkness, the tiger emerged, crossed the river, and began to follow the scent of the man it had killed, eventually tracking him right into the sleeping village. Now the tiger padded around in the silence. Where was his prey? Nowhere to be found, but in this barn…something smelt good. The tiger burst in and attacked a buffalo tied up there. The buffalo commenced to roar, alerting the whole village. People rushed to the barn, yelling, armed with sticks. Distracted, the tiger stopped attacking the buffalo and started to retreat, but not before it had grabbed a goat. In moments both tiger and goat had been swallowed up by the darkness, into which the villagers were not inclined to follow.

The next morning a young man picked up the trail of the goat. He found not only the goat, but also the tiger. The tiger attacked but did not kill the man, who managed to get back to the village. The time had come: a deputation was sent to the park authorities. The tiger, insisted the villagers, must be killed. Because the animal was now out of the jurisdiction of the park proper, the authorities had no option but to concede to the villagers' wishes.

Elephants were procured. Dhan was called in to help conclusively identify the tiger – they wanted to be absolutely sure they killed the right animal. A gun was brought by the local police.

First, Dhan went to the village to look at the pug marks. He knew what he would find. There was the unmistakable wide gap between the toes of the front left paw – it was Nuna Bhale. Then they got on to the elephants, and followed the trail away from the village. It didn't take long to find him, lying beside the long grass. The great tiger did not get up and move away when the elephants approached; he just looked at them, panting. It was as if he knew what was going to happen. He blinked and snarled. But still he did not move.

The policeman with the gun looked across at Dhan Bhadur. Was it…? Dhan nodded.

One shot rang out. The tiger convulsed. Another; then another. The tiger slumped. Nuna Bhale sighed. A cheer went up from the crowd of villagers that had followed. But that quickly stopped. For a beat or two a great silence fell. Then there was pandemonium.

Dhan told me over a thousand people came to look at the remains of the once-great tiger. Once great: now, Nuna Bhale was a wreck, a shadow of the ambitious adolescent that had set out to conquer the jungle some ten years before. One elbow was smashed; he had hardly any teeth – the big canines were gone, even the smaller teeth were missing; his claws were worn away. The once-powerful body was thin, and covered in cuts and scratches from fights with other tigers.

Nuna Bhale was fourteen: past his prime. It turned out he had been driven out of his territory by a younger, more powerful male, Munda Bhale, and was now struggling to find food, a typical set of circumstances that conspire to create a man-eater. He had lived by the sword, and now he died by the sword. In tiger terms, Nuna Bhale had had a fantastic life. The protection Dhan had given him earlier had worked, because four of the six cubs survived – and Nuna Bhale's offspring roam the hidden paths of Chitwan to this very day.

But the end had been as sad as it was inevitable.

And, of course, I never did get to make the film.

14

RUNNING WITH REINDEER

Wild, BBC2, 2007

They were coming. I could hear them in the distance. This was the climax of the film. Everything we had done so far had led up to this moment. Any second now, hundreds of them would appear out of the trees on to the great expanse of dazzling white snow in front of us. This was it.

'Where are you going to put the camera, Sam?'

'Er...'

'Sam, where are you going to put the camera? They're coming any second!'

'I...I...'

'Sam, for Christ's sake! Where are you going to put—'

'Oh, dear...' – looking up to the sky helplessly – 'there's nothing upstairs but little sugar mice!' (Translation: *I haven't a clue.*)

And there, in a nutshell, you have Irish cameraman Sam Gracie; half genius, half blithering eejit!

'Sam. Put the tripod down here. And turn over...*now.*'

Thundering around the tree line, hundreds – no, thousands – of galloping reindeer made their entrance. It was quite a sight.

We had come up to the snowy wastes of northern Norway to make a one-off special documenting the lives of the Sami reindeer herders for the BBC2 *Wild* series. Today was the last day of filming: the huge reindeer herd were coming to the end of their autumnal migration. For the Sami people with whom we had been living, this was a day of reckoning, an audit of the whole year.

The Sami are a fascinating people. Hang on – is that the right word? Race? Race of people. They used to be known as the Lapps, but today that's considered demeaning. *Lapp* is Swedish for 'patch of cloth for mending old clothes' (although how you get all that from just a four-letter word I'm not sure), and calling a Sami a Lapp might imply they are scruffy and bedraggled, and nothing could be further from the truth. The Sami are a proud race with a rich culture, and their traditional clothing is anything but bedraggled.

There are three main groups of Sami. There are those that live by the sea, who fish. Then there are the mountain Sami, who herd reindeer, and a third group who are known, prosaically but very accurately, as 'the not reindeer Sami who don't live by the sea'. Only around 10 per cent of the Sami are reindeer herders, and less than 3000 herd reindeer full time. You must never ask a Sami herder how many reindeer they own – the reindeer are their wealth and, as our fixer Jason Roberts explained, it would be like asking someone how much money they had in the bank. A bit rude. Because they follow the reindeers' ancient migration paths, the historic Sami territory encompasses parts of Norway, Sweden, Finland and Russia. As you can imagine, this has caused a few problems over the years, as the herders try to follow their migrating animals from country to country, the man-made borders being meaningless to a reindeer.

Jason had not only lived with the Sami for two years, but also spoke one of the many different Sami languages. This allowed us exceptional access. One Sami family had agreed to let us travel with them for the last stages of the autumn reindeer migration and round-up. During the film our presenter, the tough, clever and strikingly handsome Saba Douglas-Hamilton, would live and work with the herders. Effectively, she would become a Sami. Actually, it wasn't just 'our' family, because by tradition, during the round-up a number of different families will work together, in a group known as a *siida*.

The leader of the *siida* was Isak Mathis – a great bear of a man who radiated an aura of quiet authority. We joined Isak and the *siida* towards the end of the migration, the reindeer and Sami had already travelled some 250 kilometres together. Now they were approaching the outskirts of Kautokeino, a centre of Sami culture and the end of the journey.

If all went well, Isak and his *siida* would try to gather the huge herd and guide the reindeer into traditional wooden pens. There, all the animals would be given a health check, identified, and divided up amongst the different members of the community. It being winter in northern Norway, the snow lay deep and crisp and even. It was extremely cold, and getting around, even on the snowmobiles Jason had sorted out for us, was tough.

Snowmobiles can be bloody dangerous. The problem is, they are a doddle to ride – it hardly takes any skill at all. You hit the starter, push the throttle – just a thumb lever at the end of the handlebar – and off you go. There's no clutch. But in reality they are heavy, powerful and, for the inexperienced – especially riding two-up – it's quite easy to get into serious trouble. Saba Douglass-Hamilton learned quickly, and was soon fast and safe. Cameraman Sam Gracie, however, although undoubtedly fast, could not, by any stretch of the imagination, be called safe.

'Begob, that's fun!' he gushed.

'I'm not going out again unless I have my own skidoo,' said Frazer, our sound recordist.

'But, Frazer—'

'No. I'm not going on the back with Sam again – no, sorry, I'm not.'

From our base in Kautokeino, the plan was to go out and rendezvous with Isak and the members of the *siida*, so we could share the last few days of the round-up with them.

First we had to find them.

From intuition and a good understanding of the usual migration routes, the indefatigable Jason thought he knew where Isak and the reindeer would be. I was, frankly, dubious. Our little convoy set off across the dazzling snow, heading out into the vast white emptiness of northern Norway.

On a clear winter's day it's completely Narnia-like. Thick, unblemished white snow with bare birch trees poking out. The sky is clear and blue, the air cold and clean. When you stop and turn off the skidoos it is utterly, totally and profoundly silent. You can hear the pulse of your heart. Small glittering crystals of ice seem to fall gently all around – I'm not sure where they come from. Occasionally the silence is broken as snow slides off a branch and hits the ground with a muffled thud. When the wind gets up and the snow whips across your face it's rather different – but still elementally beautiful.

We drove around a bend between two snow banks, and there, slightly below us, lay a huge, flat, frozen, snow-covered lake. Jason's intuition had been correct. Spread out across the lake was the herd, and amongst them a fantastic figure.

Despite being on a skidoo, Isak Mathis still looked like someone from another time – a prehistoric hunter-gatherer, perhaps, or some junior Norse god. His huge size was accentuated by his *gákti*, the traditional costume of the Sami. These clothes are not some sort of faux-touristy confection. The *gákti* is the real thing, evolved over centuries of living in the harsh freezing conditions the reindeer-herding Sami have had to endure. There is a colourful tunic, loose and quite long, beneath which thick leggings are tucked into high boots made of reindeer skin. Around the tunic is a belt, which reminds me of Batman's utility belt because it may contain a host of useful things: a leather pouch, an antler needle case, a fire-starter kit, and it will nearly always have at least one knife hanging from it. Isak had two knives, a smaller, super-sharp one called Puukko in Samish, kept in an attractively carved bone sheath, and a huge one, known as Leuko, or *stuorraniibi* (meaning simply 'big knife'), which later we were to see being put to serious use. (Of course, at the end of the trip I had to buy a *stuorraniibi* for my ever-expanding knife collection.)

To another Sami, the *gákti* can impart important information. The detail may define where the wearer is from and, if the *gákti* is being worn by a woman, it can show her marital status. Square buttons on her belt mean, I'm married; round ones mean, 'Well, hello there..!' Rather poignantly, if a divorced man goes on wearing the *gákti* his ex made for him, it means he still pines for her and wants her back. Over his *gákti* Isak was wearing a great cape (*lukka*) of reindeer skin, which kept him warm but allowed total freedom of movement. Slung across one shoulder was a bright orange lasso which, to our amazement, he was able to throw, from his moving snowmobile, with unerring accuracy around the antlers of any reindeer he wanted to look at. Isak would hurl the lasso, dismount the still-moving skidoo, and join with the reindeer in an epic tug-of war. Once he was close enough he'd grab its antlers and wrestle it to the ground in one fluid movement.

Isak seemed particularly interested in the reindeer's ears. The reason soon became apparent. By looking at small cut marks on them he could quickly tell who owned the animal. When they are young every Sami herder – boy or girl – is allocated a pattern of ear cuts unique to them. It's sort of like binary maths: a simple system of nicks and no nicks that, in combination, allows a large number of different owners to have their own individual mark. Isak could often see the ear-cut pattern from surprisingly far off, but occasionally he would catch the reindeer just to be sure – I think partly for the pleasure of being able to use his great skill with the lasso, like the quiet satisfaction of a cabinet maker crafting a perfect joint, or a potter at her wheel. That's the trouble with working in television, you never experience the profound satisfaction that can be had by simply using your hands.

Once he'd finished, Isak undid the lasso, and both he and the reindeer would get up, shake themselves down, and go their separate ways. If Isak had been equipped with antlers it might have been difficult to tell them apart: his *lukka* of reindeer fur just blended in with the herd.

Isak's skill with his lasso allowed us to go in and film close-ups of the reindeer he had caught. While we were doing this he took hold of my wrist and pushed my hand into the reindeer's fur. Luxury! Soft beyond compare. I had read that, however much you try, it's not possible to see the skin under a reindeer's fur because the under layer is so tightly packed. As far as I could tell, this is actually true. There are two distinct layers in the reindeer's pelt: an ultra-warm under layer, like wearing an exceptionally high-quality fleece, and above that a top coat of longer hollow hairs that provides a second layer of insulation. This is tremendously efficient. If snow falls on a reindeer it just sits there, because not enough heat escapes from its body to melt it. If you look, the whole reindeer is fur-lined – its muzzle, even the nostrils themselves, covered in insulating fur. Because of this reindeer can easily handle temperatures down to -30° C.

In late afternoon, Isak and his family parked up their snow-mobiles near where the reindeer were grazing, and began to unpack for the night. During the two-week journey down from the summer feeding-grounds in the north, the Sami must sleep out with their animals. They still use a traditional structure called a *lavvu*, whose basic design has not changed for hundreds of years. They use the *lavvu* because it works brilliantly, and also, I suspect, as a re-affirmation of their culture.

Isak, his young daughter Inger, and her friend Elle-Helene, took three long poles from the snowmobile trailer, each forked at the top. When they were hoisted up, the forks interlocked to form a secure tripod. Around a dozen other poles were laid up against this first structure. Now, canvas-like material was wrapped expertly around the structure but leaving quite a big hole at the top. Isak sent us out to collect fresh springy branches of birch, which were brought inside and laid down on the snow all around the sides of the *lavvu*. Reindeer skins were placed on top of the birch branches, which now served to keep the skins off the snow. Soon a fire was crackling in the centre of the *lavvu*, the smoke climbing out of the hole left open at the top. The first of many hot coffees was poured out into the Sami's beautifully carved wooden cups. The Sami adore coffee, and seem to drink it all the time; I never did find out when and how these people from the freezing north first discovered it. They have no milk, so they use lumps of reindeer fat instead.

As darkness began to fall, the two girls, Inger and Elle-Helene, put out sets of antlers in the snow and started practising with their lassos. They were astonishingly accurate. Saba, the presenter, asked Inger if she would teach her to use the lasso. Now, Saba has been brought up in the wilds of Africa, and is immensely proficient at this sort of physical challenge, but it was clear she would never be as good as these two little girls, many years her junior: theirs was a skill born of a lifetime's practice. Even if Saba ran away from them at full speed, both the girls could easily drop a loop of their lasso over her shoulders, time after time. Interestingly, the lassos the Sami now use are made of modern materials, and are colour-coded, the different colours indicating the temperature range at which each lasso works best. Different lassos for different times of the year.

As night fell, I walked outside. The *lavvu* was silhouetted against the dying light of the day, surrounded by the skeletal structures of leafless birch trees. Contrasting with a cold, blue-black sky, the open top of the *lavvu* was lit up by a flickering warm orange glow. A little smoke curled out. Whenever anyone left the *lavvu*, a gap would open, revealing a ruddy fire-lit scene within. A big pot of – obviously – reindeer stew and potatoes (the only vegetable commonly used by the Sami) was suspended above the fire. People were lying comfortably on the reindeer skins, clad in traditional blue and red *gákti*, chatting and laughing as they sipped steaming drinks from their beautiful cups. Then the cloth door would be drawn across once more, shutting out the picture, leaving nothing but the cold night and the darkening sky.

Next morning, after more coffee, we packed up the *lavvu* and set off to find the reindeer herd once more. We moved along with them as they slowly walked towards their final destination. It was interesting to watch them feed, digging down through the snow to find the 'reindeer moss' (actually a kind of lichen) below. This part of their diet is helped by another subtle modification for living in these freezing climes, as a close look at the reindeer's feet reveals. During the summer, when the ground is soft and boggy, pads on the reindeer's feet swell up and provide extra grip, but in winter the same pads shrink right down, exposing the hard, sharp edge of the hoof. This hard edge not only allows the reindeer to grip on ice – the hoof digging in like the edge of a ski: it also allows them to dig down through even hard-packed snow to find the reindeer moss beneath (this is called 'cratering'). If you or I tried to eat reindeer moss it wouldn't do us much good, because unlike reindeer we can't digest it. Apart from a few snails, reindeer are almost unique in the animal kingdom in having a special enzyme, lichenase, which breaks down reindeer moss into useful glucose and carbohydrates.

I couldn't help noticing, as we got to know our extended Sami family, just how many of them seemed to have injuries to their eyes – even the Mighty Isak had a damaged iris. In the end, curiosity got the better of me. It turned out they had all been hit in the eye by reindeer antlers. This just seemed to be an accepted part of being a reindeer herder. I couldn't see why this might happen quite so often, but before the round-up was over I was to discover, first-hand, why this was so.

Reindeer are unique amongst all species of deer because both male and female have antlers. In keeping with other deer, the antlers are shed and re-grown every year, but the timing of the shedding is intriguing. The bulls shed their antlers in winter, usually November to December, but the females hang on to theirs until spring. In fact, pregnant cows will keep their antlers until either just before or just after calving in May. The reason for this was explained to me many years later when I was filming with a herd of reindeer up in Scotland. Antlers are weapons: if you have a weapon and the other person doesn't, you can push them around. That's exactly what happens with the reindeer. Once the bulls have shed their antlers, the females start to bully them

– sometimes they harass them so much the poor old bulls clear off, and live together in their own men-only herd where things aren't so stressy. The reason for this apparently bitchy behaviour is grounded in good biology. The pregnant females have to find food for both themselves and their unborn calves: the last thing they want is any big bulls muscling in on the best feeding areas, and having weapons throughout their pregnancy ensures they have first access to the food – a very neat bit of biology.

The migration was heading toward its climax. Up to now we had not really got a handle on how many reindeer were heading towards the pens – they had been spread out across the tundra, half-hidden amongst the birch forest. Isak, as leader of the *siida*, had decided the exact time when they would finally try to move the herd into the holding pens. The reindeer are not tame – not domesticated in the same sense as cattle or sheep. You cannot simply drive them to where you want them to go: they have to be coaxed. Using snowmobiles, but moving cautiously, the team would try to manoeuvre the lead animals towards the wide entrance of a wooden 'funnel', which would gradually narrow as they got towards the pens themselves. But if these animals got spooked, the entire herd could turn and bolt, and the whole day's work would be undone. We could hear the sound of the snowmobiles through the trees – Isak had told us where he had hoped the herd would come out. At any minute they would stream out on to the great expanse of snow before us.

'Where are you going to put the camera, Sam?'

'Er...'

Which is where we came in.

Happily, we did get the tripod set up in time, and we did film the herd pouring forth. The numbers were enormous

– somewhere around 3500 reindeer in total. Gradually, the whole cavalcade made its way towards the opening of the funnel. The lead reindeer stopped; stood; hesitated... then went on. It was going to work. The reindeer streamed into the holding pens. As night fell, the real work would start, and we were going to help.

It was a fantastic sight. Inside a circular wooden pen, some twenty metres across, a group of perhaps a hundred reindeer streamed round and round, anti-clockwise, a blur of soft browns and whites with a forest of antlers above. The whole scene was lit by floodlights and – a quirk of the extreme cold (it was -30°C now) – each floodlight seemed to be surrounded by a halo of tiny glittering ice crystals. Above this surging mass of animals, steam rose, further softening the picture. We stood, arms on the side of the pen, watching the endless stream pass. As they went by, a strange clicking, popping sound could be heard, cutting through the general grunting and muted passage of hooves. Quite a sharp snapping sound. This was yet another subtle specialisation unique to the reindeer. One of the tendons in the reindeer's foot passes over a bony protuberance. As the hoof hits the ground, and the ankle bends backwards, the tendon is pulled across the bone, producing a sharp *snap*. It is thought this snapping sound helps the migrating reindeer keep in contact with one another, even in the dark or in a blizzard.

It was time to step up to the plate and into the ring. Isak watched carefully, then turned to me, pointing at a bull. 'That one, Martin.' There was a twinkle in his eye. 'He is verrry strong!'

I knew the score. Diving in amongst the surging mass, I managed to grab the bull's antlers with both hands. Blimey, he really was strong. For a while I was dragged around, digging my heels in, narrowly avoiding Sam Gracie and the film crew as they tried to record what was going on. But back then I too was quite strong – and I couldn't be just a flabby TV producer in front of Isak. The bull slowed, and I was able to drag him across to the boss. Isak ran expert hands across the reindeer, checked the ear marks, then carefully checked his teeth. He drew out *stuorraniibi*, the big knife, and cut a sign in the bull's fur. 'OK.' Did he approve of my performance? I couldn't tell.

One by one the reindeer were caught, and brought over to Isak to examine. Most were let go again after being marked, but occasionally, after he had examined them, Isak would draw the big knife and, holding the deer tightly, plunge the blade into its flank. The reindeer seemed to die almost instantly. No struggling: one moment it was alive; the next it was gone. It was impressive. The decision turned on the state of the animal's teeth. The winter diet of reindeer moss was gritty, and gradually ground down their teeth. For a number of years this wouldn't matter, but eventually the teeth would get so worn the reindeer would not be able to feed itself properly through the winter, and starve. If Isak discovered badly-worn teeth, the animal was dispatched immediately. Not a bad way to go: a lifetime out in the wilderness, with hundreds of companions, herded into a ring one day, still with your friends – the next moment, oblivion. If I was ever diagnosed with something long-winded and terminal, I said to Isak, I would call Jason to contact him.

Many years have passed since our time with Isak and the Sami, but I still have a recurring dream. It goes like this. I am looking across a street in a very busy shopping area. Probably London – the Fulham Road, maybe? It's winter. Hordes of people are passing by, holding bags full of stuff. Suddenly there is a gap in this surging mass of humanity. The sound recedes, and there, a great stillness amongst all the movement, is a huge figure, in his *gákti* and reindeer cape, and he is looking straight at me. Our eyes meet. I know my time has come, and as he crosses the street I will welcome Isak, and wait calmly for the big knife to do its clean work.

Once the group of reindeer had all been checked over, marked and separated off for their different owners, another hundred or so would be herded into the ring, and the whole process would take place again, then again, and again. It would take three days to sort out the entire herd.

The Sami loved our presenter, Saba. Even when the camera was not on her she was right in the thick of it. I think they could sense she was, in spirit, 'one of them'. They liked the way she worked hard, and they liked her caring but no-nonsense relationship with animals. Saba was in at the heart of the action when, suddenly, there was a commotion. I will let my diary take up the story, as it turned into a rather odd incident.

17 February 2003:
The girl Inga was in there lassoing. When she went to grab a reindeer, she got a right wallop in the face, and down she went (still holding on) – a miracle it didn't take out her eye, 1 cm above the lid – blood was pouring out down her face. Saba rushed in to help. Then it got weird. An older lady stops lassoing and comes in, she cradles Inga in her arms, and begins a strange word incantation – rhythmic, constant. The injured girl relaxes visibly – shoulders go down. The old woman now runs her finger around and around just above injury – still the words come. Then suddenly she's up, and walks off to carry on lassoing. I look at the cut – rather than a gash pouring blood it's now just a thin red line? I know Saba's been putting on snow to try to help, etc. but it's a bit difficult to explain what has just happened?

It was indeed. What was not hard to explain, as we watched the Sami working right in amongst the reindeer's flicking heads and sharp antlers, was why so many of them were partially blinded.

It had been a wonderful shoot. To be allowed into the world of the Sami at this critical time – to have been invited, albeit in a small way, to help – was a unique experience. I went to bed very late on our last night in Kautokeino, after many heartfelt thank you's and sad goodbyes. I was deeply asleep when I began to dream there were people in my room. Or was I dreaming? Was I awake? Yes, I could hear muffled voices – or was that my dream? I turned over and started to drift off. Wait a moment: there *was* giggling in my room – this time there could be no mistake. I switched on the light: at the end of my bed a reindeer was peering at me. As I struggled to make sense of this bizarre apparition, another bout of suppressed giggling revealed Saba and the blasted film crew hiding just around the corner. Not only had they bribed the porter to give them a key to my room, but as I slept they had hauled the stuffed reindeer from the lobby into my room. Idiots! But the team had also clubbed together and bought me – they are terribly expensive – a genuine, beautiful Sami cup, a *guksi*, carved from a birch burl and inlayed with a piece of reindeer antler on the handle. It is one of my most treasured possessions.

15

MYSTERIES AND LEGENDS OF
THE AMAZON

Ultimate Killers, BBC1, 1999;

Wild and Dangerous, BBC2, 1998.

I've been up the Amazon quite a few times in the course of my television career, and have stumbled across some of the legendary creatures that live there. I've even managed to film one or two. The rainforest is full of magical beings. There is the beautiful Rain Goddess – a naked woman who cries to you from a rock in the river, and whose look is certain death. There is widespread belief in the Dolphin Men, who are so often responsible for the unexplainable pregnancies that occur now and then. Interestingly, exactly the same belief used to occur in the Scottish islands, but there the mysteriously pregnant women blamed the Silkies, which were half man, half seal. If the baby was born with even a little bit of webbing between its toes, well, that really let the woman off the hook.

These days, some of the legends, to our cynical European sensibilities, may be somewhat hard to credit, but one or two, which involve wildlife, are certainly worthy of closer inspection. I'm going to explore three particular creatures of Amazonian legend. First, the shoals of voracious piranha that, as everyone knows, will strip a swimmer to the bone in seconds. Next, the hideous candiru, the 'vampire catfish' that, if you go for a pee in the river, apparently swims up the stream of urine into a man's willy. And finally – strangest of all – the mapinguari, an enormous ape-like creature that lives in the rainforest, kidnaps humans and sometimes kills cattle. One way or another I have had personal experience of all three of these legendary creatures.

So first, piranha. By a marvellous coincidence, even as I write, today's papers are full of yet another piranha horror story. These are actual bits of copy from the *Daily Mail* Online:

PIRANHA ATTACK!

'70 Christmas day bathers are savaged!'

'There was no doubt what happened: the bathers had been attacked by one of man's most feared creatures, the deadly piranha fish!'

'What happened next was like a scene from a horror film.'

'Chunks of naked flesh ripped away.'

'Agonising wounds.'

'Dripping blood.'

And (journalist struggling just a bit now) one victim 'lost the whole underside of...one toe.' How frightful! A bit of his toe – gone, just like that.

Piranha are a journalist's dream. Down off the shelf comes the well-thumbed *Big Book of Biological Bobbins* and all the old clichés come tumbling out. In later reports that I read, the number attacked by 'the deadly piranha fish' had swollen to 'hundreds'.

Before my very eyes the story was growing with the telling, as so many tales of piranha do.

We wanted to try and film piranha for the 'Pack Hunters' programme in my series *Ultimate Killers*. Almost uniquely amongst fish, piranha really do hunt in packs – herring and others may live in huge shoals, but they don't actually hunt together. As part of our mission to find out more, we were going to test the 'Piranha strips flesh off the bone in seconds' claim for ourselves.

On the morning of 12 November 1999, we chugged out of the city of Iquitos in Peru, and on to the mighty Amazon, aboard our floating base the *Amazon Explorer*. On board were the film crew, presenter Steve Leonard, and our hugely knowledgeable and only slightly eccentric piranha expert, Peter Henderson. It would take a number of days to get upstream to Peter's suggested location, so we sailed up river that first day, and moored up at night in the flooded forest.

At first light I slipped out of my hammock and crept out on deck. Swathes of spectral mist drifted up from the glassy green water and swirled around half-submerged trees. A gentle hum of insects – generally non-biting in the cool of the morning; the occasional splash from a feeding fish. An iridescent, jewel-like kingfisher – which I mistook for a large insect at first – plunged into the water after a meal. Gradually, the sun started to appear through the mist, and exotic birdcalls rang through the flooded forest. Suddenly, bizarrely, large, curved pink shapes broke the surface and rolled smoothly through the water. Pink river dolphins! Pink, for goodness' sake! A wonderful sight, somewhat ruined by our showy-off presenter Steve hurling himself off the highest deck into the water for a dip.

Knowing the whole area was rich in piranha lent a certain frisson – would Steve emerge with all his limbs? Could we get an answer to the piranha legend almost immediately? The whole boat was curious. Peter had assured us that a healthy animal, human or otherwise, was in no danger from piranha so long as they were swimming strongly. If their swimming pattern was weak, or erratic, which might signify an injury of some sort – well, that would be a different matter. Steve appeared to be swimming strongly and, to general relief (tinged with only very slight disappointment), he emerged from the Amazon, dripping but intact. We weighed anchor, and the *Amazon Explorer* headed for the Rio Tigre, a tributary of the Amazon which, Peter had assured us, was particularly rich in shoals of the fearsome creatures, and so the very best place to do our filming.

Piranha are a South American speciality. They are characterised by short, highly muscular, 'flattened' bodies and, at the business end, by a set of really formidable jaws. They have very strong, very sharp triangular teeth. The upper and lower jaws fit together perfectly, like a bear trap. As Peter says, all piranha are specifically designed 'to take bites out of things'.

Although they look pretty similar, there are many different species of piranha. I asked Peter if he could say exactly how many, and he said he could not, because even now, after many years studying them, he was still finding piranha he could not identify – 'dozens', at least, he said. Piranha are not exclusively meat-eaters – some are even vegetarian – but generally they hunt fish, which include each other, if someone in the shoal is looking a bit under the weather. Even the mainly carnivorous ones will sometimes eat fruit, too. Amongst all the different species, there are just two that are the 'mighty biters', the piranha of legend. They are the red-bellied piranha and the much larger black piranha. Both go around in shoals and, given the right opportunity, will attack en masse.

When you are told about legendary creatures like piranha, the reality often fails to live up to the hype. Not, I'm pleased to tell you, in this case. When we got to the Rio Tigre, Peter brought out a small fishing-rod, and soon a real, live red-bellied piranha, one of the big biters, was flapping about in the bottom of our small boat. The piranha was about 20 cm long: we were feeling blasé – not a very big fish…

'Be careful,' said Peter.

Ha-ha, we chuckled.

'No, I actually really, really, mean it – it will take your finger off if it can. It's watching your every move.'

And when you looked, Peter was absolutely right. The piranha really was watching us. Despite it being out of the water in the bottom of our boat, its eyes were very clearly following us about, tracking our movements. This was quite a shock. But a 20-cm fish removing a finger? Again, clearly Peter was obviously serious. We became less flippant.

Steve was given instruction on how to hold a live piranha correctly, and then Peter carefully peeled back its gums with his penknife, revealing the two rows of fearsome, saw-like teeth. The piranha grinned. Suddenly, with a snap, the little fish locked its jaws on the blade of Peter's knife. The knife was stuck – it wouldn't come out. And, once the piranha did let go, there were little teeth marks on the steel blade…'They can bite through metal,' said Peter casually.

Really?

'Yes, don't be fooled. People underestimate fish.'

Fish can be a lot smarter than we give them credit for. Some cichlid fish, particularly oscars, a popular aquarium fish, are notoriously clever. Peter told me oscars recognise their owners. They become excited when the owner appears, swimming towards them, watching them, whereas if a stranger comes by their tank they're not interested.

And piranha are smart, too. Peter told us a sobering story. 'I had a feisty young cook on a boat up here once. She used to tease the piranha by dipping a bit of chicken skin in the water off the back of the boat, then whipping it away as they came to investigate. She was very good at judging how close they could get before snatching it away. One morning she went to tease the piranha as usual but, as she lowered her hand towards the surface, a piranha shot right out of the water, successfully removing both the chicken skin and the end of her finger. It was waiting: it had ambushed her, knowing the routine.'

Steve was still holding the piranha, which was eyeing him up and looking dangerous. 'He's getting a bit frustrated, so I'll just put him back with all his thousands of friends and' (thinking about future swims) 'hope his memory is not so good.' Cautiously, he placed the little piranha back in the water.

To test the stripping-the-animal-to-the-bone claims we'd brought a whole duck carcass along with us, so we attached a bit of string and lowered it into the water, not expecting much.

'Agitate it as if it was in distress,' said Peter. 'Move it about to release some blood – it's got to look like an animal struggling, perhaps with a broken wing.' Steve wiggled it. There was a pause; a thud; then another. Suddenly the water around the duck seemed to boil. Then it went quiet. We lifted the carcass out of the water. It was literally stripped to the bone. Which was very impressive.

But would a piranha do this to you or me? In most circumstances, probably not. Despite their genuine flesh-stripping potential, piranha prefer to stay in the shadows, with good reason. Otters, river dolphins and quite a few different birds will all eat piranha if they can, so it pays for them to keep a low profile.

Piranha will almost always keep out of your way, unless, as I said earlier, they sense, if an animal is in distress. If the pack finds an animal struggling in the water, it's usually a small, hungry piranha that goes in first, to take an exploratory bite. It will swim in, take a nibble, then quickly drop away into the dark, to see how the potential prey reacts. If there is a violent reaction, the piranha will hang back, but if there is little or no reaction then others will creep in in closer. Another will flash in, take a bite and curve away. Any reaction? No? Another goes in, then another: *thump, thump, thump*. The momentum of the attack builds quickly, until finally, all hell breaks loose.

As water levels recede, piranha can get cut off in drying pools, and such isolated, sometimes starving shoals are thought to be particularly dangerous. Despite their timidity they really will attack larger mammals in the water – cows, goats and even, on occasion, humans. I am surprised to discover that there have been some recent, genuine cases of apparently healthy humans not just being nipped (see the *Daily Mail* above), but actually being killed by piranha – a drunken eighteen-year-old Bolivian man in 2011, and a five-year-old Brazilian girl in 2012. So, although there has undoubtedly been a huge amount of ludicrous hype, under certain circumstances you have to conclude the legend of the piranha is broadly true.

As we moored up back in Iquitos Bay and began to unload all the filming equipment from our boats, I couldn't help noticing some girls sitting on small canoes clustered near thick rushes growing in the muddy shallows, all looking just a tiny bit bored, and each accompanied by a much older, battered-looking man.

'Peter, er – those girls..?'

'Ah, yes,' said Peter, who is a fund of information, not all of it fish-related. 'Canoe prostitutes. It's one dollar a time at the moment. So I believe,' he added quickly.

This is how it works. Man goes down to the shore, waves at a particular canoe. The old man on the back poles to the shore and picks up man. He has to be very careful, as the canoes are quite wobbly. Old man now steers canoe into the thicker part of the rushes, to allow at least a modicum of privacy, stops, and, probably, rolls a cigarette, gazing off into the distance. Man and girl become intimate – being extremely careful, as over-enthusiastic activity could mean all three ending up in the water (complete with piranhas). Old man smokes cigarette, and then poles punter and prostitute back to shore. Extraordinary.

So now our second Amazonian legend: the canero or candiru. The fish that swims up your willy. For us westerners, the legend got into full swing in 1850 with the publication of *Expédition Dans les Parties Centrales de L'Amerique du Sud*, by the explorer and naturalist Francois de Castelnau. In this book, describing a five-year exploration right across South America, the fishermen tell Castelnau of a terrible fish, the candiru, which 'springs out of the water and penetrates into the urethra by ascending the length of the liquid column' as a man urinates. Because of this candiru, the fishermen tell him, it was dangerous for a man to wee in the river. De Castelnau was no mug: he reported the fishermen's story, but said himself that the claim was 'absolutely preposterous'. But it was too late: the seed was sown – the legend of the fish swimming up the stream of wee and embedding itself inside one's most delicate parts was here to stay. However, if this had been total nonsense I have a feeling it would have been dismissed as apocryphal. To sustain such wildlife legends over the years there has to be some grain of truth in them.

The first opportunity I had to investigate this peculiar but dangerous fish was back in 1998. Here is an extract from my diary. Then, as now, I was in the fabulous rain forest, but this time in Peru. I will include bit of background to the day, to set the scene a bit.

Saturday 25 April

Flashes of lightning and a great growing 'hiss' on the forest announce another great storm – lovely sounds. I tried to record, but the DAT recorder flashes a water drop sign at me and will not work. I am sitting under my net covered in mozzie bites, all over my body, face, arms, back, elbows, hands, writing by torchlight. Up at 0600: watch a female rat making a nest in the wall, very white tummy. At breakfast a superb tayra (large thick-set stoat or marten-like animal, with a sad face) came and ran up the papaya tree – looked at us and pinched a papaya – wonderful big animal. Out with poison arrow frog researcher Rudolph, tiny frogs, lay eggs (one or two) when they hatch. The male carries them on his back to a puddle – in old bamboo or a fallen leaf – and puts them there. (Many poison arrow frogs are remarkably good parents, even continuing to look after their tadpoles once they have placed them in their little water pools.) Depart 0930 up river, many sad goodbyes to people, including nice smiley wrinkle-up-face Japanese lady (who learned Spanish in three months). Boat for many hours. Group of spider-monkeys at a clay lick beside the river – what do they get from eating the clay? They creep slowly up the vines. Now with current so much quicker. Arrive Posada Amazonas: poke boat into bank under tree and discover steps by magic. We go off to find man whose daughter really did get the candiru fish up her urethra. We find him at community festival and football match. We are not allowed to approach – stand and wait. Man comes and tells story. IT'S TRUE! Candiru really do swim up people's bits – wedge themselves in and drink blood. Poor girl (aged eight) got it swimming in river – screamed. Took the infusion of bark from the huito tree (*Genipa americana*), which kills the fish, but the bleeding was v bad and she went to Puerto Maldonado to have it stopped. Into forest to look for the vast harpy eagles...

Now, what do you make of that? It seemed the huito tree was a well-known treatment for the candiru, as though its attacks were a reasonably common occurrence (although its unripe fruit, not the bark, is more commonly used). I have subsequently discovered accounts that make it clear the huito treatment for candiru was known about up and down the Amazon as far back as 1836.

After we had talked to the man whose daughter was attacked, we tried to film the candiru, and in so doing found out something of its natural behaviour. My assistant producer Louise Osbourne set up an arrangement with the local fishermen to bring her the catfish they caught. As soon as the catfish were put into our tank, the little candiru would start to appear, swimming out from the unfortunate catfishes' gill openings. This is because the candiru, which are between 3 and 5 cm long, normally drink the blood of other fish.

I have now done a great deal of research into this rather nasty little creature. Recent scientific papers have renamed it the 'vampire catfish', both because it drinks blood, and because it's a catfish, albeit a heavily modified one. This is a normal day in the life of a vampire catfish. Catfish sits quietly on the muddy bed of the river. A larger fish swims by. Initially attracted by simply the seeing the fish, the candiru moves into attack mode. It swims up and tries – vigorously – to enter the gill openings of its intended victim. Fish breathe by drawing water into their mouths and passing it over their extremely vascular gills, where oxygen is extracted, before allowing the water to exit past their gill covers. The gill covers, or *opercula*, open and shut as this process happens. It appears the flow of fluid as it comes out of the gills helps the vampire catfish home in as it makes its final approach.

The fish under attack will often try to protect itself from these tiny predators by closing its gill covers, or in some instances by taking drastic action and stopping breathing altogether. This occasionally works, but more often than not the candiru manages to wriggle its way into the gills. Now it attaches itself to the tissue by erecting spines around its own gill covers. It's a bit like opening an umbrella with sharp points on the spokes. These spines dig into the flesh, and make it extremely difficult to dislodge the candiru once it's in position. It now makes a bee-line for the high-pressure arterial blood vessels in the gills, and inserts its needle-like teeth. Having punctured a main artery, the candiru relies on the host's own blood pressure to pump blood into its stomach, and quickly starts to swell up as the blood rushes in. The whole process only takes a matter of seconds. The most up-to-date and detailed scientific paper I have read calibrates the total time taken for the attack as varying between 30 and 145 seconds, before the candiru – now full of its victim's blood – detached itself and drifted away to digest its gory meal. Sometimes, and this is very important, if the candiru could not get into the gills, it looked for any other possible opening to invade: the same authoritative 2003 paper recounted an observation of one ramming itself into the fish's nostril to get a blood meal. It appears a hungry candiru will look for any possible opening in a potential host in order to try to feed.

So it's now clear what is happening. The candiru mistakes the human for a potential host. It moves in to attack. Remember, a steady flow of fluid shows it where to focus its final attack. In a normal host this flow is the water from the gills; in us it's the flow of urine. The vampire catfish is not (as another recent scientific paper reveals) actually attracted to the urine itself: it's just the flow of liquid. It now tries to wriggle into the opening whence the flow is coming. In a fish it's the gills; in us it's either the man's penis, or the woman's urethra or possibly vagina. Once inside, it erects its gill spines, wedging it irreversibly in the tube of the urethra, making it almost impossible to extract. Nasty.

In a fish host, the arterial blood pressure will usually ensure the candiru fills up with blood in seconds, after which it will let go and withdraw. In us it cannot find a pressurised arterial supply of blood, and will continue to dig its teeth in, looking for a suitable vessel. It does not fill up with blood, and so it does not detach. There it stays, inside the human body, waiting for that elusive blood meal, causing a great deal of distress and making a very painful nuisance of itself. So it's all a horrible mistake. But there is no doubt it does happen.

Louise tells me she pickled one of the candiru in alcohol, to take home to show her boyfriend. If she ran her thumb around the candiru's head by the gills, she told me, she could feel the sharp spines. All in all, you'd have to say the candiru, the 'vampire catfish', has few redeeming features. I'm trying to think of one…. No: nothing comes to mind. It's bad to the bone.

Interestingly, most of the convincing cases involving humans seem to be women not men – and in the vagina, not the urethra. This was noted even in the very early days. Paul le Cointe gives a rare first-hand account from 1891. Not only was this candiru lodged in a woman's vagina, but he was able to remove the fish himself, pushing it forward first, to release the spines, then turning it around and then extracting it. In one intriguing report in the November 1941 *American Journal of Surgery*, a missionary, the Reverend Edgar J. Burns, was involved in ten human/candiru cases over a seven-year period. The Revd Burns made quite detailed notes. Of the ten victims, four were mature women; three were girls between the ages of ten and sixteen; one was a mature male; and the other two were boys aged twelve and thirteen. In most cases the victims were female, presumably because the vagina is a wider and more accessible opening than the end of a penis. In the case I discovered for myself, the father told me his daughter had to go to hospital in the town of Puerto Maldonado. I have contacted this hospital, and they confirm they really do have to deal with a small but steady stream of candiru cases.

So I strongly recommend keeping your swimming costume on while bathing in the Amazon.

Now for the third, and certainly the strangest, of my Amazonian legends: the fabulous mapinguari. The mapinguari is a cryptid – a creature whose existence has been suggested, but is not yet recognised by scientific consensus – think yeti, bigfoot or Loch Ness Monster. Accounts say the mapinguari resembles a giant ape, with long powerful arms that can tear trees apart. If it stands up on its hind legs, which it does if threatened, rather like a bear, it is supposed to stand over seven feet tall. The mapinguari is covered in thick, matted fur, and is reputed to smell awful. In 1937, the slaughter and partial dismemberment of dozens of cows was blamed on a mapinguari, so they are considered carnivorous.

OK, at first sight this is surely total nonsense – but please hear me out.

We had come to Tefé in Brazil, to try and find a man called Honis who was doing research on caiman, the large freshwater crocodilian. His method of catching caiman was to leap into the water and wrestle them into submission, all in the cause of science. He sounded like a very good subject for a programme about people whose work was, as the title of my proposed series went, *Wild and Dangerous*. 'Despite seven hours in a small metal speedboat,' it says in my diary, 'couldn't find Honis the caiman fighter or his lovely pregnant wife with piranha-nibbled fingers – v disappointing.' To put it mildly. We'd been sold a pup. We found his floating lab OK, way out on the Amazon, but we never found the man himself.

Other bits of the recce were more rewarding. For instance, we did find, and eventually film, the lady who had been attacked by a giant anaconda, and had scars to prove it, which is another story – but while I was in Tefé there was…something else.

Our contact was a slim young English academic, Will Crampton, who was a freshwater fish expert. Will appeared to be on close terms with a lot of stunning Brazilian beauties. I must be careful what I say about him here (although my diary makes pretty sensational reading, Will!) because I recently discovered he is now a terribly respectable academic – an associate professor, no less – at a prestigious university in the USA. But back then – what do they say? 'As we grow old the sins we most regret are the ones we did not commit'? Anyhow, just before I left to travel back home, Will took me to a teeming market – it was trinket heaven. At one stall he stopped, and yet another extremely attractive girl came out from behind the counter to walk with us. 'You might be interested in what she has to say,' said Will. 'Let's go back to my flat.'

Over a cup of coffee an astonishing tale unfolded. This girl was originally from a small village deep in the rainforest. One day, she said, a hunter arrived – by river – with something distinctly odd. There was a tremendous buzz, and the whole village, young girl included, turned out to see what the hunter had in the bottom of his canoe. There, she said, was a huge body, bigger than a human, covered in hair from head to toe. Half man, half monkey. In a bizarre twist, she said the creature also appeared to have a ring on one finger – but it was definitely not human. She said this was the legendary mapinguari – a strange creature known the length of the Amazon, a giant that stalks the rainforest, luring humans deep into the darkness, never to be seen again.

Now I'd heard and dismissed the legends, but here was, as far as I could tell, a genuine eye-witness. Her description seemed uncannily close to the other accounts of the mapinguari. Why would she make it up? I wondered.

'What happened to the mapinguari,' I asked.

'It started to smell really bad, so the hunter threw it into the river.'

What I would have given for a single photograph.

Some people think the mapinguari is a folk memory of a now-extinct rainforest animal, perhaps a giant ground sloth – but still, many years later, this chat in Will's flat intrigues me. What had that girl actually seen? Why the weird addition of the ring?

Peter Henderson, the piranha expert, had also heard many stories of the mapinguari, and when I asked him about it very recently, this is what he wrote to me:

> Did you know that there used to be a researcher at Manaus who was convinced that the giant ground sloths were still alive, and this explained the legends? I once travelled to Tefé and out into the forest with him. He was heading out to investigate a recent reported observation. He seemed perfectly rational, and almost believable, until he told me that the reason they were not known to science was because they emitted a substance that made us lose our memories! So no one can ever recall where they saw them, which explained the lack of evidence.

I wonder if the researcher had perhaps been watching *Men in Black* and the flashy thing? I love legends, me!

16

CONVERSATIONS WITH *MAHOUTS*

Over thousands of years, we humans have developed remarkably close relationships with a number of different animals. How these relationships started will always be a mystery. In a place called Ain Mallaha in northern Israel there is a grave. It's not possible to say if the person in the grave is a man or a woman, because the pelvis has been damaged, but from the teeth it's an older person. There are two remarkable things about this grave. First, it's 12,000 years old, and secondly, the human lying there is reaching out his or her hand to touch the body of a small puppy that has been carefully buried with them. The poor-quality black-and-white photograph I have seen of the grave is strangely touching. This burial site is often cited as the earliest evidence for the domestication of dogs.

Did we choose the dogs, or did they choose us? Current thinking is that dogs, or wolves as they were then, started to live alongside our human ancestors because we provided a ready supply of scraps from which they could scavenge. The more friendly wolves did better and got more scraps, and eventually the domestic dog evolved.

Dogs may have chosen us, but we must have chosen the horse. What a phenomenal leap of the imagination it was to consider the possibility of jumping up on to the back of this large wild animal and riding it, instead of trudging around on our own two feet.

But who on earth was the first person to come up with the idea of riding around on the back of an elephant? Now, that's the man or woman whose hand I would like to shake. A ruddy elephant, for goodness' sake! It's a barking idea – I mean, where do you start?

The first evidence for humans using captive elephants seems to be carvings on soapstone seals in the Indus Valley, which extends through parts of present-day Afghanistan, Pakistan and India. These seals depict a variety of animals, including elephants, one of which has a cloth over its back, and three others which appear to have ropes around their torsos, just behind the front legs. It's not conclusive evidence – no one is actually sitting on them – but it looks as though the people living in the Indus Valley were using captive elephants around 4500 years ago. Battle elephants were certainly widespread 3000 years ago.

I have to keep stopping myself writing 'domestic elephants' because, despite our immensely long shared history, elephants have never been 'domestic' animals in the sense of them being bred by humans. Throughout all this time, nearly all elephants brought into service by ancient or modern civilisations have been captured from wild populations, and this remains true to the present day. So elephants are not 'domesticated' like dogs or horses; they are 'captive animals'.

Perhaps because of this fact, elephants are never the cuddly creatures you might imagine if you have been brought up on a childhood diet of Babar the elephant stories and *Dumbo* DVDs. When you look into an elephant's eye you never get the feeling of domestication; there's always the sense of uncertainty – yes, that's the word: you never quite know what an elephant might do – and because of their huge size and immense power, I've always been particularly careful around them. Sometimes elephants are really good guys; other times they can be terrifying and truly terrible.

I've come across elephants many times making films over the past thirty years. I think I was the first to film elephants swimming from underwater (chapter 12). I once escaped from a flooded national park riding on the back of a swimming elephant – she was using her trunk as a snorkel to breathe, and I was holding my suitcase above my head. I have watched an elephant smash whole trees to matchwood in a demonstration of terrible fury, come face-to-face with the aftermath of an elephant's very deliberate killing of a child – one of the worst experiences of my life – but I have also reconstructed true stories of loyal elephants rescuing their mahouts from certain death in a tiger attack. So what should we make of this complex giant?

To find out more, and put some of my contrasting experiences in perspective, I recently spent time in an elephant camp in Nepal, and met up with two highly experienced mahouts, Gun Bahadur Kumal and Dhan Bahadur Tamang (whom we have already met as the key witness in the story of the man-eating tiger in chapter 13).

Let's head down to the elephant camp. There are four elephants tethered around us, picking up rice straw in their trunks, tapping it gently against their front legs to shake off dirt before slipping it into their mouths. Three are of medium size and one, in her own shelter, is a huge female. Mahouts are working around us, some bringing in creaking buffalo carts piled high with rice straw, others preparing elephant sandwiches, and still others taking the elephants off down to the river for their daily bathe. This is a perfect place to get chatting to the two old-timers.

So, Gun (pronounced 'Ghoon'): how did you become a mahout?

'My father died from a snake bite when I was seven years old, so I had to work to support the family – my brothers and sisters, my mother and my grandmother. I wanted to stay at school but we could not afford it, not possible – so I just had to work in the fields and looking after cattle, very hard time.

'Then, when I was seventeen, I went to Tiger Tops [a safari resort in Chitwan National Park – see chapter 13] and ask for work, and I got a job as a mahout, but number three mahout' [bottom of the mahout hierarchy]. The elephants were used for guests during the day, so I had to go out at night to cut grass for them – all night: start at 10 o'clock and come back at 5.30, maybe 6 o'clock, to prepare the elephants for their day's work.'

How much did you get paid at this time, Gun?

'I got 170 Nepali rupees per month – back then that was about twenty US dollars – and no food.'

How do you mean no food?

'No food from employer, had to get food from home every day.'

So when did you start to work directly with the elephants?

'First experience not good!' (Laughs.) 'Elephant tries to kill me!'

What happened?

'I got on elephant first time and she tries to break my leg by rub against tree – first my right leg, so I pull my leg up out the way, then other leg…Then she runs, runs right through thorn bushes, I am all cut and bleeding, lost everything – my knife, *ankush* [the short metal hook all *mahouts* carry to try to control the elephant], everything – but still sitting on her. Then she runs at a low branch and knocks me off. Other elephants had to come to get her – very bad – but we had a very good relationship in the end. She was called Gulab Kali [all female elephants in Nepal are called Kali, and *gulab* means 'rose']. I was with her one and a half years.'

How about you, Dhan? When did you become a mahout?

'I was just thirteen years old when I started. My first elephant was Sundar Prasad. He was very big male elephant [in Nepal male elephants are called either Prasad, Badur or Gauj, and *sundar* means 'beautiful']. Female elephant more friendly than male, but I had to start with a male. He was very big, maybe 9 feet 6 inches tall. I was small – to me he's look like Everest!'

Can you remember how much you were paid back then?

'Yes, it was 1969, and I got 160 rupee – nowadays top mahout is getting maybe 100 dollars a month, and he gets three meals a day, his accommodation and a uniform.'

Gun, do mahouts move around from one elephant to another fairly regularly?

'No, no! Stay with same elephant long time – must get to know each other: elephant only react to own mahout's voice, not anyone else. I was with one elephant, Christian Badur, for thirteen years.

Do you have to try and dominate the elephant? How would you describe the relationship?

'Friendly relationship, close relationship. But sometimes even after thirty years together relationship can become dangerous.'

So how do you mahouts control your elephant?

'With your feet, and by words.'

What, real words? How many words does the elephant understand?

'Here in Nepal twenty-seven words of command, understand them all.'

Like what?

'Break branch; grab; twist; drink; suck and spray; kneel; back leg kneel – so I can get up; front leg lift – many, many words! So *Khol* is kneel; *Dthar* is grab; then *Thurr*, break; and *Hick! Hick! Hick!* make him charge…'

Would the elephant understand if I said the words of command?

'No. Well, yes – he would understand, but not obey. Only obey his own mahout.'

And how about your feet?

"You push behind both ears to make the elephant go forward [this seems to be a constant movement], push his left ear to go right, right ear to go left, rub his shoulders with you heel to make him go back.'

So when you start you have to learn all this, and you and the elephant have to get to know each other?

'Yes, but three men work with each elephant, so the elephant already knows the two others, and takes maybe ten days to get to know you – sometimes never like you. Three different level, senior man called Phanit work with guests, second man Pachhuwa cut grass, sometimes with guests, third man Mahout – bottom man – make sandwiches, cut fodder, clean stables.'

So the bottom man is the mahout? I thought he was top man?

'No, mahout bottom man, then, after maybe three or four year, you can move up, six or seven if you are slow. But can be dangerous being promoted.'

Why dangerous?

Then both men told me a grim story. There were two elephants in the camp, a male and a female, and they very much disliked each other. Contrary to popular belief, when elephants meet, they don't immediately bond in a cosy intimacy. They can be very particular about who they like and associate with. In the wild, Asian elephants move in closely related sisterhoods, generally six or seven individuals led by an older matriarch – the males live apart from the female herd. Although the sisterhoods will associate with other groups, they tend to keep to their own. In this case, for whatever reason, these two really didn't like each other.

One day, one of the mahouts looking after the male elephant was promoted. This promotion entailed him moving up a level, but in order to do so he had to move across and work with the female elephant.

Generally, the three-men-per-elephant system works well because, when a new mahout is introduced, the elephant is still familiar with its two existing handlers, and this allows a 'soft introduction' of the third person. But in this case things went badly wrong. On the very first day in his new position, the mahout tried to introduce himself. The elephant allowed him to approach; all seemed to be well. But then, without any warning, she suddenly grabbed him with her massively powerful trunk, gathered it around his neck and, despite the shouts and entreaties of the other mahouts, she began to push the unfortunate man into the ground with an appalling force, eventually breaking his spine.

The mahout was rushed to hospital in Kathmandu but, despite the best efforts, he could not be helped. He was paralysed, and before long died. Dhan and Gun speculated that the female recognised the smell of the male she disliked so much on the new mahout, and that was what had turned her against him. Elephants are said to have a sense of smell four times better than a bloodhound: not sure about that, but they definitely have a very good sense of smell. I was horrified by their account of this apparently unprovoked attack.

Which elephant did that terrible thing? I asked. 'This one,' they chorused, waving at the huge female elephant just behind us – the same one I had just been stroking and trying to blow down her trunk. *She'd* killed the mahout? Ambivalent feelings – do you see what I mean? There's a sort of moral ambiguity about elephant behaviour. Neither mahout appeared particularly concerned about the attack. It seemed they just accepted this as part of the mahout's life.

I noticed a man sitting down apparently making small bird's nests out of straw. 'Dhan, what is this man doing?'

'He's going to making sandwiches for his elephant.'

As well as grass, rice straw, sugar cane or other fodder, depending on the season, the elephants all get their sandwiches. First, a handful of rice straw is carefully selected, and the loose ends are whisked away. Then, using his foot to work against, the mahout begins to curve the straw around to make a neat 'nest'. Into the cup of the nest he scoops a handful of a rice, chickpea and molasses mixture from a large pile. He then pushes the straw inwards to make a roof over the nest, and continues to wrap it up. The sandwich is finished off by wrapping a fresh green sugar cane leaf around it, and finally the ends are neatly twisted and tucked away. It is mesmerising to watch: each sandwich created with wonderful dexterity, then tossed into a pile.

How many sandwiches must he make? I asked Dhan.

'For her [the big female behind us], 150 every day: 50 in the morning, and 100 before she goes to bed.'

The attitude the mahouts have towards the wild elephants living free in the forests of Chitwan is another example of the ambivalence elephants seem to engender. As Gun, Dhan and I discuss the actions of a wild bull elephant named Valentino, currently at large in the park, from our conversation, try to decide if you would consider wild elephants 'goodies' or 'baddies'– because I'm damned if I can work it out…Now, Gun, you tell me there is a wild bull elephant in the area right now who has already killed eight people?

'Yes – Valentino! Very angry bull. Always attacks people. First attacked some soldiers, killed one, and another man saved by his rucksack, stopped Valentino's tusk going in 'is back. Very aggressive.'

Dhan: 'I think maybe someone has upset Valentino some time, make him so angry.'

'Call him Valentino because he came to Tiger Tops elephant camp on Valentine's Day 2009 – first time we saw him, coming to find the females.'

What do you do when a wild bull like Valentino comes into the camp?

'Everyone just back off, leave the females to him, but he won't ever force them. They come into season every ninety days, and then Valentino come and take them away. Last time he took his girl away for nineteen days, he drove away the mahout and they went off. But then Valentino brought her back. When he left, she tried to follow, but he did not want her, he came back and they stood together talking, lots of talking, then she came back to her mahout. Mahout offered her a sandwich, she took and then she stayed.'

'Talking'? When you are on an elephant's back you often hear their low rumbles as they communicate with each other. Unlike the shattering din of a proper trumpet, the rumbling seems quite quiet, but these low rumbles appear to travel remarkable distances. In 1984, American scientist Katy Payne was watching the elephants in Washington Park Zoo in Portland, Oregon. It suddenly occurred to her that, rather than *hearing* some of the rumbles the elephants were making, she was actually *feeling* them in her body. She began to wonder if the elephants might be using really low sound frequencies – well below the sounds we humans can hear – to communicate. Research showed Katy's hunch was absolutely correct, and that these very low-frequency sounds, or infrasound, travel far further than the higher-frequency sounds we normally hear, which is ideal for long-distance communication between widely separated groups of elephants. The rumble calls vary in intensity: mothers make very soft rumbles around their calves, but females can also produce extremely loud rumbles announcing their sexual availability. Experiments have shown the rumble calls can travel at least four kilometres, and perhaps twice this distance – even in dense forest. The distance the rumbles travel depends on the atmospheric conditions, and they travel furthest in the evening and at night.

Valentino, the rogue bull elephant, is undoubtedly very dangerous to humans, but he appears, on occasion, to be a blessing to other elephants. 'Three years ago,' Dhan continues, 'this elephant [a smaller one we are now standing beside], Sundar Kali, got stuck in a swamp. We tried all day to get her out, no good, tried everything. We left her at 2 a.m. at night, and came back at 6 a.m. next morning with a crane, but no elephant! She was gone. There were prints of a wild elephant all around. It was Valentino – somehow together they pull her out. We found her a day later, all fine.'

So when a wild bull like Valentino comes into camp, everyone just gets out of his way – but what happens if they meet him, or any wild elephant, when they are out on safari with one of the working elephants?

Gun: 'If it's wild female she usually runs off. If it's a bull he may charge us – got to get away, make a run for it. I got chased by a big bull – made my elephant run, then across the river to get away, but he followed – thought we got away, but suddenly, ambushed! Had to cross the river again – try to run. He chased us over five kilometres – two clients on elephant with me – very scared' (laughs).

Part of the reason I suspect the mahouts don't seem to mind the wild bulls like Valentino is the possibility they may impregnate their elephants. A big powerful wild bull is probably going to help produce a good calf. If the camp can generate its own calf, that's great, because buying an elephant is extremely expensive – as I write, the cost is between $50,000 and $60,000. But Dhan tells me, if I'm interested, there is a special offer on right now: 'If you buy two you get a free camel.' Mmm – tempting.

The elephant's own biology throws a degree of uncertainty into their behaviour at the best of times. At certain times of the year bull elephants enter a state of heightened sexual excitement. They dribble urine constantly, and secrete a sticky fluid from temporal glands on their heads. Their testosterone levels soar, up to sixty times the normal level, and they become extremely aggressive and unpredictable. This state of almost sexual frenzy is known as *musth* (Hindi for intoxicated). It appears female elephants prefer these furious bulls as suitors.

A working bull elephant may come into *musth* perhaps once or twice a year – but it's unpredictable, which of course makes it even more dangerous. When he thinks he can detect the first signs of *musth*, a mahout will try to moderate the effects by reducing the bull's food intake, feeding it herbal medicine, and making him work extra hard. But often this is not enough, and sometimes for safety reasons bulls in *musth* have to be chained up. I have come across this in India, and it's frightening to see just what a *musth* elephant looks like: furious, crazed, smashing anything he can get hold of to bits, no holds barred – an elephant at absolute full power.

Although most books say decisively that female elephants do not undergo *musth*, that's not what Dhan and Gun tell me. They say females do experience a similar period of hormonal change, but it only lasts two or three days, and happens roughly every three months, depending on the individual. It's only during this time that they are able to conceive.

It might have been just such a *musth* bull elephant that was responsible for a dreadful incident I was called to in Assam, India. I was in Kaziranga National Park as part of my BBC2 *Wild and Dangerous* project. Kaziranga is, I think, the most wonderful reserve I have ever had the good fortune to visit – teeming with fantastic wildlife. But living close to all this wildlife can exact a terrible price. One morning, the senior park officer told me there had been an incident with an elephant – would I like to come and see? Yes, of course, said my TV producer self, not understanding what this 'incident' might mean. When we arrived there was a scene of devastation: a building destroyed and, from a small hut, the terrible cries of weeping women. 'Elephant came and killed son. He's in there – do you want to see?'

'No, no, thank you.'

An elephant had come out of the jungle in the night, smelt the food stored in the top floor of the house, and started to destroy the building to get at it. As the family ran out, trying to escape, the elephant appeared to make a specific bee-line for the young son, who he grabbed. Elephants can kill humans in a number of ways: the trunk is fantastically strong, as we have seen; the tusks, of course, can stab; but the preferred method, Dhan tells me, is to use the feet, and stamp, and rub, and stamp again. The awful remains of the child were in the hut.

Why did the elephant behave so aggressively? Was it a bull in *musth*? Perhaps it had had very bad experiences with people in the past. I was ashamed at intruding on this tragedy, and we left as soon as the park officer had done his official duties. Living in the vicinity of wild elephants is fraught with danger.

But then again, on the same *Wild and Dangerous* trip, I was told a story of two *mahouts* who were out collecting fodder. One man was up a tree cutting branches; the other was on the ground collecting grass. They had chained their elephants to the nearby trees, which turned out to be an almost fatal mistake. Suddenly, a tiger sprang out of the long grass where it had been hiding, knocking the mahout to the ground. The tiger then began to play with the man, letting him crawl away, before pouncing and dragging him back. The man up the tree was paralysed with terror and could do nothing to help, unlike the mahout's elephant, which was trumpeting and showing every indication of wanting to come to his aid. But, of course, the elephant was chained up. The mahout knew that if he could only release his elephant, it might save him – but every time he tried to get to the chain, the tiger grabbed him and dragged him away. It was a horrible game of cat and mouse. Eventually, the tiger left the mahout alone long enough for him to crawl across the clearing and slip the chain. The moment it was free, the elephant charged the tiger repeatedly, driving the big cat back. The tiger did not go away completely, but stayed close by, snarling and swishing its tail, so the elephant then placed itself between its mahout and the tiger, exactly as female elephants will do to protect their young. Eventually, the elephant helped the badly injured mahout up on to its back, and they both retreated. The mahout owed his life to his elephant.

So, two striking examples of the elephant's ability to both take human life and protect it – and it's not as simple as 'Wild elephants are dangerous; working elephants are safe', because, as we have seen, working elephants will sometimes take human life, too. Elephants are wonderful, complex, massively powerful animals, and must always be treated with the upmost respect, and, I would personally add, with a healthy dose of caution.

To my surprise, both Gun and Dhan had spent time abroad, looking after elephants in unexpected places. Perhaps none more unexpected than Gun's experience.

One day back in 1984, the owner of Tiger Tops, where Gun had now been working for many years, asked him if he'd be willing to take on a challenge. Quite a big challenge, it transpired, because he would have to use all his skill to try and control two elephants that had apparently run amok. They had rejected their handlers and were now out of control. Oh, and there was just one other thing – they were in Alaska! Incredibly, this was true. The owners of the zoo were at their wit's end: they had been all around the world – across the USA, Thailand, India – trying to find someone to help, but no joy. Finally, they had come to Tiger Tops. Gun was given three days to make up his mind, and in the end he said yes. A fateful decision because, as it turned out, he would not return home for many years. What Alaska in winter must have seemed like to this small Nepali man I cannot imagine.

When Gun arrived in Alaska the situation had deteriorated still further. The head of the zoo had been attacked – thrown across the floor into a wall, breaking two ribs and an arm, and had been knocked unconscious in the process. The head keeper had been injured by a blow from the elephant's trunk, and a third employee had been hit, too. No one could approach the elephants.

Gun sat down and looked at them, trying to work out what to do. He had to try and establish some sort of connection. During the day, the zoo was very noisy, and it was impossible for him to talk to the elephants – so he determined to work nights. Once the public had gone and the zoo was quiet, he began his campaign: talking quietly in a soothing voice; giving them food treats; letting them get used to his smell. It took six months of patient work before the elephants accepted Gun and he could go in with them without being attacked. Two months later, they would sit, kneel and lie down at his command, and not long after this, Gun was able to climb up and ride them. They no longer attacked people. It was a triumph. Gun stayed in Alaska with the elephants for a total of four years.

But what did you eat, Gun?

'Cook for myself! Everybody want some!'

In 1989 it was Dhan's turn to perform a similar miracle when he was called to a wildlife park in the south-west of England. They too had elephants they could no longer control. Once again, after eight months' patient work, Chikky and Millie had calmed down and made friends with Dhan, who became very attached to them, especially Millie.

Both Dhan and Gun are now heading for retirement, after a long life both as *mahouts* and as exceptionally skilled naturalists in the jungles they love.

But what happens to elephants when they get old? Like us, they retire when they are sixty-five, 'maybe still do little bit work till they are seventy.'

Finally, I ask both men for some favourite memories as mahouts.

Gun (after thinking for a long time): 'In the river, sit on elephant, sunny day, peaceful. Elephant selects clean water and sucks it up, lifts his trunk and gives me water into my hands to drink. If I go to sleep on his back, he wake me up with trunk very carefully.'

Dhan: 'When my first elephant died, very upset, did not want to work any more. I still think about Sundar Prasad so many years later. But best time with Millie throwing twigs at me – she was so darling,' he says wistfully.

17

AFRICAN WILD DOGS

Botswana, 2005; *Incredible Animal Journeys*, BBC

Throughout this book I have drawn extensively on my old diaries, but for the last chapter I thought I would use actual quotations from them rather more freely. This is because I'd like to give more of a feel for what it's like, day to day, on location, and I think the diaries, although written in haste, tend to give a reasonable sense of this. Please forgive me if it's a little unguarded at times.

This shoot was in 2005, and we had gone to Botswana, to the Okavango Delta, to share the lives of a pack of wild dogs, some of which had been fitted with radio collars (or else you wouldn't have a hope of finding them). To be honest, I was stretching my *Incredible Animal Journeys* brief a bit here, because wild dogs don't undertake an actual migration like all the other animals we featured in the series. Yet wild dogs' entire lives are pretty much one long incredible journey. They just never stop, covering around 40 kilometres day after day – they are endlessly nomadic. Wild dogs are among the most fascinating animals I ever filmed, but they have been terribly persecuted by man, and are now endangered.

'Wild dogs hunt in packs, killing wantonly far more than they need for food, and by the methods of the utmost cruelty.'

Nothing makes my blood boil faster than reading some destructive, biased nonsense about animals. Such accounts, moreover, are often designed to give people who kill animals for pleasure some sort of justification for their actions. Am I being unfair? What I've just quoted is a perfect example of what I'm talking about. Although written in 1956, the piece it introduces is significant because its author, R. M. Beres, was at the time Director of Uganda's National Parks, so when such a senior official makes pronouncements, others – especially in the same field of park management and wildlife – will sit up and listen. Such a statement would have a profound effect on attitudes, and perhaps even on conservation policy. The article, in *Oryx* magazine, is about African wild dogs.

> *Lycaon* [the wild dog's Latin name] does not kill quickly, as the lion does, but often starts to devour the antelope, which is his victim, before life is extinct. They do more damage than almost any other *carnivorae*, for when they enter a particular stretch of country the disturbance they cause is so great that, for the time being, all the buck are driven out: indeed, a strange absence of antelope from an area is often the first sign of the wild dogs' presence. A particularly unpleasant characteristic is that they will, without hesitation, turn upon any member of the pack that falls by the way, through wound or sickness, and show no reluctance to consume their own kind.

As John McNutt says in *Running Wild*, his excellent book about African wild dogs...

> apart from the first five words, this piece of natural history reporting, dating back only to 1956, is nonsense...Not a single

sentence describing wild dogs is accurate. The paragraph is presented as fact, and thereby contributes to further entrenching
the various myths that abound in our collective understanding
of these maligned animals.

As well as, I would suggest, helping to justify their wholesale
killing by farmers and so called 'conservationists' like Carl Akeley,
who took great pride in killing entire packs of wild dogs. This
attitude has been responsible, at least in part, for the wild dog's
shocking decline, from an estimated 500,000 individuals to
perhaps 3000 to 5000 today, and has helped ensure the African
wild dog is now classified as endangered by the IUCN, the
International Union for Conservation of Nature. During our
time in Botswana, in trying to keep up with the wild dog pack,
we would discover for ourselves how wildly off the mark Mr
Beres really was.

Nowadays it's hard to find a wild dog pack at all, let alone one
to try and film. Luckily, in Botswana there was a long-running
study that might, with a good deal of luck, allow us to share the
dogs' lives. Our first filming, to set up the story, was on a train.

9 February
We go on the train from Gaberone to Francistown. Departs on
time at 10.00 and gets in at 4.30 p.m. Dear old Badger [Giles
Badger – researcher] and Trevor drive the car at breakneck speed
to set up, and get shots of our train passing at various points
along the way. Unfortunately, the map is a load of bobbins, and
a number of RVs just don't work out. However, four do, which
is a great bonus.

Reading this all these years later I feel a little bit guilty. Thanks,
Giles! You deserved that beer.

From Francistown we picked up more cars and drove to Baines' Baobabs. Baobabs are huge, long-lived African trees with enormous trunks. Thomas Baines was an artist and explorer who painted 'his' baobabs on 21 May 1862 as he was passing through. The Royal Geographical Society who hold the original sketch kindly allowed me to examine it, which revealed that all the recorded references to this picture that say he painted it on 22 May are one day out. Baines wrote the date in the corner of the sketch, even noting that it was painted 'p.m.'. It is said that if you look at the Baines painting and then at the trees today, over 150 years later, you can't tell the difference. (One branch has apparently fallen off!)

Baines' book, *Explorations in South-West Africa*, published in 1864, doesn't tell us if he left any letters in the baobabs. He might have done, because in the early days of exploration huge baobabs were used as letterboxes. Explorers going into the interior would leave letters in a secure landmark, on the understanding that any explorers coming out on their way home would collect them. I love this gentlemen's agreement. I wonder how long some of these letters took to get home to loved ones? We left some letters up the baobab on our visit, but there must be fewer gentlemen around these days, because our letters never made it home. Mind you, it was only nine years ago that we posted them, so they may still turn up.

That night we camped out.

Camp is delicious, v lux. Own tents, little bed, bar of soap. Fine mess tent, fab. Film chatting around fire to introduce team, Mike, Neuman, Steve and all.

This was the team for this trip:

Steve Leonard: vet, presenter, wag.

Me: worried producer/director.

Simon 'Wagger' Wagen: cameraman – 'The camera's bust again, we can't go out today'. Get on with it, you old misery!

Jake Brockman: sound recordist; my best friend.

Giles Badger: researcher, ex-gamekeeper and old Africa hand.

Mike Holding: awesome bush pilot (got licence aged 18); wild dog expert; cameraman; hard taskmaster, but all-round good bloke who would be crucial to the success of our mission.

Neuman: bushman, lion tamer and apparently telepathic tracker.

11 February, Friday
Five-hour drive to camp, but not for me because I fly the aeroplane there! Mike hands me the controls, and he gets in the back to look for a microphone. Quite scary but v v exciting in a tiny plane. We dodge huge storms, we find three wild dog packs from the air using telemetry – Mike is genius at this. Thirteen dogs by a small pool, dozens of elephants (literally) below. Two hippos. Mike gives me a little lesson – exhilarating. I bring us around to land after buzzing the dirt strip, and Mike takes over on the final approach, warning me what we will have to do if an animal runs out. Amazingly gentle landing.

My diary entry may be fairly cool, but I had never flown an aeroplane before. Mike simply asked if I wanted to try, gave me a very brief lesson, then handed me the controls of his slightly battered 1965 Cessna 182 and disappeared into the back. 'Oh, yes,' came his muffled voice, 'don't forget the aeroplane doesn't know which way up it is, so keep an eye on that dial with the wings on it.' Now, er… exactly which dial did he mean?

Despite my almost total ignorance, it was interesting how much more relaxing it was to have the controls in my hands as the small plane bucked about, rather than helplessly experiencing the turbulence as a passenger – somehow my destiny was literally back in my own hands.

The telemetry I mention in the diary entry was crucial. Mike and the research team had perfected a brilliant system for finding the pack. He would pick up the signals from the dogs with radio collars from the air, do some lightning triangulation, and pass on their position to the ground team, who would then attempt to find the dogs in an assortment of reasonably battered vehicles. Written down like that, it sounds fairly easy, but driving through the dense scrub and Mopane Forest, actually trying to find the wild dogs on the ground, was extremely tricky. The very next day, however…

> 12 February. Chesney and the boys.
> Shake down all morning, fixing gear. Marvellous birds all around the camp. We went out p.m. to have our first go at finding the dogs. A huge surprise when we did! All the aeroplane/GPS/ telemetry comes together, and there they were, Chesney and the boys, all lazing about doing absolutely nothing. As evening fell we filmed the dogs playing 'wild dog rugby' with a big lump of elephant poo. Saw croc in small pool. Camp fire, ate, bed.

Steady, Martin – not too fast! Who on earth are 'Chesney and the boys'? This was a small breakaway group of wild dogs (names given by the research team) – a fascinating ongoing mini-drama, quite separate from the ups and downs of the main pack.

A wild dog pack is like a living organism: it is born, it grows, and eventually it falls apart, but hopefully not before it has given birth to one or more new packs. The membership of the pack is continually changing. Through the year, members of both sexes will leave or die, pups will be born. At the heart of the pack are a dominant male and a dominant female, who probably started the pack in the first place. This dominant pair are usually inseparable: they stick together through thick and thin.

But not in the case of Chesney. Poor old Chesney: he had been the dominant male in his pack, but his partner, the dominant female, had taken up with a younger man, and Chesney had been kicked out. Remarkably, four of Chesney's sons had decided to go off with their dad, leaving the relative safety of the pack, and striking out in a small group. Chesney, as Mike said, had got custody of the kids. Which was a mixed blessing. The youngsters were not old enough to be proper hunters: Chesney was going to have to find food for the whole lot of them. If anything happened to him, things would become extremely serious. What this little group needed now were some unrelated females to join them, both to help Chesney hunt and, perhaps, to have a chance of starting up a brand new pack.

> 13 February. Punter and Jones.
> Find Punter and Jones's pack (I can't really believe the system works, but it does). The pack is there, but no Punter and Jones. Have they gone already?

Punter and Jones were the second story we hoped to follow. Over the past few weeks, before we arrived, Mike had been watching the pack, and he now thought Punter and Jones, two young males, were on the verge of leaving, to try and start a new pack of their own. A new pack starts when a male or several males from one wild dog pack join up with a female or several females from another. Finding each other can be tricky. It's all done with smell.

When I take my pet dog Pip out for a walk, she spends a large part of our wanderings either sniffing interesting signals left by other dogs or leaving scent signals of her own – remarkably frequently. A really good smelling session, to get the full story of the scent, seems, at least in Pip's case, to take an average of sixteen seconds – you might like to try this with your dog. Dogs live in a world of smell. As they travel around their territory, the wild dog pack leaves scent marks all the time. From these, other wild dogs in the area can tell a great deal about their neighbours. They can certainly tell the sex of individuals, their age, and perhaps how many of them there are, too. Scent marks can alert younger dogs to the presence of potential mates nearby. This olfactory alert may be the trigger for them to leave their own pack, and try to join up with suitable neighbours to start a new pack of their own. At other times they may just go for it, and set off, leaving their family and travelling long distances to try and rendezvous with another pack.

Mike was pretty certain Punter and Jones were just about to make the break – and this morning they were nowhere to be seen. We filmed the pack for a while and then…

Suddenly Neuman comes back from listening, away from the cars – 'Elephants coming'. Soon we hear the awesome grumblings and odd crashings of nearby elephants, but invisible in the trees all around us. Fantastic and fabulous sounds – deep subsonic (?) lows, shrieks, rumbles, trumpets – crashings – silence. We stand up on vehicles, and soon vast grey shapes can be glimpsed all around us – then a face, a back. We are, it transpires, completely surrounded – a bit scary. How would we feel right now if we didn't have any jeeps to get into? Eles mysteriously disappear – then a lot of yipping and yelping – Punter and Jones are back!! Our heroes are filthy, covered in mud, exhausted, unfed, and Punter has a cut – excellent!!! 'Always keep your heroes in trouble'!!

Wild dogs' greetings are a delight to watch – they just seem so enormously pleased to see one another. There's tremendous yelping, sniffing, tail-wagging and excitable rushing around. The other members of the pack seemed overjoyed at the return of the wanderers.

So Punter and Jones hadn't gone yet. But this was normal: they would continue to come and go until, one day, they would meet some girls and never come back.

You can always tell when a brand new pack has just been formed, because the females behave in an unusual way. They are all over their new partners, constantly sniffing, greeting and rubbing themselves against the boys – even lifting them right up off the ground by squirming underneath their legs, a behaviour you never otherwise see in wild dogs.

15 February, Tuesday.
Up at 0430 – supposed to leave at 0500 but car work took us to 0520. Exquisite sunrise – mist all over Africa, dead trees loom. Tall grass w layers of mist then sun peeps up, sending dazzling shafts through the mist – can't resist filming passing shots, but snatched, as we are on a mission for dogs. Mike gets in a roaring bate up in his plane, as we are a) late, b) lost!! We can't find dogs, frustrating. VV good sequence with Neuman tracking and interpreting: 'One dog here…now more dogs. Chasing impala…impala stopped here, then ran on, now a hyena joined them, etc. amazing. Mike arrives and has words.

Then:

> Bump bump bang! What's that noise? Water pump coming off (vehicle). V serious, but Mike thinks it will struggle on a few kms. Set off. Twenty feet later, the wheel snaps off the other car – the whole swivel hub assembly, now we're stuck. Major car disaster.

Driving around through the Mopane wood trying to keep up with the dogs is desperate for any vehicles. Much of our time during the shoot was spent just trying to keep the vehicles going. While we worked on the broken wheel, Mike told me a story.

Mike works closely with John 'Tico' McNutt, the academic who started the Botswana wild dog research project back in 1989. Like Mike, Tico is also an experienced bush pilot, and able to detect the dogs' radio collars from the air. One morning, he was about to take off from the grass strip with four passengers and a full load of fuel. It was midday, hot, and, Mike says, a 'fairly average flying scenario'.

Tico has finished all his pre-flight checks, and it's time to go. Then he notices a giraffe in the undergrowth beside the runway. The giraffe looks busy, so Tico thinks it's OK to go ahead. He taxis out, throttles forward, and the plane starts to gather speed. But then he notices the giraffe has broken into a run, right alongside the plane. It still seems OK, because the giraffe is well off to one side. Just as Tico is approaching take-off speed, the giraffe changes direction – and runs straight out on to the runway.

The aeroplane is now just a few feet off the ground, but the giraffe is on a collision course. Tico pulls up the stick, to try to gain height fast and avoid the giraffe. Up, up – the stall warning alarm is bleeping furiously – up, up. *Whack!* The plane hits the giraffe's head, stalls, then smashes down on to the runway. The impact instantly throws Tico, his researcher and the other passengers straight out of the cockpit, taking the glass with them. What was, just seconds before, a perfectly serviceable little aeroplane is transformed, in an instant, into a mass of twisted debris, awash with aviation fuel.

Incredibly, all the humans survive (unlike the giraffe), with nothing more than bruises. One of the passengers in the back misunderstands the stall alarm – 'Gee! I could hear you blowing the horn at that giraffe but he jus' wouldn't get outta the way!'

Mike got Tico back up in the air the next day in his own plane – too much thinking-time might have put him off flying for a bit.

> 17 February
> Woken in the middle of the night by tremendous crunchings
> of surprising rhythm. Giles says each mouthful is like a box of
> cornflakes being crushed – it's a big noise from a very, very big
> animal.

I peeped out. There was a hippo – generally considered the most dangerous of all the large African animals – breakfasting just outside my tent. I could literally have reached out and touched him, but I did not. It's odd, the sense of security a thin layer of canvas gives you against hippos, lions or hyena.

> Up at 0445 and away at 0500 on the dot – bit of tension between
> Mike and me about being ready on time.

Mike was, of course, right. If we wanted to film any serious wild dog action – a hunt, for instance – we had to be with them very early. This is because wild dogs generally hunt at first and last light. A hunt is usually initiated by the hungriest dog, who will get up and attempt to get the others interested by walking around whining and twittering. Gradually, the whole pack will be roused, and the level of excitement mounts. Eventually they all head off, walking to start with, then moving into an easy trot. The hunt is not a co-operative effort, in the sense of dogs working together to ambush or cut off prey; success doesn't require the whole pack – a single dog is quite capable of killing on its own. One female lived alone for more than eight months, regularly killing impala.

When prey is sighted, the trot or run becomes a sprint. Now the pack will spread out. We followed a number of hunts and, not surprisingly, when the dogs moved into top gear, sprinting through sometimes thick cover, it was extremely difficult to follow what was going on. The intended prey will jink and turn to try and escape one dog, but this may bring it within striking distance of another member of the pack. Now, at this critical point, let me remind you what Mr Beres said:

> Wild dogs hunt in packs, killing wantonly far more than they need for food, and by the methods of the utmost cruelty: *Lycaon* does not kill quickly, as the lion does, but often starts to devour the antelope, which is his victim, before life is extinct.

Complete rubbish. He obviously never saw wild dogs in action. They kill their prey in seconds, by disembowelling them with their razor-sharp teeth. They go into the belly, extract the vital organs, and it's all over. Wild dogs never kill far more than they need for food, either.

Once the prey is down, any members of the pack who are not actually at the kill will be called in by a specific *Hoo* call, which can carry over two kilometres. They also seem to have some sort of extraordinary telepathy. I have seen dogs separated from the rest of the pack during a hunt trotting along, then suddenly stopping. They pause, extremely alert, then very deliberately turn, and run off at high speed in a totally different direction – presumably responding to some signal utterly incomprehensible to us watching humans.

Sometimes, the successful hunter will seek out the rest of the pack and lead them to the kill. It is vital the kill is eaten as fast as possible, for fear of being driven off by larger animals like hyena and, in particular, their mortal enemy, the lion. Younger dogs are always given first access, while older dogs keep watch, before they get their turn to feed – there is a logic to this. As Tico says, 'a pack of wild dogs on a kill is organised, co-operative, fast, efficient and quiet.'

Once they get the food inside their stomachs, where it can no longer be stolen from them, they can move on or, if it's the breeding season, return to the den. Wild dogs are very adept at regurgitating food for pups, for other dogs who have been left guarding pups, or even, remarkably, for members of the pack who may be injured. These animals pick up some horrific injuries, both from running at high speed during hunts, and from fights with hyena and lions. I have seen some ghastly wounds on still-living dogs, wounds that must mean the poor animal is in agony. But even a wounded animal is valued by the pack – they can still look after pups, or be a useful pair of eyes to look out for danger. Accordingly, injured animals will be fed by the returning pack. We had first-hand experience of this.

One of the dogs we met in Okavango was called Skree or, latterly, Hopalong. She was called Hopalong because she had a badly broken leg. This dog, completely unable to hunt for herself, survived for over two years because of the constant support of the pack. Now, what was it Mr Beres had to say?

A particularly unpleasant characteristic is that they will, without hesitation, turn upon any member of the pack that falls by the way, through wound or sickness, and show no reluctance to consume their own kind.

Complete rubbish again.

19 February, Saturday.
Caught in extremely violent storm returning from hippo pool. 43 hippo in a puddle, so so content in bubbling mud and poo bath. Storm quite something, flashing lightning in towering clouds, coalescing into a vast black wall full of violent blasts of light and forked bolts. 'Don't worry,' says Neuman, 'we will get back to camp before—.' Er, no! Unbelievable downpour, no windscreen, so Steve and Neuman get it proper, but nowt compared to me in the (open) back. I bought a special raincoat before coming out – do I have it with me? Not once the three times we've been caught in the thumping rain – turnip!

Skree, the dog with a broken leg who has survived two years with pack support, never made it back to the pack yesterday – this may be the end.

20 February, Sunday.
Lying in bed listening sleepily to Mike setting off to film at 0430. It's totally delicious – cozy minutes tick by, my bed is blissful inside my tent. The francolins yell and woodland woodpeckers make sweet mellifluous sounds. Every minute becomes more and more precious as time ticks away toward my alarm – we're going out with Neuman to find lions, the place is crawling with them.

Lions seem to have an almost pathological hatred of wild dogs – going out of their way to try to attack them. More than half of all wild dog youngsters are killed by lions.

But lions are not a problem for Neuman, our bushman tracker, who tells us he used to go out and drive the lions off their kill so he and his family could get a square meal of zebra, kudu or whatever the lions had brought down. How, asks presenter Steve, do you go about taking food from under the noses of a pride of hungry lions? How did you drive them off?

'You pretend: you raise your hands; shout; clap your hands; bang sticks together.'

'And this is obviously without a gun – this is with just sticks and spears?'

'Yeah, sticks and spears. You don't have to use them – I mean, you just bang them together, and then go on and charge them.'

'And how many? Fifteen, twenty of you?'

'Well, no – two, three…I did it myself with my younger brother.'

'How old were you?'

'Ten.'

'You chased lions off a kill when you were ten years old, with your younger brother?'

'Yes. Pretend yourself big – take a stick. Of course they can see your height, but if you put something big there [holds a stick up above his head], you are much bigger.'

'And you chased them off a kill?'

'Well, I mean, if we need fresh meat…'

'Oh, so you take some of theirs. They must have just been sat watching you?'

'Yeah, you take your little piece then go. They look at you and say, "Naughty you – don't come back again!"'

21 February, Monday.

Find scorpion in Giles Badger's bed. Watch African fishing eagle flit over pond in front of camp, swing down talons and grab fish, then give it to female – wonderful. Need to focus hard on Punter, Jones and Chesney for rest of trip. We set out in the evening down the road, and suddenly Neuman is stopped, and gesticulating in car ahead – what is it? Where is it? 'Leopard!' mouths Steve. We peer ahead – where, where? Suddenly realise it's not ten feet from the front of the car – AMAZING! It's utterly gorgeous – it was stalking impala, but now sauntering along the road ahead of us. The graceful sweep of its tail – such a stunning animal – it slips off into the undergrowth – my third ever leopard. 'My favourite animal,' says Neuman.

22 February, Thursday.

Giles has injury on his mouth; Si has injured his wrist holding camera in bumping car. Jake is bleeding. Crossing ground at speed it's almost impossible to film. Steve becomes very ill. To bed. I get v down.

23 February, Wednesday.

Up at 0430, depart camp at 0530 after coffee and rusk around fire.

Sometimes members of the team would have been up all night trying to keep tabs on the pack, so that we could find them fast in the morning, without Mike having to fly and locate them all over again. It didn't always work, because the dogs could slip away unseen. These all-nighters were perhaps the hardest job of all, but everyone on the team was up before dawn, stumbling out of tents, then sitting quietly around the fire, which we coaxed back to life. A coffee pot would be steaming, and there would be the smell of roibos tea. For a little while everyone would just watch the fire and sip their drink, but then we'd be off – all, that, is except our presenter Steve, who was feeling delicate that day…

Steve still very ill: says his back was so painful in the night he nearly came to wake me up at 3 a.m. – jessie! Poor Giles and Graham [one of Mike's team] are still on the dogs, having been awake all night with them. Unfortunately, before we can get to them the dogs are up and running, so we bounce across potholes, trees, scrub, etc. following. Catch up, but no chance to rest, we are all off – 'Go go go!' screams Mike, and we do…except my car. In the middle of the chase, just as the dogs go into top gear, the Jeep sputters to a halt. Arse! As Graham and Neuman try to fix the fuel pump, the radio tells us the whole story, as the other cars close in on the hunt. Get amazing kill sequence, as the dogs fight off the hyena at a huge impala kill – superb footage: most unusual. Dogs, two hyena, jackals, vultures, all there, and a two-camera shoot. Exciting! I couldn't ask for more. At 0930 it's back to camp for breakfast and medals. Steve now up and bored.

Wild dogs are constantly pestered by hyena. It's a numbers game – if there are four dogs to each hyena the dogs can drive them off, up to a total of four hyena. Any more than four hyenas, and the dogs will give way. On the other hand, if a single lion turns up, the dogs will back off immediately. Lions are just too strong.

After the action in the mornings we generally, like the dogs, tried to rest in the middle of the day.

23 February, Wednesday (still)

It's now so so so hot – wash smalls. Shower, and the small chap who cadges fags comes out as I go in. He has a huge willy – makes me feel v v small. You could tie a knot in it, or tie up a yacht. V odd to walk to shower (a fair walk) looking around for lions – a v real possibility. What to do if I come face to face with one? Strong winds and oncoming storm wash out p.m. We have to try to locate Chesney tomorrow a.m.

We were running out of time to wrap up our main stories.

Wednesday the 23rd had already been full of incident and interest, but there was more to come. Each night we had supper in the mess tent, which was open at one end. There were quite a few of us, and the table fitted snugly inside the tent. Jake, Steve and I are vegetarian, but on this night the meat eaters were having a leg of lamb which, once they had had their cut, was put on a small table between the back of my chair and the side of the tent. We were all busy discussing the events of the day by the light of the hurricane lamps, when I became aware that we had been joined by an uninvited guest. Squeezing down between the backs of our chairs and the side of the mess tent was a bloody great bristling hyena – just inches away from us all. It was heading for the leg of lamb. There was a moment of stunned realisation, as everyone clocked what was happening, then uproar – chairs falling over, people jumping about, crockery flying. The hyena, discomfited by the fuss, made a lunge for the lamb, which it missed, instead managing to grab the metal serving plate, on to which it hung with grim determination as it backed off and made its exit. Bold or what?

24 February.
Depart at 0500 to look for Chesney. Find him. He is limping.
Only one adult with him – worried.

25 February.
Up at 5 to find Chesney for the last time, to see if he's OK.
Scary wake-up call from roaring lions, apparently just outside
my tent – my, what a din! Off at 0530 – Mike is already airborne
in the dark. His engine starts to cut out, and he looks around for
somewhere to land – all he can see is…dark! Scary. Eventually
he leads us to Chesney. Neuman uses sign from kites, hyenas
and tracks to lead us to dogs. They stink! Hyena is with them. V
happy, as all dogs v tight round tummies – 'tight as a drum' – so
despite injury Chesney is still feeding them all, awesome dog.
     Charged by elephant, then back for breakfast at 0950.
     The last time we catch up with the main pack. Punter and
Jones are still there, up front, leading the kill. Are they really
going to go? Then Neuman notices something. Amongst the
mayhem of the kill there is a subtle change that only Neuman,
perhaps Mike, would notice. The dominant female is behaving
unusually, the other dogs are reacting to her slightly differently.
Is she perhaps a little bit more plump than just a good meal?
     Neuman says quietly, 'The female is pregnant.'

Which was the end of Punter and Jones's chance to strike out
on their own. When the dominant female becomes pregnant, it
signals a radical change in the pack's behaviour. For a while these
restless animals come to a halt. The female chooses a suitable
site – an old warthog den, or perhaps an aardvark hole – which
she tidies up a bit. Then, one day, after a ten-week pregnancy,
she disappears underground, only to reappear a couple of days

later, considerably slimmer, having given birth to up to nineteen pups (the average is ten). The entire pack now rallies round, to help guard the pups, and act as a food delivery service, bringing them meals they are only too keen to regurgitate in response to the pups' whines. Their enthusiasm gradually wanes as the pups become increasingly demanding. Everyone helps out, which is not surprising, because they are all related. Even though the other females are not allowed to have pups themselves, they help out, because the dominant female's pups are their nephews and nieces, or close relations, anyway. So because the dominant female was pregnant, Punter and Jones were going nowhere. Over the next few weeks and months, they would close ranks with the other members of the pack to help with the domestic chores. For Punter and Jones, the window of opportunity had just shut.

Our time with the wild dogs was drawing to an end.

26 February, Saturday.

Up at 0445 – now ridiculously tired. Most exhausting is juggling everyone's egos. I throw a bit of a wobbler at camp, and have to go to the bog, with its unbearably hot seat and sauna-like atmosphere, to cool off. A dung beetle is down the hole – groggy with joy.

We go out filming in the afternoon. Get back, and surprised to find total turmoil in my tent – everything scattered everywhere, and all plastic bags ripped. The bloody baboon has got in my tent. Luckily, the camp guard heard a zip being undone, then suddenly thought, 'Hang on, they are all out filming – what's all this?' He rushes out and screams at the baboon, which carelessly gallops out. I was very lucky, because they usually shit everywhere, and ejaculate too – ugg.

27 February, Sunday.

Lovely lie-in till 0600 – really feels it. I think we will look back and think, did we really lie in our tents and listen to hippos munching and crunching just feet away? Lions roaring just outside the camp, Hyenas nicking food before our eyes in the mess tent, etc? Neuman 'reads the morning paper' for us for the last time, to see what has been going on during the night in camp whilst we slept: hyena walked right by fire, into mess tent, then out (after a relaxing lie-down) not two feet from Steve's tent.

We filmed in the morning, then out again in the afternoon to try to get some final pick-ups – then as evening fell we go out for final drive by glorious hippo pool. We are all silent for ten minutes, and I lie on my back and watch the stars appear, trying to comprehend my distant African ancestry.

I was trying to imagine the dawn of humankind, which, if the anthropologists are right, happened here in Africa some two million years ago. So go back far enough, and all of us are African.

The sandy ground is very hot. The hippos grunt, birds cry – a vast croc cruises across the water. Last supper, and for the last time the delightful Margaret our cook comes out (with hat) to us sitting around the fire: 'I would like to tell you for supper tonight there is…lamb, and, for the vegetarians, cottage pie with lentil squash and cauliflower…but first…[we all chorus, as she says the same thing every night] *Souuup!!*' What recipe book does Margaret use to cook over her great fire and big iron grid? 'Mrs Bee-ton!' Honestly! After supper I make a small speech tho drunk and very, very, very tired. At the end I read a quote from *The Fruit Palace* by Charles Nicholl:

'All journeys are like a dream: you snap awake at the end, wild-eyed and dusty, and try to carry the memory of it into your life.'

ACKNOWLEDGEMENTS

It would have been very difficult to write this book without the generous help of many people, some of whom I must have driven to distraction with my endless badgering. Thank you all for your patience and for lending me your memories. In particular I would like to thank Jason Roberts, Lloyd and Rose Buck, Leo Dickenson, Scott Tibbles, Scott Stockwell, Andy Rowell, Andy Montriou, Richard Ganniclift, Louise Osbourne, John Roberts, Professor Uwe Schmidt, Peter Henderson, Dr Rob Bierregaard, Elizabeth White, Doug Allen, Dr John Takekawa, John Melton, Bob Drury, Jessica Pailthorpe, Dr Wendy Darke, Dahn Bahadur Tamang, Gun Bahadur Kumal, Mike Holding, Ali and Shaun Morris, Tim Martin, Steve Leonard, Giles Badger, Stu Armstrong and Mary Colwell. Special thanks to my editor at Little, Brown James Gurbutt, for his enthusiasm and guidance throughout this project. James is a man who knows that good red wine is a medicine well in advance of modern medical science.